Country
New England
Inns

Country New England Inns

by
Anthony Hitchcock
and
Jean Lindgren

New, Revised Edition

BURT FRANKLIN & CO.

Country
New England
Inns

Introduction

PEOPLE ARE DRAWN to New England for many reasons. Some are attracted by the long coastline with its variety of beaches. Others love the inland areas with their myriad lakes, forests, rolling hills, and mountains. Sportsmen enjoy New England the year round for its hunting, fishing, boating, skiing, swimming, mountain-climbing, or hiking. Artists come to paint; writers, to write. Theater-lovers come for summer theater, and history buffs come to observe the lessons of the past represented in the thousands of museums, historical societies, and historic sites that are found in every corner of these states. For our part, we find ourselves drawn back by some even more deeply rooted force, perhaps from our childhood. One of us was born and has spent the better part of his youth in New England, and the other has summered there for many years. For whatever reason and in whatever season, you will find New England a most compelling place. It is unlikely that you will fail to return. Many never leave.

If you have decided to go, here are some helpful suggestions. First, choose your season and area with care. If you cannot cope with snow, you will certainly know not to select a winter weekend. It is not so well known, however, that the early-spring mud season makes travel on back roads in the three most northerly states trying at best. If you plan an April trip to a remote inn, be sure to ask if local travel will be a problem.

We also suggest you write early for literature about inns that interest you. We have deliberately omitted a rating system, because tastes in old inns vary widely from the very informal to the elegantly formal. Read the brochures, look at the pictures, check the maps, and determine if the inns will actually meet your needs. Inns are not at all like motels. Each has special qualities that can be one's personal pleasure but not necessarily another's. Do not hesitate to call an innkeeper and discuss your requirements. Most innkeepers are highly understanding of the needs of their guests. If you are seeking an old-fashioned, small country inn that is secluded, with few outside distractions, ask before you go. We have purposely included a wide range of inns, from the simplest to small resorts.

We also point out that the quoted rates at all inns described in this book are subject to change. Be sure to ask what the current rates are and what they include. Many inns automatically add a service charge of from 10 to 20 percent that covers all gratuities. The more expensive rooms are the ones with the best views, most elegant bathrooms, and fireplaces or other special features that you may or may not want. If your room is described as having a fireplace, be sure to ask if it can actually be used; some are merely decorative. If you have a working fireplace, ask if wood is included in the room rate. One inn we stayed at (and did not include here) charged us extra for the fireplace and then added two charges for wood delivered to our door. We had forgotten to ask in advance. Please also note that some 1978 rates are listed. Those inns did not respond to our request for updated rates in time for this edition.

We also suggest you ask if your room rate includes meals. We have listed daily room rates as based on the American Plan (AP; all three meals included), the Modified American Plan (MAP; breakfast and dinner included), or the European Plan (EP; no meals included except, in some cases, a light continental breakfast of rolls and coffee or tea). Variations on these themes are spelled out in the individual inn listings. We prefer the European Plan where it is offered, because it leaves us free to dine at a variety of local restaurants. However, in some locations this would be no particular advantage, and a greater value is often obtained from the American Plan inns.

Children and pets present special problems for many inns. Unlike motels, inns often have antique furnishings, and the layout of an inn's interior may not be conducive to younger visitors or potentially obstreperous pets. If either children or pets are *not* welcome at an inn, it has been mentioned. However, these regulations often change, and it is imperative that families traveling with children or pets inquire in advance. Pets may often be placed in local kennels for the night.

A wealth of travel information can be obtained free of charge from the highly organized state and local chambers of commerce as well as from several promotional organizations serving the New England area. One of the best sources is the New England Travel Council, a division of the New England Council. The Travel Council operates the newly formed New England Travel Club, which offers touring assistance and discount travel coupons to its members. For complete information, contact the New England Travel Council at 1000 Statler Office Building, Boston, MA 02116. Its telephone number is 617-542-2580. Discover New England is another Boston based promotional organization that will provide useful travel information. Discover New England operates a New York City office that has helpful brochures and a friendly staff. Its address is the New England Vacation Center, 1268 Avenue of the Americas, New York, NY 10020, and its telephone number is 212-757-4455. Ski reports are available from this office during the winter months.

The single best source of state information in compact form is on the back of each state's official road map. These are issued by the respective state departments of transportation but are usually shipped by the state tourism office of the division of commerce and development in each state capital. All these departments offer extensive vacation-planning material in addition to the maps and will be glad to steer you to individual areas' chambers of commerce, which are listed in this volume in the introductions to the individual states.

For the convenience of readers, this book is organized by state and into regional subsections within most states. Within the regional subsections, the listings are alphabetical by the names of the towns and villages and, under each town or village, by the names of the inns. For those seeking a description of a particular inn, there is an Index of Inns at the end of the book. In the introductions to towns and villages, points of interest appear printed in italics, to indicate that the particular attraction is described in detail in one of the three companion volumes in this series: *Country New England Sightseeing and Historical Guide*, *Country New England Sports and Recreation*, and *Country New England Antiques, Crafts, and Factory Outlets*. These three books describe hundreds of things to do and places to see throughout the entire New England area.

The inns described in this book were chosen for their inherent charm, based partially on their architectural style, location, furnishings, and history. The information incorporated here came from several sources: our personal knowledge of inns, recommendations by people we deem reliable, and our own surveys of innkeepers. We have made every effort to provide information as carefully and accurately as possible, but we remind readers that all listed rates and schedules are subject to change. Further, we have neither solicited nor accepted any fees or gratuities for being included in this book or any of the other books in this series. We have tried to be highly responsive to reader suggestions arising out of the first edition of this book. Should readers wish to suggest corrections for future editions or offer their own comments, we welcome their correspondence. Please write to us in care of our publishers, Burt Franklin and Company, 235 East Forty-Fourth Street, New York, NY 10017.

Have a good trip.

JEAN LINDGREN
ANTHONY HITCHCOCK

Connecticut

CONNECTICUT was frequently explored by trading parties dispatched from the Dutch trading colony based on the island of Manhattan. The first permanent settlement consisted of Puritans who had left Massachusetts under the leadership of Reverend Thomas Hooker in the year 1633. In 1639, the "Fundamental Orders" were written. Most historians believe this document to be the world's first written constitution, outlining as it did the basic form of democratic government that was to prevail within the state. The publication of this important document lead to Connecticut's being called the "Constitution State." Connecticut sent many of its finest men to fight the British in the American Revolution. One of them, General Israel Putnam, shouted the now famous "Don't shoot until you see the whites of their eyes" at the battle of Bunker Hill. Other well-known Connecticut citizens who contributed to the American effort during the revolution were Nathan Hale and Governor John Trumbull, and Benedict Arnold, before he went over to the British.

During the nineteenth and twentieth centuries the tremendous expansion of trade industrialized the Connecticut coastline communities from Norwalk to New Haven and along much of the Connecticut River. Much of interior Connecticut, however, remains surprisingly rural and draws a tourist population in all four seasons, as do many coastal villages.

To obtain useful travel information, contact the State Department of Tourism at the following address: Connecticut Department of Commerce, Division of Tourism, 210 Washington Street, Hartford, CT 06100. The telephone number is 203-566-3977. One particularly helpful publication is "Connecticut, So Much, So Near."

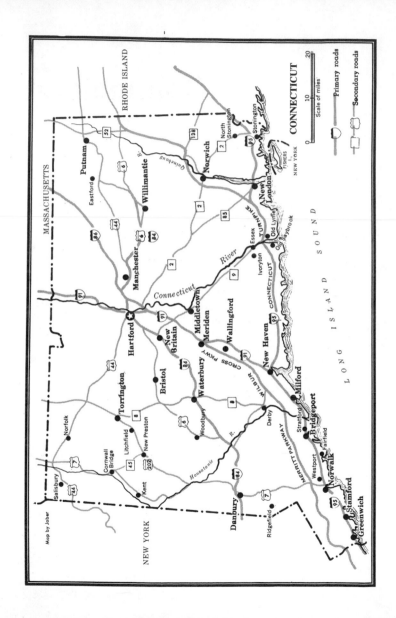

Eastford, Connecticut

Eastford is a tiny village (population 900) in north-central Connecticut. It is most noted for the success story of Albert Buell, who started a small gloxinia business with a few leaf cuttings and a packet of seeds in 1944. Today, *Buell Greenhouses* is one of the country's major growers of both gloxinias and African violets, with sales in excess of three hundred thousand plants annually. Within driving distance of Eastford is the *University of Connecticut* at Storrs, with its Jorgensen Center for theater and music. *Caprilands Herb Garden* is in nearby Coventry. Here, Adelma Simmons presides over a thriving herb business and serves luncheons featuring talks on herbs along with herb-accented meals. The Eastford area provides a variety of opportunities for cross-country skiing in the winter and hiking or exploring back roads in the warmer months.

GENERAL LYON INN

Route 198, Eastford, CT 06242. 203-947-1380. *Innkeepers*: John and Dorothy Bowen. Open all year.

The General Lyon was the first New England inn we visited, a number of years ago, and it has retained every bit of its charm during our many return visits. To arrive at Eastford and the General Lyon is to step back into the days when stagecoaches stopped there on the Boston-to-Hartford run. The inn, which shared its beginning with the nation's in 1776, was renamed for General Nathaniel Lyon, an Eastford resident killed in the Civil War. His funeral was attended

by fourteen thousand people, including members of Lincoln's cabinet who stayed at the inn. Later, the famous bandit Sam Bass stayed at the inn and inscribed his name and the date on one of its windows.

The inn is now furnished in eighteenth- and nineteenth-century antiques that give it a genuinely old feeling. The bedrooms are simple, and all share bath facilities. No attempt has been made to modernize unnecessarily. Most of the furnishings of the inn have been passed from owner to owner.

Meals at the General Lyon are an example of true Yankee cooking at its best—pot roast, roast lamb, baked stuffed flounder, or lobster casserole, for example. The innkeepers are experts on herb gardening and herb cookery and frequently have herb dinners throughout the year featuring interesting talks and fine dining.

The General Lyon will appeal to any traveler who enjoys a quiet lodging and simple country food. The inn operates a small antique shop in an adjacent building, with a selection of reasonably priced American antiques. Pets are not permitted, but children are welcome. *Room Rates*: Single rooms are $12; double rooms are $16. Reservations are required. *Driving Instructions*: Take Route 44 to Phoenixville and turn north on Route 198 to Eastford and the inn.

Essex, Connecticut

Because Essex is located on the banks of the Connecticut River, it is helpful to tour the environs by boat. Several excursion companies offer river cruises, including Riverboat, Inc., of Essex, and the New England Steamboat Line, operating from East Haddam, Haddam, and Old Saybrook. A pleasant day trip involves taking the ferry from Chester to Hadlyme to explore the opposite shore of the river, including the *Gillette Castle* and *State Park*. *Goodspeed Opera House* in nearby East Haddam, a grand Victorian building, spawned a number of fine theatrical productions that went on to Broadway fame, including *Annie*. Essex has a number of fine antique shops, including the *Connecticut Mariner*, which features antique nautical items.

GRISWOLD INN

Essex, CT 06426. 203-767-0991. *Innkeepers*: William and Victoria Winterer. Open all year except Christmas Eve and Day.

The Griswold, in continuous operation since 1776, is one of the loveliest inns in this country. Each public or guest room is decorated with such impeccable good taste that the effect is breathtaking. This remarkable inn contains not only some of the finest guest accommodations and dining facilities but also a fascinating collection of marine art displayed on its walls. There is, in addition, an extensive library housing a collection of reference material concerning the history of firearms.

Perhaps the most famous room in the inn is the Tap-Room. This handsome, paneled room features a pot-bellied stove that crackles during the winter months. The room was built in 1738 as an early schoolhouse in Essex. It was rolled to the Griswold in the late eighteenth century on a bed of logs. Food is served in seven dining rooms, including the Covered Bridge dining room constructed from components of an abandoned New Hampshire covered bridge. The room's decorations include a collection of Currier and Ives steamboat prints and a number of temperance banners. Food here is proudly served and always perfectly fresh. The menu features a choice of six appetizers and a large number of seafood, meat, and poultry entrées. Full dinners, including appetizer, entrée, salad, vegetable, and potato, range in price from $6.50 to $14.00.

The twenty guest rooms are decorated with equal care and include many brass beds and lovely wallpapers. Air conditioning has been added in deference to some modern tastes, but never will a telephone or television jar you from your restful sleep. Personal touches are the rule here; do not hesitate to ask for an extra pillow or two if you wish. Most rooms have private baths. *Room Rates*: Rooms range from $18.50 to $26.50 daily (EP, including continental breakfast). There is a private suite for $32.50. *Driving Instructions*: Take exit 3 from Route 9 (exit 69 on the Connecticut Turnpike) to Essex Village.

Greenwich, Connecticut

Greenwich is one of the oldest settlements in Connecticut, dating from 1640 when it was purchased from the Miossehassaky Indian tribe by two agents of the New Haven colony, who named it after Greenwich, England. These agents were not the first Europeans to set food in the area; a regiment of explorers headed by Captain Adrian Block—for whom Block Island was later named—had stopped in what is now Greenwich in 1614 while on an exploratory mission out of the Dutch trading settlement on Manhattan Island.

Today Greenwich, just 30 miles from Manhattan, has a population of 63,200 and contains several important places of interest. *Putnam Cottage* is a prerevolutionary house maintained by the DAR and open to the public. The *Bush Holly House* is the headuarters of the Greenwich Historical Society; it houses the Society's museum and a fine display of antique farm tools and household utensils. Also in Greenwich is the *Museum of Cartoon Art* and the *Bruce Museum*, with its displays in the areas of natural history, physical science, and American Indian studies. The National Audubon Society is particularly proud of the *Audubon Center*, with its 447-acre nature preserve, noted for an abundance of wild flowers and an excellent self-guiding nature trail.

THE HOMESTEAD INN

420 Field Point Road, Greenwich, CT 06830. 203-869-7500. *Innkeeper*: Richard F. Perchak. Open all year.

The Homestead Inn, on a hill overlooking Greenwich, has twenty-five guest rooms. The main part was built in 1799, and the dining room was added in 1859. The building has been carefully restored by its present owner and his predecessor. A wide, sweeping veranda, complete with wicker and lounge chairs, gives a Victorian air.

The inn is decorated with period antiques. Each room is different, but all have such modern conveniences as a private bath and television. There is a fireplace in the parlor to warm guests in the winter. Outside are many old shade trees on wide lawns. Summer guests can enjoy lunch served at poolside. The chef has spent the winter of 1978–79 completely revising the menu. When the restaurant re-opens in March of 1979, the inn is expected to offer French-continental menus. *Room Rates*: Because the inn recently changed hands, current rates were not available in time for publication. It is imperative that reservations be made well in advance for lodging. *Driving Instructions*: The inn is three minutes from Greenwich. Take Route I-95 to exit 3. Turn left at the railroad bridge and go two blocks to the end. Turn left again and proceed ¼ mile uphill.

Ivoryton, Connecticut

Ivoryton was once New England's center for the ivory trade, from which the town derived its name. Elephant tusks, shipped from far-off Zanzibar, were transformed into organ and piano keys in the local factories. The Pratt Read Company, which manufactures these, is still in operation today, although it now uses materials other than ivory, happily for the elephants. The village is the home of the *Ivoryton Playhouse*, on Main Street, a summer theater.

There is much to do in the surrounding area. A few miles to the north, on the Connecticut River, is the town of Haddam, with its now famous *Goodspeed Opera House*, where such Broadway musicals as *Man of La Mancha* and *Annie* were born. Farther up the river and on the opposite bank are the *Gillette Castle* and the state park. At the river's mouth is Old Saybrook, with its many antique stores and its annual sidewalk art display, held in late July. A comfortable drive away are *Mystic Seaport* and the *Mystic Marinelife Aquarium*.

COPPER BEECH INN

Main Street, Ivoryton, CT 06442. 203-767-0330. *Innkeepers*: Robert and Jo McKenzie. Open all year, closed Mondays.

The Copper Beech Inn has a renowned restaurant, which has been praised by restaurant reviewers from nearly all the major magazines and newspapers that cover the central-Connecticut region. Few people know that the inn also contains five guest rooms.

This Victorian mansion, dating from 1898, has gained a reputation for its unusually large menu, which can best be described as country-French classic. Diners are served in four well-appointed dining rooms furnished in Queen Anne and Chippendale antiques and decorated with old paintings and prints. One dining room is actually the mansion's former greenhouse, which was converted to a four-season eating place by using carefully treated glass to reject unwanted heat in the warmer months. Diners can choose from a selection of foods that includes nineteen appetizers, four soups, and nineteen entrées. Entrées are served with fresh vegetables, salad, and a small loaf of French bread. The dessert menu lists twenty-one items. There is a well-thought-out seven-page wine list that includes offerings ranging in price from $5.50 to $150.00 (for a 1949 Chateau Latour Pauillac) per bottle.

The inn's five double rooms contain their original cast-iron bath-tubs in their private baths. *Room Rates*: Rooms are $30. *Driving Instructions*: The inn is on Main Street 1½ miles west of Route 9, exit 3 or 4.

Kent, Connecticut

Kent is located near the western border of Connecticut, about midway between the northern and southern boundaries of the state. This scenic area is dominated by nearby Lake Waramaug and the spectacular foothills of the Lower Berkshires. Some have called this area "little Switzerland." Although much of Lake Waramaug is privately owned, the public is offered access through the state park. History buffs and tool collectors will enjoy the *Sloane-Stanley Museum*, founded by Eric Sloane in conjunction with the Stanley Tool Company. *Kent Falls State Park* is known for its beautiful waterfalls.

CONSTITUTION OAK FARM

27 Beardsley Road, Kent, CT 06757. 203-354-6495. *Innkeeper*: Deborah Devaux. Open all year.

Constitution Oak Farm is a 200-acre working Holstein dairy farm with accommodations in its two-story farmhouse, which dates from 1830. Unlike some farms that offer housing for guests, the emphasis here is on overnight accommodations in a guest-house atmosphere. The farm does not offer extensive participation in agricultural activities. Many of the overnight guests have been referred to the farm by the local inns, which often become overcrowded. In addition, many travelers prefer the simple and restful accommodations to the more commercially oriented inns. Indeed, there are no tennis courts, swimming pools, or organized recreational activities here. But there are five guest rooms and two public rooms furnished with pieces dating from the mid- to late 1800s. Two of the guest rooms have private baths. There is a wide porch that faces the sitting rooms and what are called dining rooms although the farmhouse does not offer meals. This is a peaceful back-road vacation or holiday alternative. Pets are not permitted. *Room Rates*: Rates vary from $20 to $28 for a double room, according to bath location. Single-room rates are available. *Driving Instructions*: Owing to the farm's back-road location, it is best to request driving instructions when making reservations.

Litchfield, Connecticut

Litchfield was purchased from the Tunxis Indians for 15 pounds sterling in 1716 and incorporated by the Connecticut Colonial Assembly in 1719. The land was formally settled by a group of sixty families the next year. During the American Revolution, Litchfield was a major supplier of cannons and munitions made in its several foundries. For years the town was an important stagecoach stop for both the Albany-New Haven and the Boston-Hartford lines. Industry never developed in Litchfield as it did in the many mill towns of New England, because it is located at too high an elevation to have any useful source of water power that was so abundantly available to towns in the river valleys. Today, the quiet village has a population of only 7,500, less than double the population of 1810.

Litchfield is one of the best-preserved examples of an eighteenth-century village in America, largely *because* it was bypassed by the Industrial Revolution. The town offers a number of tourist attractions including the *Litchfield Law School*, the first such school in America, where Tapping Reeve taught law to, among others, Aaron Burr in 1775. More than a thousand pupils passed through this school, including two vice-presidents of the United States. The *Litchfield Historical Society* contains four galleries of art and historical artifacts, as well as a "Please Do Touch" exhibit for children. Also in Litchfield is the *White Memorial Foundation*, its 4,000 acres open for public recreation, with facilities for swimming, fishing, boating, hiking, cross-country skiing, snowshoeing, and more. Part of the grounds are devoted to the *Litchfield Nature Center and Museum*, with its wildlife dioramas, nature trails, and special *Braille Nature Trail*.

THE MEETINGHOUSE INN

West Street (Route 202), Litchfield, CT 06759. 203-567-8744. *Innkeepers*: Chris and David Marr. Open except Christmas.

The Meetinghouse Inn was constructed in 1760 atop a hill in historic Litchfield. Originally a farmhouse, it has undergone many renovations—one such by Colonel Albert Lamb in 1900. He turned the inn into the magnificent Georgian colonial building it is today. The Meetinghouse is set off by 4 acres of gardens, flowering shrubs, and shade trees. Ten colorful guest rooms are available. All are uniquely decorated, each with a private bath; some also have fireplaces. There are three distinctly different dining rooms and a taproom with an enormous copper bar. The two main dining rooms contain antique-filled cupboards, chandeliers, period prints, and fireplaces. Overlooking the tree-shaded lawns and terrace, the glassed-in porch filled with hanging plants is the third dining area.

The inn features traditional New England fare with a Continental flavor. The specialties are stuffed Cornish game hen, a special house sirloin steak Tallyrand, escallopes of veal Lafayette, and roast duckling. *Room Rates*: Single rooms are $35, and double rooms are $40. A suite is $67.50. *Driving Instructions*: The inn is nine-tenths of a mile from the Litchfield green on Route 202.

New Preston, Connecticut

New Preston is located on Lake Waramaug, one of the largest and most beautiful lakes in the state. It is surrounded by the foothills of the Berkshires, which abut its shore. Biking, hiking, or driving around the lake is a memorable experience. The back roads of New Preston abound with colonial homes and well-kept farms. Water mills and covered bridges dot the area. During the Revolutionary War, this area's many ironworks with water-powered mills manufactured cannon and other arms for the American troops.

The lake provides year-round sports activities, including fishing, skating, and boating. For spectators, there are the *Eastern Women Sprints Regatta* (crew racing) in mid-May and the *Illumination of the Lake* in early July. Antique-carriage rallies, marathons, fairs, and auctions are just some of the varied entertainments the area around New Preston and Lake Waramaug has to offer the visitor.

BOULDERS INN

Route 45, Lake Waramaug, New Preston, CT 06777. 203-868-7918. *Innkeeper*: Peter G. Franklin. Open all year. All meals are served from mid-May through October only; open for bed and breakfast the rest of the year.

Up in the Berkshire hills, on 230 acres of woods and lake frontage, sits the Boulders Inn. Built in 1895, the inn has been run by the Lowe family for four generations. Richard Lowe's grandfather supervised the oxen that dragged the huge fieldstones and granite lintels to the site. Large windows overlook Lake Waramaug and the surrounding hills. About 500 feet of private shore provides excellent swimming, with a sandy, gentle slope for children and a deep-water float for swimmers. The waters are well stocked for guests who want to fish, and boating, sailing, and canoeing are available. Riding stables offer scenic trails and instruction. The property includes a large barn with an open fireplace, lounges, a snack bar, and games. In warm weather, its large doors open onto a terrace where weekly cookouts are held, and traditional barn dances are a regular feature in the 60-foot structure.

In winter, Boulders has a toboggan run and a ski slope with a 500-foot ski tow. Snowshoers and cross-country skiers blaze the snowy trails for hikers. For those who love the outdoors, the lake and pond provide ice-skating and ice-fishing; other guests prefer to relax by the crackling hearth and enjoy the winter scenery.

The main building contains a blend of antiques and comfortable furniture. The inn's bedrooms have views of the lake and the countryside. Six spacious rooms have private baths, antique furnishings, and new beds. In addition, there are several cottages on the property, bringing the total number of rooms to twenty-three.

The dining room (in season) offers selection of meals that are generally traditional American restaurant fare, such as steak, stuffed shrimp, baked chicken, roast duckling, and pot roast. There are also the less frequently seen curry of lamb and crabmeat Sycamore, a blend of crabmeat, artichoke hearts, Swiss cheese, and a sherried cream sauce. *Room Rates*: American Plan (in season only) is $25 to $40 per person. Double rooms are $30 to $44, depending on the season. *Driving Instructions*: Take Route 202 to Route 45 North. The inn is 1½ miles up Route 45 on the right.

HOPKINS INN

Hopkins Road, New Preston, CT 06777. 203-868-7295. *Innkeepers*: Beth and Franz Schober. Open from May through October; meals available April to January, except on Mondays.

The Hopkins Inn, also on Lake Waramaug, was built in 1846, although the barn section predates the main house. The inn was owned and operated continuously by members of the Hopkins family for more than a hundred years (until 1954). There is a terrace for outdoor warm-weather dining overlooking the lake. The cuisine is mostly continental, and diners may choose from the ten to fifteen items that are listed daily on the dining room blackboard. Both luncheon and dinner are offered to the public, but breakfast is available to inn guests only. Pets are permitted, within reason. *Room Rates*: Double rooms with private bath are $20 to $23. *Driving Instructions*: The inn is ½ mile west of Route 45 on North Shore Road.

THE INN ON LAKE WARAMAUG

Lake Shore Road, New Preston, CT 06777. 203-868-2168. *Inn-keeper*: Richard Bonynge Combs. Open all year.

The Inn on Lake Waramaug also sits on a hill, surrounded by sloping lawns and fields and towering sugar maples, overlooking Connecticut's second largest natural lake. Built between 1795 and 1815, it has operated as an inn and tavern since 1860. The main building is furnished with pine and cherry antiques, and houses collections of pewter, brass, and copper. Daguerreotypes, cupboards filled with lace fans, and silver tea services add to the atmosphere of the inn. With the addition of several new colonial-styled guest buildings, an indoor heated swimming pool, and porches and terraces on the old building itself, the inn has become a family resort. Nowhere is this resort atmosphere more evident than in the pool building with its whirlpool lagoon, sauna, snack bar, barefoot bar, and a connecting game room. There is a tennis court with professional lessons available in the summer months, as well as volleyball, bandminton, and croquet. Guests can have free, unlimited golf at a nearby club.

Though the inn may appeal more to the activity-minded than to those seeking a small, quiet country place, one can certainly stay at one of the inn's rooms dating from the 1800s and also enjoy the amenities of the resort, such as the recently added summer cart rides and winter sleigh rides, with the vehicles drawn by Chester, Happy, and Merrylegs—the inn's ponies. The inn also sponsors numerous events throughout the year, including wine-tasting evenings, family picnics on the beach, Wednesday-night bingo, a Fourth of July clambake, and much more. Pets are permitted. *Room Rates*: July, August, weekends, and holiday weeks, double rooms are $30 to $40 per person, MAP. Rates for the rest of the year are 10 percent less. Single occupancy rates are slightly higher. European plan is available at certain times and under certain conditions. Write or phone for information. *Driving Instructions*: Between New Milford and Litchfield, go off Route 202 at Route 45. Take Route 45 to the north end of Lake Waramaug. Turn left onto Lake Shore Road. The inn is about three-quarters of a mile down the road.

Norwalk (and neighboring New Canaan)

Norwalk, a city with a population of 77,000, is located in southern Connecticut between Stamford and Bridgeport. The city has always been an important industrial area and now is a suburban center as well. The Silvermine area, which derived its name from an early settler who falsely believed that he had discovered silver there, has retained its country feeling.

Norwalk itself boasts the *Lockwood-Mathews Mansion*, which is open on a limited basis to the public while the grand building is restored to its former condition. The *Silvermine Guild of Artists* in nearby New Canaan has several galleries open all year; it sometimes sponsors special art shows. *Old MacDonald's Farm* on Route 1 in Norwalk is an 8-acre amusement park with tame animals and other entertainments for children. Nearby New Canaan is also the home of the *New Canaan Bird Sanctuary and Wildlife Preserve* with its 18 acres of trails, bridges, and ponds. *The New Canaan Nature Center* has a number of nature displays and greenhouse exhibits. The *New Canaan Historical Society* maintains several old buildings housing museums that display such things as antique pewter, tools, costumes, and the work of John Rodgers, a nineteenth-century sculptor.

SILVERMINE TAVERN

Perry Avenue and Silvermine Avenue, Norwalk, CT 06850. 203-847-4558. *Innkeeper*: Francis Whitman. Open all year, except Tuesdays in winter.

Four buildings make up the Tavern group—the Coach House, the Old Mill, the Country Store, and the Tavern itself. The buildings are furnished in antiques, Oriental rugs, and primitive paintings. Each guest room has its private bath and authentic antique beds (three have canopies). Several rooms have balconies overlooking the millpond. A waterfall contributes to the charm of the 200-year-old building called the Old Mill. Crackling fireplaces in winter, leafy shade trees in summer, and colorful foliage in autumn all create an atmosphere of warm New England hospitality.

The Tavern has several dining rooms overlooking the swans on the millpond and the wooded banks of the Silvermine River. Decorated with unusual kitchen utensils and primitive portraits, it is very popular with tourists. The menu features traditional New England fare: shore dinners, Boston scrod, steaks, and chicken. The Tavern is particularly proud of its Indian pudding. Pets are permitted but are their owners' responsibility. *Room Rates*: Single rooms are $17 to $20 plus tax; double rooms are $29 to $32. *Driving Instructions*: Take exit 39 on the Merritt Parkway (Route 15). Proceed south on Route 7 to the first traffic light, then turn right on Perry Avenue. Follow Perry for 1½ miles to the inn.

Old Lyme, Connecticut

Old Lyme is a summer art colony and home of the *Lyme Art Association*, with its year-round gallery and special Art Association shows held annually from Memorial Day weekend through mid-June, late June through July, and early August through mid-September. The *Florence Griswold House*, built in 1817, is a Georgian mansion housing a collection of paintings and murals by members of America's oldest artists' colony, as well as antiques, dolls and other toys, and rare china.

BEE AND THISTLE INN

100 Lyme Street, Old Lyme, CT 06371. 203-434-1667. *Innkeepers*: Gene and Barbara Bellows. Open all year.

Gene Bellows once made a lovely dulcimer for Barbara. Now you can enjoy her singing and playing while you similarly enjoy Gene's thoughtfully prepared evening meals at the Bee and Thistle Inn. The inn is a quiet, relaxing country home that was built in formal colonial style in 1756 and remodeled in 1938. Several porches and fireplaces have been added over the years. The inn has two parlors with fireplaces, a dining room, and ten guest rooms. Dinners are served to guests and to the public from a simple menu that changes every four months but includes about four regular dishes, such as scallops with pignola nuts, veal Viennese, New York sirloin, a special chicken dish, or fresh fish of the day. There are also a nightly chef's special, homemade soups and chowders, and a small but well-prepared selection of desserts, including a highly acclaimed frozen chocolate mousse

and peach Melba. All meals are cooked to order and artfully presented. Complete dinners range from about $9 to $14 depending on choices from the à la carte menu. The inn serves breakfasts, in bed if you wish, with selections including fluffy omelets, English muffins, and imported jams. Pets are not permitted. *Room Rates*: Double rooms are $30 to $36; single rooms are $5 less. *Driving Instructions*: From the south, take Route I-95 to exit 70, turn left off the ramp, then right at the stoplight. From the north, take exit 70 off I-95 and turn left off the ramp. The inn is the third building on the left.

OLD LYME INN

85 Lyme Street, Old Lyme, CT 06371. 203-434-2600. *Innkeepers*: Kenneth and Diana Milne. Open all year.

The Old Lyme Inn was built as a private mansion in 1850 and restored by the Milnes to its original style, with French Empire furnishings; it is included in the National Registry of Historic Buildings. The inn has five guest rooms, each with private bath, all decorated in the same French Empire style. The parlor, with its marble fireplace and sofa, can be used for dining by small private parties. There is also a cocktail lounge that features a 16-foot Victorian bar. A mid-nineteenth-century atmosphere prevails in the blue and gold dining rooms, providing a perfect setting to enjoy fine provincial French cooking. The menu takes advantage of fresh, seasonal foods, and the meals are all cooked to order; even the French pastries are baked on the premises. An extensive collection of French wines compliments the menu. For guests there are many nearby attractions, such as the *Goodspeed Opera House*, the *Gillette Castle*, *Mystic Seaport*, and the *Mystic Marinelife Aquarium*. The Connecticut River and the Long Island Sound provide good boating and swimming. In summer, guests are given passes to the town beach. Pets are permitted. *Room Rates*: Single rooms are $27; double rooms are $30. Reservations are required. *Driving Instructions*: Take the Connecticut Turnpike (I-95) to exit 70. The inn is within view of the turnpike.

Old Saybrook, Connecticut

The first Europeans to visit the Old Saybrook area were led in 1614 by the Dutch explorer Adrian Block, a representative of the Dutch trading colony in what is now Manhattan. Block returned to the Connecticut River many times on trading voyages, but no settlement by Europeans was made until 1636, when a fort was built by Lion Gardiner (later of Gardiner's Island, New York). The original patents that granted rights to settle this land were given by King James I to the Earl of Warwick, who then formed a syndicate to colonize his holdings. The heads of the syndicate were viscounts Saye and Sele and Lord Brooks; it is from these men that the name of the town was taken. The first submarine ever used in combat was built in Old Saybrook in 1775 by the inventor David Bushnell. It was a wooden craft whose lone occupant turned the propeller by hand.

Today Old Saybrook is a town of 9,200 people. The area has fine boating in both the Connecticut River and the Long Island Sound, and there are several marinas and a *Town Beach*. The annual *Outdoor Art Show* is held the last weekend in July. The *Old Saybrook Historical Society* maintains a small museum.

CASTLE INN AT CORNFIELD POINT

Hartland Drive, Old Saybrook, CT 06475. 203-388-4681. *Innkeepers*: David Garfield, Ron MacDaniel, and Fred Lucia. Open all year.

The Castle Inn, a 38-room stone mansion, is situated on a cliff overlooking the Long Island Sound. Built at the turn of the century as a private residence, the inn was recently purchased by Garfield, MacDaniel, and Lucia. They have launched a major renovation project, and the building is now well on its way to recapturing its former

elegance. The big public rooms are wainscoted, and stained-glass windows have been added to the lounges and dining room. The main rooms are furnished with Victorian antiques. The fifteen guest rooms (all with private baths) have been redecorated with wall-to-wall carpeting, and most have antique furnishings. The second- and third-floor rooms offer a scenic view of the water. The mansion is constructed of massive beach-stone walls, with some exposed in the dining room. The menu features local seafood, beef, and a variety of coffees, including Jamaican, Irish, French, and Italian espresso. The restaurant is open to the public for lunch and dinner and serves a Sunday buffet brunch from 11:00 A.M. to 2:30 P.M.

A 70-foot pool is available for guests' use in summer. Within walking distance are two beaches, tennis courts, a golf course, and boating facilities. Pets are not permitted. *Room Rates*: Double rooms upstairs are $29.95; rooms downstairs are $24.60. Continental breakfasts are included in the room cost. *Driving Instructions*: Take Saybrook's Main Street to Maple Avenue, then turn right and continue to stop sign. Take a left to the first right turn, and follow the road to the inn.

Ridgefield, Connecticut

Settled in 1709, Ridgefield is a charming colonial town. Old houses line the tree-shaded Main Street. *Keeler Tavern*, also known as the Cannon Ball House because of a ball still buried in a corner post, is located on Main Street. The tavern, which has a fine collection of antique furnishings, sells jams, preserves, and craft items in its shop. Also on Main Street is the *Aldrich Museum of Contemporary Art*, with its sculpture garden. Ridgefield has an annual Antique Car Rally and Show in September.

STONEHENGE
Route 7, Ridgefield, CT 06877. 203-438-6511. *Innkeepers*: David Davis and Douglas Seville. Open all year.
Stonehenge is a large white brick and fieldstone farmhouse that was built in 1832. Swans, Canadian geese, and mallards glide on the lily-covered trout pond. The inn is surrounded by 10 acres of lawns and big shade trees. There are two large guest rooms with fireplaces in

the farmhouse and six rooms in the shady annex; all are furnished with antiques.

Known for its splendid cuisine, Stonehenge serves unusual food at breakfast, lunch, and dinner. Appetizers include its own smoked sausage with mustard wine sauce, smoked trout, and shrimp in beer batter with a pungent fruit sauce. Main course specialties include fresh brook trout, roast rack of lamb, pheasant and venison in season, and (given five days notice) roast suckling pig. A weekend at Stonehenge, only 1¼ hours from New York City, is a quiet, restful way to enjoy haute cuisine. No pets permitted. *Room Rates*: Rooms are $35 to $45. Reservations are required. *Driving Instructions*: The inn is off Route 7 in Ridgefield.

WEST LANE INN

22 West Lane, Ridgefield, CT 06877. 203-438-7323. *Innkeeper*: Maureen M. Mayer. Open all year.

The West Lane is one of Connecticut's newest old inns. The original building was constructed in the early 1800s as the home of one of the wealthy landowners of that era. It has an impressive columned porch running along the entire front with a central bow window on the second floor. The inn is set behind a broad lawn and flowering shrubs framed by a stand of majestic old maples. Inside, the tone is of quiet elegance, with rich oak paneling, deep-pile carpeting, and a cheerful crackling fire on the hearth in the lobby. Off the lobby on one side is a breakfast room, and on the other side is the office. There are fourteen oversized guestrooms that have either one king-size or two queen-size beds, as well as private bath, climate controls, color television, and radio. Some of the rooms have working fireplaces, and some baths have continental bidets.

The elegant dining room features public luncheon and dinner but breakfast for guests only. The evening menu is prix fixe at $18.25. Although this is considerably more expensive than many inn menus, the charge gives the diner a choice from an extensive range of Continental dishes. Appetizers include terrine of game with Cumberland sauce, Westphalian ham with fresh figs, chilled mussels in mustard sauce and herring salad Goeteborg, among a total of nine choices. There is a daily hot or cold soup course and then a choice of seven entrées that include frogs legs sautéed with mushrooms, medallions of veal, duckling à l'orange, lobster and sweetbreads, and on Saturdays only, Beef Wellington with Bordelaise sauce. Dinner is concluded with a choice of dessert served from a wagon or from among several ice cream and custard dishes, as well as tea or coffee. For those who do not wish such a large meal, there is an à la carte menu that includes all the dishes mentioned and a number of other offerings. The luncheon menu is almost as large. It offers several cold dishes, including steak tartare, that range in price from $2.50 to $9.75. Pets are not permitted. *Room Rates*: Rates are $40 single or $50 to $60 double. *Driving Instructions*: Take Route 35 (West Lane Road) to about a mile west of the center of the village of Ridgefield.

Salisbury, Connecticut

Salisbury, a small village in the far northwestern corner of Connecticut, is a most attractive place to explore. Nearby are *Mount Riga State Park* and the northernmost part of the *Housatonic State Forest*. Salisbury is a short drive from the Massachusetts Berkshires, with their skiing and points of historical interest.

WHITE HART INN
Junction of routes 41 and 44, Salisbury, CT 06068. 203-435-2511.
Innkeeper: John D. Harney. Open all year.
Located on the village green in Salisbury, the White Hart Inn was built in 1800 as a private residence but has been in continuous service as a hostelry since 1867. The inn is actually a three-building complex consisting of the original 1800 building, an adjacent annex that was also built as a residence and at one time served as a private girls'

school, and a more modern seven-room motor court–type building next to the inn. Guests therefore have a choice of accommodations in several styles. All rooms are comfortable and have private baths and telephones. Ten of the inn's rooms are air conditioned.

The inn employs an Oriental chef, so the menu offers an interesting combination of Oriental, continental, and American cuisine. Among the many dishes are Buddha's ten-ingredient vegetables, sliced pork with oyster sauce, mixed meats in hot spicy sauce, shrimp with cashews, tea-smoked-flavor duckling, rainbow trout Bretonne, tournedos of beef Bordelaise, and broiled filet mignon. These are only a small sample of the thirty-two different entrees available, which are priced from $5.95 to $9.95. Pets are permitted.

The inn maintains an old-fashioned country store within the main building, complete with potbelly stove and bayberry candles. Also available for sale are old lamps, maple sugar, cheddar cheese, and more. *Room Rates*: All rooms are European Plan. In the inn and annex, single rooms are $16 to $20; double rooms are $18.50 to $24.50. Motel rooms are $2 to $4 additional. Reservations are required on weekends. *Driving Instructions*: The inn is located on the village green at the junction of routes 44 and 41.

Stonington, Connecticut

Stonington is a lovely seacoast town noted for its abundance of small shops and tiny restaurants, many with the accent on Portuguese cooking. *Whitehall* is a country mansion restored and furnished with antiques by the Stonington Historical Society. The *Old Lighthouse Museum* of whaling gear, tools, firearms, and early stoneware is housed in the oldest lighthouse in the state. Nearby, in the village of Mystic, are two of Connecticut's most famous tourist attractions—*Mystic Seaport* and the *Mystic Marinelife Aquarium*. Reserve a full day to see them both.

PENTAWAY BED AND BREAKFAST
Al Harvey Road, RFD 2, Box 57, Stonington, CT 06378. 203-535-3333. *Innkeeper*: Helena Farrell. Open all year.
Pentaway is a 200-year-old, shingled ten-room colonial home set on 2 acres of stone-walled lawns surrounded by 8 acres of woods in

Stonington, and our candidate for the most beautiful village in Connecticut. The name of the inn means "cowpath" and refers to the time when the land was part of a working farm. Since then, the place has been attacked by Indians, been operated as a speakeasy, and served as the home of an apothecary who carved his initials and "Rx" on the wooden front door. Guests have private parking and entrance, a sitting room with television and a fireplace, a breakfast room with a fireplace, and the use of the swimming pool and a pool house with its own kitchenette. Furnishings throughout Pentaway are a combination of antique and contemporary, with house plants abounding. Bedrooms have old-fashioned tiny-print wallpapers, and rocking chairs. Two guest rooms have a private bath, and two share a bath. One bedroom has its own fireplace. The one meal served is breakfast, for the guests only, and it often features blueberry pancakes and French toast. Pets are not permitted. *Room Rates*: Rates during the peak tourist season are $30 to $35 per room, double occupancy, including breakfast. Off season, rooms are $5 less. *Driving Instructions*: Take the North Main Street–Stonington exit off Route I-95. Follow the Pequot Trail toward Old Mystic and cross the highway. Al Harvey Road is to the immediate right; Pentaway is the first house on the left.

Woodbury, Connecticut

Woodbury is a lovely old New England town with a large number of houses that predate 1750 and that have been restored to their original state. Among several points of interest is the *Glebe House*, birthplace of the American Episcopacy and site of Samuel Seabury's election as the first bishop of the Episcopal Church in America. Part of this building has been restored to represent a home of the period in which it was built (1740), and part is a church museum. Also in Woodbury is the *Flanders Nature Center*, an 830-acre sanctuary with walking trails and special environmental displays. The town has a number of excellent antique shops. It is a short drive from another New England village, Litchfield (described earlier).

THE CURTIS HOUSE
506 Main Street, South Woodbury, CT 06798. 203-263-2101.

Innkeeper: Garwin Hardisty. Open all year. Restaurant is closed Christmas Day only.

The Curtis House first opened its doors in 1754, and has been in continuous operation ever since. It is reputed to be the oldest inn in the state. The main house has eight rooms with private baths and fourposter canopied beds. Six other rooms share a common bath, and are furnished with period antiques "wherever practical." On wintry evenings, cheery fireplaces blaze in the public room.

The dining room is open to the public. It serves lunch and dinner featuring a large seafood selection and a flaky chicken pot pie. In the mornings, coffee, toast, and juice are served to guests.

For a vacation or a weekend stay, such activities as swimming, boating, and horseback riding are available nearby. The town of Woodbury also has some thirty antique shops for browsing or buying. No pets permitted. *Room Rates*: Without private bath, single rooms are $8; double rooms are $12. With private bath, singles are $12 to $15; doubles are $18 to $20. Tax is additional. Reservations are recommended. *Driving Instructions*: Take Route 6 to South Woodbury.

Massachusetts

MASSACHUSETTS is no stranger to exploration. Probably visited by Norsemen in the year 1000, it was certainly visited by John Cabot in 1497 and 1498. He and all early navigators were drawn to this area because of the abundance of cod off its shores. This gave the ships a welcome chance to refill their stores before continuing their way along the coastline. So grateful for the cod was Bartholomew Gosnold, the coastal explorer, that he named the now famous Cape for it. The first settlers here were, of course, the Pilgrims, who had been compelled to leave their homes in England to seek religious freedom. After landing in Provincetown in 1620, they wrote the Mayflower Compact, a model for part of the Constitution when it was written many years later.

Although the early years of the Massachusetts Bay Colony were characterized by peaceful relationships with the mother land, the strain developed soon and reached a pinnacle by the early 1760s, when a series of repressive trade and taxation acts inflamed residents of the colony. In 1770, British soldiers fired on a crowd of angry citizens, further inflaming the Massachusetts residents. The Tea Act of 1773, which followed the earlier Stamp and Sugar Acts, was virtually the last straw. Just two years later, the "shot heard round the world" was fired at Lexington and Concord, and the American Revolution had begun. In 1780, the constitution of the Commonwealth of Massachusetts was drawn up and ratified. It is the oldest constitution still in use today. The name Massachusetts, incidentally, was taken from the Algonquin tribe living to the south of Boston.

Massachusetts is divided into several sections, each of which has a special appeal to tourists. In the western part of the state are the Berkshires with their summer music festivals and winter sports cen-

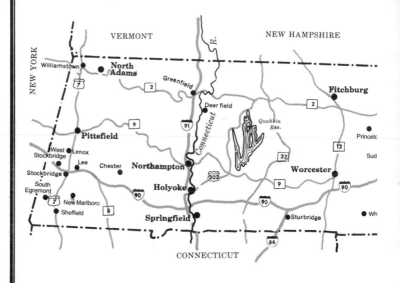

MASSACHUSETTS

Scale in miles

Primary roads

Secondary roads

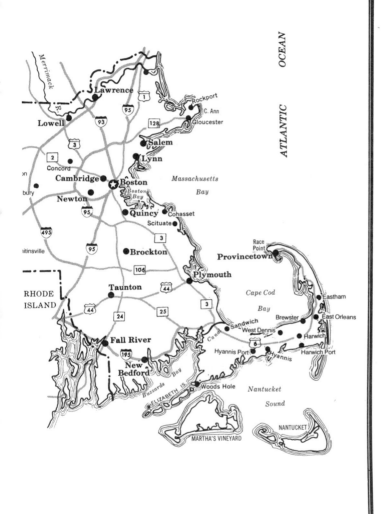

ters. The central part ranges from Amherst, with its colleges, to Worcester, the state's second largest city. The eastern portion is dominated by Boston and its suburbs but remains remarkably rural within a short drive of the Hub, as Boston is known locally. Cape Cod is probably the best-known vacation spot in the East.

To help you plan your vacation, we recommend that you contact the Massachusetts Department of Commerce and Development, 100 Cambridge Street, Boston, MA 02202. Its telephone number is 617-727-3205. Its staff will be glad to send you their vacation planner. Chambers of commerce in particular areas can also be helpful.

WESTERN

The Berkshires (including Lee, Lenox, New Marlboro, South Egremont, Stockbridge, and environs)

The Berkshires make up a mountain-and-lake region of extraordinary beauty and variety. The Maine-to-Georgia *Appalachian Trail* runs the length of Berkshire County, with miles of cross-country hiking and skiing trails.

In the mid-nineteenth century, gentlemen from New York and Boston began buying up Berkshire farms, and by the 1880s nearly a hundred fabulous mansions had been built in and around Lenox, the "inland Newport." The quiet, rural places attracted many artistic men and women throughout the years. Nathaniel Hawthorne and Edith Wharton came to Lenox, and Mark Twain and Herman Melville came to the surrounding area. Norman Rockwell lived and painted in Stockbridge. His work can be seen at the *Old Corner House. Tanglewood*, where Hawthorne wrote, is the summer home of the *Boston Symphony Orchestra* and the *Berkshire Music Festival*. Ted Shawn's *Jacob's Pillow*, site of the foremost dance festival in the world, is located in Lee. *Hancock Shaker Village*, a restored Shaker settlement dating from 1790, lies north of Stockbridge and just west of Pittsfield. The area abounds with wildlife sanctuaries, theaters, playhouses, museums, and historic houses.

In the fall, the Berkshires are ablaze with autumn foliage. Soon to follow are the snow and its accompanying skiers. There are several ski areas, all within an easy drive from the villages. Most of the large ones have snow-making facilities.

For nonskiers, there are hills and lakes for sledding, ice-fishing, skating, and snowshoeing. Weekends in winter are great for sports participants and spectators alike. The Berkshire Vacation Bureau has brought together many different winter events staged annually by the resorts and local organizations into one enormous *Berkshire Winter Carnival*. The events are held in January and early February, mostly on weekends.

For antiquers and sightseers, there are many antique shows, fairs, and festivals throughout the summer and fall. One of the biggest is the *Berkshire Craft Fair*, held in Great Barrington in August. A wide selection of antique and craft shops can be found in the Berkshire villages and along the winding back roads.

Deerfield, Massachusetts

Deerfield is a designated national historical site. Settled three hundred years ago, it was, for a while, the farthest outpost of New England's frontier. The settlement was twice devastated by Indian raids, once by the Bloody Brook Massacre of 1675, and again, in the French and Indian Wars, by the Deerfield Massacre of 1704. The town was re-settled and became an agricultural center in western Massachusetts. The past was not forgotten, and in 1952, Mr. and Mrs. Henry N. Flynt founded *Historic Deerfield* on mile-long Old Deerfield Street. Historic Deerfield, Inc., maintains eleven old houses, a research library, and an active education program focused on the arts in early America, the culture of the Connecticut Valley, and Historic Deerfield itself. The town is the home of the Eaglebrook School, the Bement School, and Deerfield Academy, a boys' preparatory school built around the village green and founded in 1797.

DEERFIELD INN

Main Street, Deerfield, MA 01342. 413-774-3147. *Innkeeper*: Jerry Jacobsen. Open all year, except for three days at Christmas.

Open the front door to the Deerfield Inn and you are likely to be greeted by the cheering aroma of freshly baked pies and cakes. You are welcome to enjoy afternoon tea while a guest at the inn, and this is a good time to explore its public rooms. The inn was built in 1884 and now stands at the mid-point of historic Old Deerfield Street. Many of the street's houses and buildings are owned and maintained as museums by Historic Deerfield, Inc. The inn, with its two-story, white-columned porch, is shaded by large trees. It is decorated with antiques, and portraits of stern ancestors peer down from the walls. The fourteen guest rooms have private baths, starched white curtains, and flowered wallpaper. The dining room serves three meals daily, as well as afternoon tea. The room is filled with Hepplewhite and Chippendale furniture and set off by a crystal chandelier. The menu includes veal à la Oscar, trout, individual rack of lamb, and prime ribs. Pies are turned out in almost every imaginable variety, and the inn's cheesecake is a tradition. Entrées, including salad and vegetable, run from about $7 to $13, with appetizer and dessert extra. There is a popular dinner buffet Thursday evenings, and brunch is served Sunday mornings. No pets permitted. *Room Rates*: Single rooms are $28 to $30; double rooms are $30 to $32. *Driving Instructions*: Take routes 5 and 10 (the same road) to Deerfield.

Greenfield, Massachusetts

Greenfield is a neighbor of Old Deerfield. Several rivers join the big, meandering Connecticut near Greenfield. It is an area of rivers, mountains, and many state parks and forests. In the summer there are concerts at *Shattuck Park*. The *Mount Mohawk Ski Area* has, in addition to alpine skiing, indoor ice-skating.

RITE VIEW FARM
493 Leyden Road, Greenfield, MA 01301. 413-773-8884. *Innkeeper*: Mrs. Ida Wright. Open all year.
Rite View is a real working dairy farm where the milk is pumped fresh from the cow to the bulk tank. The nineteenth-century farmhouse is situated on 230 acres of rolling fields, pine groves, and woodlands, all ideal for some peaceful hikes. Guests enjoy Mrs. Wright's up-country fare served family style in the kitchen. Three bright guest rooms overlook the fields of corn and hay in summer and the snowy vistas in winter. Most summer and winter activities

are available within an easy 5- to 10-mile drive from the farm. No pets permitted. *Room Rates*: Including two meals, for adults, $17 per day; for children, $12 per day. *Driving Instructions*: The farm is 3 miles north of Greenfield. Take Main Street to Conway Street to Leyden Road.

Lee, Massachusetts (see The Berkshires)

MORGAN HOUSE
   33 Main Street, Lee, MA 01238. 413-243-0181. *Innkeeper*: Tony
   Ferrell. Open all year.

The Morgan House, built in 1817 as a private residence, was converted to a stagecoach inn in 1853. Early guests included Buffalo Bill, Robert E. Lee, and President Ulysses S. Grant. In 1974, Mrs. Nat King Cole bought the Morgan House and restored it to its original charm. The inn has seven guest rooms, each furnished with Victorian beds, quilts, and rockers, and decorated with flowered wallpaper. The dining room features such up-country fare as Yankee pot roast and Irish lamb stew. Meals are served family style. A glassed-in sun porch off the bar is open year-round.

   Nearby Tanglewood, ski areas, antique shops, and many theaters make this centrally located inn a convenient stop. No pets permitted. *Room Rates*: Double rooms are $27 July through October, $15 to $20 in the off season. Reservations are requested. *Driving Instructions*: Take Massachusetts Turnpike exit 2 (Lee), then Route 20 to Lee.

Lenox, Massachusetts (see The Berkshires)

GATEWAYS INN AND RESTAURANT

71 Walker Street, Lenox, MA 01240. 413-637-2532. *Innkeepers*: Gerhard and Lilliane Schmid. Inn and restaurant open all year. The Gateways is known both for its elegant and attractive rooms and for the superb continental cuisine of its chef-owner, Gerhard Schmid, winner of several gold medals at the 1968 and 1976 International Culinary Olympic Competition. The Gateways was the fabulous summer mansion of Henry Proctor of Proctor and Gamble, who built the "cottage" in 1912 in the heart of Lenox. The inn today has lost none of its magnificence; the rooms are colonial in style and are furnished attractively with antiques. There are seven working fireplaces in the dining rooms, sitting room, and bedrooms. The ten guest rooms all have private baths. A complimentary breakfast is served to guests. Dinner is available to the public as well as the guests and is definitely the highlight of any stay in Lenox. No pets please. *Room Rates*: Rates range from $28 to $70 for a double (EP), according to location, size, and time of year and week. *Driving Instructions*: Take Massachusetts Turnpike exit 2 (Lee). Follow Route 7 north through Lee and turn left onto Route 183 toward Lenox. The inn is in the center of town.

THE VILLAGE INN

16 Church Street, Lenox, MA 01240. 413-637-0020. *Innkeepers*: Richard and Marie Judd. Open all year.

The Village Inn is located in the center of historic Lenox, one mile from Tanglewood. Built in 1776, the inn has twenty-five guest rooms, all decorated in true colonial fashion with antique furnishings and wallpapers of that period. During the winter, open fireplaces add a glow of warmth and cheer to the lounges and the dining room. The wonderful concert organ in the front reception room is played for fortunate guests by Richard Judd, a professional organist turned innkeeper. Both the dining room and the pub below it are open to the public for breakfast and lunch. No dinners are served at the inn. The Judds prepare a variety of crepes, quiches, salads, and sandwiches. The pub, Poor Richard's Tavern, captures the atmosphere of Ben Franklin's time with its hand-hewn bar and big fireplace. No

pets please. *Room Rates*: From $17 to $29 at all times except: July and August at $29 to $47, and September and October at $25 to $35. *Driving Instructions*: From the west take Route 23 east to U.S. 7, then north on 7 to Lenox. From the east, take Massachusetts Turnpike exit 2, then U.S. 20 to Lenox.

WHEATLEIGH

West Hawthorne, Box 824, Lenox, MA 01240. 413-637-0610. *Innkeepers*: A. David Weisgal and Florence Brooks-Dunay. Open all year.

In the heart of the Berkshires, bordering a lake, and lawns and gardens, stands Wheatleigh, a sprawling Italian Palazzo. Patios, porticoes, and terraces surround the chateau, which is situated on a 22-acre estate. The centerpiece is Wheatleigh, built in 1893 by industrialist H. H. Cook as a wedding present for his daughter, who married Count de Heredia. The multimillionaire New Yorker is reputed to have paid $1 million for the mansion. About 150 Italian artisans were said to have been imported to carve the mantels, ceilings, and walls. Wheatleigh combines the beauty of a European hotel with the comfort and elegance of an Edwardian-American home. The public rooms at Wheatleigh include a Great Hall with original Tiffany windows and a winding staircase as well as a library with a new bar. These rooms have carved fireplaces, as do many of the guest rooms. Some guest rooms have balconies with views of the lake and grounds; they are furnished with antique sofas and canopied beds, and have marble bathrooms. Breakfast is served to guests only, but the inn's dining room is open to the public for lunch and dinner.

Dinner at the Wheatleigh is a special event, with a most unusual menu that changes daily. Each nightly offering consists of a modest number of appetizers, entrées, and desserts, all of which show both inventiveness and care in preparation. Dinner recently started with a choice of spinach quiche, eggplant caviar, shrimp Arnaud, or mushroom bisque. Entrées included baked fish amandine, beef ragout in Bordeaux wine, Japanese tofu and broccoli, and steak au poivre. Thus, diners could choose between the more familiar steak or the delicate vegetarian offering of the tofu preparation. Desserts included the popular David's cheesecake and a number of other sweets, as well as Camembert. Prices are à la carte, with a complete indulgence ranging from $10.75 to $17.00 (for the shrimp-steak-cheesecake combination).

Music, theater, art, dance, sports, and antique shops all abound in the surrounding area. The Tanglewood Music Festival is within walking distance. Swimming and tennis are available on the grounds. To stay at the Wheatleigh is an unforgettable experience.

Pets not permitted, and the inn generally prefers not to have children. *Room Rates*: Winter rates are $80 per couple, per night, MAP, on weekends, and $45 per couple, per night, breakfast only included, on weekdays. Summer rates were not available. *Driving Instructions*: Starting in Stockbridge at the Red Lion Inn on Route 7, go up Prospect Hill Road, bearing left past Stockbridge Bowl and Music Inn up the hill 5 miles to the Wheatleigh entrance on the right.

New Marlboro, Massachusetts (see The Berkshires)

THE FLYING CLOUD INN
South Sandisfield Road, New Marlboro, MA. Mailing address: Box 143, Star Route, New Marlboro, MA 01230. 413-229-2113. *Innkeepers*: Diane and Bob Rolfs. Open December 20 through March 20, and May 5 through October 31.
The Flying Cloud, one of the most widely publicized inns in the

United States, has received rave reviews in many magazines, newspapers, and guidebooks. Despite its well-deserved acclaim, the inn remains a secluded colonial retreat in the heart of the Berkshires. All the rooms are furnished with antiques, and one features a 1790 four-poster bed with an antique log-cabin quilt. The main portion of the farmhouse was built by shipwrights in 1771 and sits in the middle of 200 acres of meadowlands.

The dining room features fresh vegetables from the organic garden, onion and cheese pies, roast barbecued lamb, fruit cake, crumbly apple pie, and home-baked breads and rolls. The inn also has an excellent wine selection. Dinners are served family style and only to inn guests (and their guests).

In the summer there are two tennis courts—one a very fine clay court—and swimming in the spring-fed pond. In winter, cross-country skiing, skating, and snowshoeing are available. The nearby Appalachian Trail can be hiked in any season. No pets please. *Room Rates*: Including two meals, gratuities, tennis in summer and cross-country skiing in winter, rates range from $40 to $50 per person, Friday through Sunday, and slightly less Monday through Thursday. *Driving Instructions*: Take Route 23 to Route 57. Go 7 miles on 57 to New Marlboro, then turn right onto South Sandisfield Road and go 3 miles to the Flying Cloud.

Sheffield, Massachusetts

In 1724, a group of Mohegan Indians sold a tract of their land for three barrels of cider, thirty quarts of rum, and $460. The new owners divided the land into two townships: Sheffield was part of the lower Housatonic township. The first white settler, Matthew Noble, arrived alone in 1725, and the first settlement in the Berkshires was on its way. Today Sheffield is one of the leading agricultural communities in Berkshire County. The town has many interesting old homes: The *Colonel John Ashley House*, built in 1735, is the oldest house in the county and a fine example of eighteenth-century architecture. Adjacent to the Ashley House is *Bartholomew's Cobble*, a National Landmark, a natural rock garden overlooking the Housatonic River. There is also a covered bridge over the river. The *Westenhook Gallery* on Route 7 is open during the summer months.

IVANHOE COUNTRY HOUSE

Route 41, Sheffield, MA 01257. 413-229-2143. *Innkeepers*: Mr. and Mrs. Richard Maghery. Open all year.

The Ivanhoe Country House was built in 1800 on the Appalachian Trail at the foot of a mountain. The inn is quiet and comfortable, with many antique furnishings. There are five guest rooms, one with a working fireplace and one with a complete kitchenette. A continental breakfast with cocoa and homemade blueberry muffins is provided. For other meals the Magherys recommend several nearby

restaurants and inns, including Stagecoach Hill in Sheffield and the Old Mill in South Egremont. There are 25 acres of grounds at Ivanhoe for all kinds of outdoor activities, including sledding in the winter. The surrounding area offers an enormous assortment of activities year-round for all interests, from antiquing and sightseeing to skiing and canoeing. *Room Rates*: Weekends and holidays, single rooms are $18 to $24; double rooms are $20 to $26; the room with kitchenette is $30. Weekdays, rooms are $4 less. All prices are EP. *Driving Instructions*: The inn is located 3½ miles south of Route 23, on Route 41.

STAGECOACH HILL INN

Route 41, Sheffield, MA 01257. 413-229-8585. *Innkeepers*: Ann and John Pedretti. Open all year; restaurant closed Wednesdays. The Stagecoach Hill Inn is a handsome brick building that was constructed in the early 1800s as a stagecoach stop. The public rooms of the inn are highly reminiscent of an old English inn. The dining room has red walls with lanterns, chintz curtains, portraits of the royal family, and old English hunting prints. The pub predates the rest of the inn and is a romantic, dark paneled room with a blazing fire in season. In keeping with the pub atmosphere, English beer is on tap. Dining at the inn features food carefully prepared by John and Ann, both fine cooks. The menu features fresh seafood, veal dishes, and steaks. Roast beef with Yorkshire pudding is available on Saturday evenings. Also popular are the traditional steak and kidney or steak and mushroom pies, as well as New England oyster pie.

Accommodations are currently offered in a large cottage known as "the poorhouse," which is located behind the inn. The name was derived from a less cheerful use of the building many years ago. Accommodations are also available in a series of chalets on the property. The owners plan to renovate a number of original rooms in the inn itself for overnight accommodations in the near future.

Butternut Basin and the *Catamount Ski Area* are just a few minutes away, and mountain climbing and cross-country skiing start at the doorstep. In the summer, Tanglewood and Jacob's Pillow are an easy drive away. Pets not permitted. *Room Rates*: Single rooms are from $22, double rooms are from $25. *Driving Instructions*: Take the Massachusetts Turnpike to the Lee exit, Route 7 to Great Barrington, then Route 41 South for 10 miles.

South Egremont (see The Berkshires)

THE EGREMONT INN

Old Sheffield Road, South Egremont, MA 01258. 413-528-2111.

Innkeepers: Robin and Rudyard Propst. Open all year.

The Egremont is another old stagecoach inn. The oldest section was constructed in 1780, and the living room was once the stables, reflecting a day when housing for the horses was as important as housing for the people using them. The huge fireplace was once a blacksmith's forge. The inn was greatly enlarged during the Victorian era. The main dining room was added after World War I and has a distinct 1920s feeling. A swimming pool and tennis courts are even more recent additions.

The inn is located on what was once part of the Albany–Boston Post Road system, and the grounds slope down to Goodale Brook. Across the road from the inn are two enormous buttonball trees planted in 1812 by Peter Goodale. The inn is just down the road from the site of Shay's Rebellion, one of the first taxpayer's revolts in history.

Although the inn is one of the area's oldest, it has been altered to incorporate certain twentieth-century conveniences, such as private baths for each of its twenty-three guest rooms and its two-bedroom suite. However, other modern conveniences, such as television or telephones in the rooms, have been omitted on purpose. Although there is air conditioning, it is unobtrusive. The bedrooms are old-

fashioned in appearance and very comfortable. The public rooms have fireplaces, and the broad porch contains rockers as well as tables for dining in warm weather. A ski-touring center at the inn has gently rolling wooded trails, as well as certified instruction; equipment rental is available. The inn serves three meals daily to guests and the public. Pets are not permitted, but children are welcome. *Room Rates*: Range from $35 to $48, double occupancy, EP. Less in some seasons. *Driving Instructions*: Take Route 23 directly to the inn in the center of South Egremont.

Stockbridge and West Stockbridge, Massachusetts (see The Berkshires)

THE RED LION INN

Main Street, Route 102, Stockbridge, MA 01262. 413-298-5545. *Innkeeper*: Betsy M. Holtzinger. Open all year.

The Red Lion is the grande dame of old colonial inns. First built in 1773 as a small tavern and stagecoach stop for vehicles serving the Albany, Hartford, and Boston runs, the inn was greatly enlarged in 1862. Although the Red Lion has had several owners, it was owned from the Civil War until the early 1960s by members of the Treadway family. Over the years, various modernizations have occurred without disturbing the basic charm of this long-term resident of the Berkshires. It should be noted, however, that this is not a small country inn; the Red Lion currently offers 103 rooms for overnight accommodation of its guests.

The inn has an extensive collection of antiques that grace its public rooms and greatly add to the feeling of the past. The tavern is paneled in old wood with the warm patina of age. There is a feeling of grandeur in both the dining room and the parlors with their Oriental rugs and grand pianos. In its long history, the inn has been host to five presidents of the United States. It is easy for the visitor today to see why.

All meals at the Red Lion are open to the public. Breakfasts are $3.00 to $5.50, and luncheons may be simple sandwich affairs for under $5.00 or more formal meals featuring meat, poultry, or fish and ranging from $3.50 to $6.00 with salad. Dinner at the Red Lion features twenty or so entrées, including such specialties as entrecote with herb butter, veal à la Oscar, stuffed pork chop, three different lobster dishes, or scallops in mushroom and wine sauce. There is also a modest list of appetizers and a good selection of desserts. A complete dinner with appetizer and dessert might range from $10 to $17. Pets are permitted for a daily surcharge of $7.50. Children are always welcome. *Room Rates*: Rates are seasonal and vary for double rooms from $34 to $55. *Driving Instructions*: Take exit 2 on Massachusetts Turnpike to Lee. Follow Route 102 to Stockbridge.

WILLIAMSVILLE INN

Route 41, West Stockbridge, MA 01266. 413-274-6580. *Innkeepers*: Lenora and Stuart Bowen. Open all year, except November until the day before Thanksgiving.

The Williamsville Inn is near the base of a 2,000-foot mountain. Christopher French built the old farmhouse in the late 1700s. He had lived 100 yards away on the Williams River, but the neighboring Indians were so noisy he was forced to move his family up the hill. Later, Mr. French deeded all but the front room, a room over it, and the cellar beneath to his son. He retained possession of his section of the house until his death. The Christopher French Room is now a favorite guest room.

Today the inn is a quiet home on ten landscaped acres with a swimming pool, tennis courts, a trout pond, and twelve guest rooms, all with private bath. The spacious rooms are furnished with antiques. There are eight working fireplaces, two in guest rooms. The candlelit dining room has a big fieldstone fireplace, adding a special glow on cool nights.

The Williamsville is well known for its French country cuisine prepared by innkeeper Lenora Bowen. An article by Andy Merton and Gail Kelley in *Boston Magazine* (October, 1977) described her as "a marvelous French chef. . . . her veal dishes are especially recommended. . . . flavors delicate and delightful. In fact we judged the food here the best on our trip, just topping LeJardin, Stafford's-in-the-Field and the Arlington Inn, all of which are worth a trip for the food alone." *Room Rates*: During July, August, October, and holidays the double rooms are $48, EP. Off season the rate drops to $34. *Driving Instructions*: The inn is 4 miles south of West Stockbridge. Take the Massachusetts Turnpike exit 1, turn left on Route 41.

CENTRAL AND EASTERN

Andover, Massachusetts

Andover is a town of lovely tree-shaded streets and lanes with expansive white colonial homes, little shops, and the 450-acre campus of Phillips Academy. The town of Andover was established in 1646 when settlers purchased the land from the local Indians for $30 and a coat. The Phillips Academy, founded in 1778, has many historic buildings on its campus; the *Robert S. Peabody Foundation for Archaeology* contains New England exhibits; the *Addison Gallery of American Art* traces American history with paintings, sculpture, and decorative crafts from colonial times to the present. There are many other historic sites in the town.

The area abounds in craft and antique shops; the North Andover Center has a great many thrift and antique shops in one place. Hiking, picnicking, bird watching, and star gazing are offered in the surrounding parks and forests. The *Harold Parker State Forest, Ward Reservation*, and the peaceful *Cochran Bird Sanctuary* are all in Andover. For winter sports, the *Boston Hills Ski Area* is 4 miles away.

ANDOVER INN

Chapel Avenue, Andover, MA 01810. 617-475-5903. *Innkeeper*: Henry Broekhoff. Open all year.

The Andover Inn is located on the campus of Phillips Academy with its ivy-covered buildings. Built in 1930, the white-columned brick structure contains thirty-three guest rooms. The recently redecorated inn blends warm woods and comfortable furnishings with modern conveniences. The many fireplaces in the public rooms add a warm glow to the inn's colonial atmosphere. There are also fireplaces in the two suites.

The Andover Inn's restaurant is open to the public for all meals. The menu is varied, with seafood, beef, and a continental selection of veal and game dishes. The special day is Sunday, when Chef Oudheusden features a rijsttafel, an Indonesian feast combining rice nasi with a large number of delicious side dishes, such as roast pork with peanut sauce, fruit in hot sauce, beef, shrimp, and fish in various sauces, and much more—an exciting meal. Small pets are permitted. *Room Rates*: Double occupancy with bath is $37, with shared bath, $29. *Driving Instructions*: Take Route 93 north to exit 15 (Route 125). Go 4 miles on Route 125 to Route 28 North. Andover Inn is on the right-hand side on the campus.

Concord, Massachusetts

The shot heard 'round the world was fired at *Old North Bridge* here. The area abounds in Revolutionary War historical sites, as well as houses occupied by such literary lights as Nathaniel Hawthorne, Louisa May Alcott, and Ralph Waldo Emerson. *Thoreau's Cabin* is, however, a replica. The *Concord Antiquarian Museum*, with Paul

Revere's famous lantern and much more, is another popular stop for tourists. *The Wayside*, home of Hawthorne, Margaret Sydney, and the Alcotts, is open to visitors. There are a number of interesting antique and crafts shops in the area, including the *Sneak Box Studio*, where Charles Murphy may be seen carving his famous decoys.

THE HAWTHORNE INN

462 Lexington Road, Concord, MA 01742. 617-369-5610. *Innkeeper*: Gregory Burch. Open all year.

The Hawthorne Inn was built in 1870 across the street from a home once occupied by Nathaniel Hawthorne. The famed New England writer planted a number of pines, two of which survive today on the old path to the mill brook beside the Hawthorne Inn.

The Hawthorne, originally a private home, was converted to a small inn in 1976 by Gregory Burch, and it now offers five guest rooms, all with shared baths. The rooms have been carefully restored and decorated with antique furniture, beautiful handmade quilts, and some of the innkeeper's paintings and other art. Burch has inserted wonderful leaded-glass transoms over the doorways, and he has sanded and finished all the floors. The inn is presided over by a handsome striped cat, Ratface. The complimentary breakfasts include a selection of freshly baked breads and wild-berry turnovers. *Room Rates*: Single rooms are $18, doubles are $25, including breakfast. *Driving Instructions*: The inn is three-quarters of a mile east of the town center on Lexington Road, across from the Nathaniel Hawthorne House, Wayside.

Princeton, Massachusetts

At the turn of the century Princeton was a resort town in the Wachusett Mountains. The old inns are almost all gone now, but the lovely common and the handsome old summer homes remain. From the summit of Mount Wachusett 2,006 feet up, there is a spectacular view of the surrounding countryside. The *Wachusett State Park* offers horse trails, picnic sites, hiking, skiing, and recreational vehicle trails. *Mount Wachusett Ski Area* is off Routes 2 and 140. The Massachusetts Audubon Society maintains the *Wachusett Meadows Wildlife Sanctuary*.

THE INN AT PRINCETON

Mountain Road, Princeton, MA 01541. 617-464-2030. *Innkeepers*: Elizabeth Sjogren and Suzanne Reed. Open all year, except January and February.

Built in the early 1890s, the twenty-three-room Inn at Princeton was originally the country summer home of Charles Washburne, founder of American Steel and Wire. The old mansion is situated on 12 acres of mountainous woodlands with a view of the Boston skyline. The five spacious guest rooms are each attractively decorated with Victorian pieces in keeping with the inn, which has been painstakingly restored by Elizabeth and Suzanne and furnished with a blend of turn-of-the-century antiques and modern decor. One enters the building through an enormous front door, nearly 5 feet wide and 8 feet high. There are four downstairs fireplaces, including a beauty in the hall. Off the center hallway is a living room and two dining rooms.

The Inn at Princeton is known for its country-classical cuisine and

features such specialties as paupiettes de veau, duckling à la Montmorency, veau sauté aux morilles, and deliciously rich desserts. Dinners are available to the public on Wednesdays through Saturdays, reservations necessary. No pets or children. *Room Rates*: Rooms are $35 to $45. *Driving Instructions*: Follow Route 31 from Holden to Princeton. In town take the Mountain Road up to the inn.

Rockport, Massachusetts

First settled in 1640, Rockport is a harbor town north of Gloucester on the Massachusetts coastline. The village has long been a thriving artists' colony, rivaling Provincetown on Cape Cod. There is a very active, tourist-oriented shopping area that is a collection of historic fishing shacks and more substantial buildings located on a tiny spit of land and breakwater known as Bearskin Neck. Here the shopper can browse in many craft and art galleries as well as a country store and a number of small restaurants and seafood stores. The famous fishing shack "Motif No. 1," a favorite of painters, was, sadly, washed away by the surf during the cruel winter of 1978. In the village itself is the *Rockport Art Association*, with its gallery of graphics, painting, and sculpture all contained in the Old Tavern Building. *The Sandy Bay Historical Society and Museum* has exhibits covering mineralogy, Indian Artifacts, quarrying artifacts, and marine life, among others.

OLD FARM INN

291 Granite Street, Rockport, MA. Mailing address: Box 590, Rockport, MA 01966. 617-546-3237. *Innkeepers*: The Balzarini family. Open April through mid-November.

The Old Farm Inn is situated between Halibut Point and Folly Cove on the northernmost tip of Cape Ann. The date of the farmhouse is estimated to be 1799, but a house has been on the site since 1705. In the early 1900s, Antone Balzarini, an immigrant from Italy, rented the farm and raised dairy cows and twelve children there. The family later moved down the road. In 1964, one of Antone's sons, John, and his family bought the old place. The Balzarinis restored the farmhouse and furnished it with antiques, including the much-used big black iron stove. They added on a dining room overlooking a meadow where ponies graze and an outdoor terrace, and converted the old barn into guest rooms. The dining room has beamed ceilings, open hearths, and floor-to-ceiling windows. The Old Farm Inn specializes in fresh locally caught seafood. For dessert there is Indian pudding baked in the iron stove, and Uncle Charlie's rum bread pudding. Rockport is a dry town, so bring your own spirits and the restaurant will provide setups.

Guests can enjoy the inn's 5 acres of lawns and meadows, with towering trees and abundant flowers, or hike along the winding coast road to downtown Rockport, one of New England's most charming seacoast towns. No pets permitted. *Room Rates*: July through September, rooms are $20; off season, they are $16. Reservations are suggested, especially July through September. *Driving Instructions*: Route 128 to Gloucester, then follow signs to Rockport. Turn left at Railroad Avenue, follow sign to Pigeon Cove (about 2 miles).

THE RALPH WALDO EMERSON INN

1 Cathedral Avenue, Rockport, MA 01966. 617-546-6321. *Innkeeper*: Gary Wemyss. Open from Memorial Day to mid-October. The Emerson began life in 1806 as a tavern and was moved a half mile in 1840 (when the town went dry) to a location in a "better part of town" to get the carriage trade. In the 1850s, Emerson and other notables of the time summered here when it was known as the Pigeon Cove House. In 1870, it was moved to its current location on the ocean. The Wemyss family purchased and renovated the inn in 1964, renaming it for Ralph Waldo Emerson.

The Emerson is a thirty-six-room traditional nineteenth-century resort hotel furnished with antiques of the period. Overlooking the ocean are big terraces complete with wicker rockers and potted geraniums. The spacious grounds are perfect for croquet, horseshoes, badminton, or just strolling. There is also a heated salt-water swimming pool and saunas. The inn serves three meals a day to guests and the public in the summer months only. Rockport is still a dry town, so no liquor is served, but it is allowed in one's room. No pets please. *Room Rates*: Rooms are about $48 per day for two people, MAP, or $28 for two, EP. Before July and after Labor Day, rooms are available at slightly reduced rates. *Driving Instructions*: Take Route 128 to Route 127 and go 1½ miles north of downtown Rockport to the inn's sign on Phillips Avenue (on the right).

Scituate, Massachusetts

Scituate is a pretty, popular seacoast village on Boston's south shore. It has several important historical attractions, including *Cudworth House*, with its huge caldron and 250-year-old loom; the *Mann Farmhouse and Museum*, with its artifacts dating from the early 1600s; the *Stockbridge Mill*, a restored working gristmill; Lawson Tower; and Scituate Lighthouse. The *Scituate Arts Festival* is held in late July, and *Heritage Days* take place annually in mid-August, with clambakes, band concerts, pancake breakfasts, and more family-oriented events. The village offers numerous opportunities for swimming, fishing, boating, and tennis. Nearby Cohassett, Hingham, and Marshfield are equally popular with visitors.

INN FOR ALL SEASONS

32 Barker Road, Scituate, MA 02066. 617-545-6699. *Innkeeper*: Elaine Wondolowski. Open all year.

Currently situated in a quiet residential area of the village, the inn was originally built about two centuries ago as the barn for an English garrison. Although its fame has centered around its outstanding kitchen, the inn also offers seven guest rooms, each decorated with Victorian and other antiques. Each guest room shares a bath, and some have special touches, such as the veranda off the Red Room, the wicker furniture of the Wicker Room, the quilts and iron beds in the Patchwork Room. Public rooms include a Victorian parlor with its fireplace and three noted dining rooms. The menu is extremely well thought out and is noteworthy for its abundance of individually prepared items. Soups ($1.50) include French onion, clam stew, and a special of the day. Appetizers ($2.50 to $3.50) include mushrooms Sam Ward (served under glass with broiled ham, a crouton, and special sauce), pâté maison, quiche, escargots, and cheese Helene (french fried Gruyère served on fried parsley). There are eleven entrées ranging in price from $9.50 to $13.00, including an individual beef Wellington, a crab quiche Pompador, stuffed pork chops, chicken breast Duglere, and several other selections. Entrées include vegetables, bulgur, or potatoes, as well as salad. Desserts are $1 to $2, with no special surprises. *Room Rates*: Rooms are $27 to $34, double occupancy. *Driving Instructions*: Ask for a map when placing your reservations.

Sturbridge, Massachusetts

The town is most famous for *Old Sturbridge Village*, a re-created town of the 1790–1840 period. As they do the work of early New Englanders, costumed personnel talk with tourists. In addition to the actual working farm village, there are craft work, exhibit galleries, a visitors' center, and shops selling the craft products and period merchandise. *Wells State Park*, off Routes 20 and 49, offers swimming, boating, horseback riding, cross-country skiing, and other recreational activities.

PUBLICK HOUSE

On The Common, Sturbridge, Massachusetts 01566. 617-347-3313.
Innkeeper: Buddy Adler. Open all year.

The Publick House was built two hundred years ago to serve coach travelers on the colonial Post Road. The tavern and barn were constructed by Colonel Ebenezer Crafts, an officer who drilled his cavalry troops on the Common during the Revolutionary War. The inn, completely restored and expanded in 1937, is listed in the National Registry of Historic Places. An enormously popular place, then and now, the Publick House offers twenty-one guest rooms, each with the furniture and decor of the colonial period. Some of the rooms have beamed ceilings and wide plank flooring, and all have modern bathrooms and air conditioning. The Penthouse Suite has large rooms for either two couples or a family. It has beautiful fan windows in both rooms, with views of the Common and the inn's grounds. The original ballroom, with its dome ceiling, fireplace, and noticeably slanting floor, is used for private functions and as a lounge for guests wishing to watch the inn's television set.

The Colonel Ebenezer Crafts Inn is the Publick House's annex, built in 1786 on a hill beside the inn. The house was recently restored, and it retains the wonderfully charming atmosphere of its beginnings. Its rooms are furnished throughout with period antiques. The innkeepers, Patricia and Henri Bibeau, will gladly give guests a tour of the rooms. There is a complimentary breakfast of juice, freshly baked muffins, and coffee or tea, and in the afternoons there are complimentary candies, cookies, fresh fruits, and tea. Other meals are available at the Publick House down the hill. The Colonel Ebenezer Crafts Inn is a peaceful place, and we recommend that guests

wishing to be away from the bustle of the Publick House request rooms here.

Back at the Publick House, there are five dining rooms and two cocktail lounges to serve the many tourists who come to the historic inn and *Old Sturbridge Village*. These rooms are furnished with antiques and reproductions of the period. Three of the eight fireplaces in the public rooms are in use. Hearty yankee meals are offered in the dining rooms. Visitors may choose from a large menu including thick roast beef with onion popovers, roast Cornish game hen with wild rice stuffing, and baked lobster pie. For dessert, there are deep-dish apple pie with chunks of Vermont cheddar cheese, mince pie, and Indian pudding with a scoop of vanilla ice cream.

Holidays and winter weekends are very special here. Guests are treated to horse-drawn sleigh rides through the village, with hot buttered rum and roasted chestnuts by a roaring fire at the end of the ride. Wild-game dinners, including venison, mince pie, and apple pan dowdy top off the day. Arrangements should be made well in advance for these weekends, especially those of Thanksgiving and the twelve days of Christmas. The winter weekends continue from January through March. *Room Rates*: Rates vary according to season and time of week, but the range is from $28 to $36 double occupancy. *Driving Instructions*: Take the Massachusetts Turnpike to exit 9 or Route I-86 to exit 3. The Publick House is on The Common on Route 131.

Sudbury, Massachusetts

Sudbury was first settled in 1638 by a group of Englishmen and was primarily an agricultural village for many years. Today Sudbury is a suburban village about 20 miles west of Boston on the old Boston Post Road, now Route 20. Most famous as the home of Longfellow's Wayside Inn, the village boasts an enjoyable, picturesque *Wayside Country Store* with an old-fashioned nickelodeon. A short distance away in neighboring Southboro is one of our favorite country stores, the *Willow Brook Farm*, with its herd of buffalo and its store filled with old-fashioned and newer products, including a meat department that specializes in prime aged beef, buffalo meat, and a variety of game in season. This is an enjoyable stop for people of all ages. Neighboring Framingham is home of the *Garden in the Woods*, with its extensive collection of wildflowers. Historic Concord and Lexington are just 10 to 15 miles away.

LONGFELLOW'S WAYSIDE INN

Wayside Inn Road (off Route 20), Sudbury, MA 01776. 617-443-8846. *Innkeeper*: Francis Koppeis. Open every day except Christmas.

The Wayside Inn is a place of such beauty and history that words do not do it justice. The inn is a designated National Historic Site. To stay here is to stay at a great museum. It is the oldest inn in America. Originally the Red Horse Tavern, the name was changed following the publication of Longfellow's *Tales of a Wayside Inn*, which were based on his knowledge of the Red Horse. This inn was run by four generations of the Howe family for almost 200 years. It was purchased, along with 5,000 surrounding acres, in the 1920s by Henry Ford, who completely restored it and reproduced a water-powered gristmill that operates today grinding meal for the breads served at the inn. Ford later built a replica of a typical New England chapel nearby, and it is currently popular with members of every faith for weddings. In 1928, Ford purchased a one-room schoolhouse, which had been the real school of Mary and her little lamb in the early 1800s. He moved the school from its original site at Sterling, Massachusetts to its present location near the inn.

Built in stages, starting in 1702, the inn is an extraordinary collection of exposed timber rooms with original paneling and museum-

quality antiques. There is, refreshingly, no television or radio. The ten guest rooms, each different and special, have been modernized to give each a private bath. When you are here, it is hard to remember that the center of Boston is only twenty-five minutes away. The rural quality is made possible by the tract of surrounding land that Ford purchased to protect the inn. For the day visitor, the common rooms of the inn are open for inspection daily, although there is a very small fee to help support the museum. Shortly before his death, Ford deeded the entire property to the Wayside Inn Corporation.

The Wayside Inn restaurant is one of the most popular eating places in this area. House specialties include roast duckling, stuffed fillet of sole with lobster sauce, and deep-dish apple pie.

Pets are not permitted. *Room Rates*: Single rooms are $20; double rooms are $25. *Driving Instructions*: Take the Massachusetts Turnpike to Route 495, go north to Route 20 East; 8 miles to Wayside Inn (1 mile after the turn at Wayside Country Store). From the east, take Route 128 North to exit 49, go 11 miles west on Route 20.

Whitinsville, Massachusetts

Whitinsville, located in the Blackstone Valley, is an interesting example of an old mill town with mills and turn-of-the-century mill housing along the Blackstone River. Once the home of the Whitin Machine Works, the leading manufacturer of textile-mill machinery, Whitinsville has many large homes and mansions built by wealthy mill owners in the late 1800s. Massachusetts is in the process of constructing a $1 million state park along the Blackstone River in Whitinsville. It is hoped that it will be completed in 1979.

THE VICTORIAN

583 Linwood Ave., Whitinsville, MA 01588. 617-234-2500. *Innkeepers:* Martha and Orin Flint. Open all year.

The Victorian, a mansion on a 50-acre estate, was built in 1871 by a wealthy mill owner. The inn is perfectly preserved. The theft of $2 million of the estate's antiques so discouraged the previous owners, the Whitins, that the place was sold. Two graduate students, with no inn experience but with lots of ideas on how to run an inn and restaurant, bought the estate. Their ideas were apparently excellent: The rooms are lovely and the food delicious. The inn is a strikingly beautiful Victorian mansion, with walnut and mahogany woodwork set off by tasteful and luxurious wall-coverings. From the inn's fine etched Victorian glass doors to the several chandeliers to each drape, rug, and chair, the effect is elegant, formal, and delightful. The seven guest rooms are large and inviting, and four have characteristically roomy bathrooms furnished with modern fixtures. One room has a working fireplace, and three have king-size beds.

Dinner may be taken in any of three dining rooms, with menu selections showing a strong French influence. The list of appetizers changes daily but usually includes a quiche (perhaps shrimp or mushroom), one of several crepes, ceviche, onion soup, or escargots. There are always at least four such preliminary offerings and often as many as eight. Entrée specialties include frogs legs Provençal, oysters Florentine, fillet of sole stuffed with salmon mousse and coated with a cream and duxelle sauce, suprême de volaille, fricassee of rabbit,

and five or six other offerings, including lobster and prime ribs for
those who cannot stray from the tried and true. Salad is served after
the main course in the continental manner. Prices for the complete
meal range from $10 to $15. *Room Rates:* Rooms are $25 to $50.
Driving Instructions: Take Route 122 south of Worcester and turn
south on Linwood Avenue.

CAPE COD AND THE ISLANDS

The Cape, as it is always called by natives, has long been a vacation
favorite on account of its coastal villages and rural landscape, just a
short drive from the heart of Boston. It was discovered in 1602 by
the English explorer Bartholomew Gosnold, who first called the Cape
"Shoal Hope," but changed its name when his crew caught a particularly impressive load of codfish.

Visitors to the Cape will be treated to a host of attractions in the
many towns on this hook-shaped island separated from the mainland
by the Cape Cod Canal. There are, in fact, so many attractions that
visitors are urged to read with care the many entries in the three
companion books in the Compleat Traveler series. In addition, excellent travel information is available from the Cape Cod Chamber
of Commerce, Mid-Cape Highway, Hyannis, MA 02601. Summer
visitors who plan to spend any appreciable amount of time on the
Cape should investigate the incredibly complete guidebook *The
Family Guide to Cape Cod* by Bernice Chesler and Evelyn Kaye
(Barre Publishing, Barre, Mass., 1976). This is one of the finest and
most comprehensive guides to a geographical region available today
and is most helpful to those who wish to see the Cape in detail.

Discussions of special attractions on the Cape are included in the
town descriptions preceding each inn listed here. The attractions
listed here fell outside those town limits but are some of the high-
lights of any visit to the Cape. As a matter of orientation: The Cape
has three main roads running for part or all of its length. These are
Route 6 (the Mid-Cape Highway), Route 6A on the north shore, and
Route 28 on the south shore. Visitors who prefer a quieter tour of
the Cape will be happier following the last two routes.

For a number of years it appeared that the Cape's frail environment would succumb to the tremendous inroads of tourism. To a

degree, this has happened and is likely to continue. However, in 1961 the federal government established the *Cape Cod National Seashore*, which now controls over 25,000 acres of prime shoreline. In addition to the visitors center mentioned in the section on Eastham, there is the Province Lands Visitors Center in Provincetown, where tourists can get maps and descriptive literature.

In Bourne there is the *Aptuxet Trading Post*, which is a replica of the first trading post, built in 1627 by Plimouth Plantation. Brewster is the home of the *Cape Cod Museum*, with its excellent exhibits in the area of natural history. There is also the *Drummer Boy Museum*, a guided tour of twenty-one historical life-size paintings of the American Revolution. Brewster is also the home of the *New England Fire History Museum*, which contains a fine collection of antique fire engines. The *Chatham Railroad Museum* is a hit with railroad buffs, and the *Old Windmill* in Chatham is still in operation. Falmouth, birthplace of Katherine Lee Bates, who wrote "America the Beautiful," has the *Falmouth Historical Society* museums, which maintain exhibits of paintings and whaling memorabilia. At Woods Hole are three oceanographic institutions that are open to the public at various times. Hyannis, the summer home of President and Mrs. John F. Kennedy, has a memorial to the late president—a 12-foot stone wall bearing the presidential seal and offering a peaceful view of the surrounding harbor. At Mashpee there is the *Wampanoag Indian Museum* and the *Old Indian Meeting House* at the Indian Cemetery.

Sandwich is the home of *Heritage Plantation of Sandwich*, a 76-acre display of Americana housed in replicas of American buildings. In addition to the general exhibits, there is an antique auto museum, a military museum, and a museum of the arts and crafts. The *Sandwich Glass Museum* chronicles the production of the now famous glass factory from 1825 to 1888. An extensive doll museum is housed at the *Yesteryears Museum*, also in Sandwich. South Wellfleet was the site of the first wireless station in America and of the first transatlantic wireless message, sent by Marconi in 1903. The *Wellfleet Bay Wildlife Sanctuary* has several hiking trails. The *Aquarium of Cape Cod* at West Yarmouth has the usual array of trained animals performing in the water, to the delight of young and old. Also in Yarmouth are two historic houses open to the public—*Thatcher House* and *Winslow-Crocker House*, next door.

Brewster, Massachusetts

Brewster is located on the north coast of Cape Cod on the Cape Cod Bay with its calm, warm waters. (For swimming, it is recommended that one wait until afternoon for the warmest water.) Brewster is noted for its cemeteries, among other things. The *First Parish Church* is the site of the graves of sea captains and early settlers. There are also a great many museums and other historical sites. The *Cape Cod Museum of Natural History* has nature trails, live animals indigenous to the Cape, and many interesting exhibits and lectures. Another wonderful nature trail is the *Wing's Island Trail,* a walk through the marshes to Wing Island—a peninsula on the bay. *Nickerson State Park* has forests, inland fresh water lakes, and trout-stocked ponds. The area offers all manner of outdoor sports available to the public.

INN OF THE GOLDEN OX

Old King's Highway (Route 6A), Brewster, Cape Cod, MA 02631. Mailing Address: 1360 Main Street, RD 1, Brewster, MA 02631. 617-896-3111. *Innkeeper:* Charles Evans. Open all year. The restaurant is closed Mondays in summer and open only on weekends in winter; call to check first.

Overlooking Cape Cod Bay sit the Inn of the Golden Ox. Originally the home of the First Universalist Church of Brewster, the building was constructed in 1828. The inn has four guest rooms sharing two baths. The rooms all have the charm and quiet of an Old World inn, as does the restaurant. All rooms in the Golden Ox are furnished with antiques. The restaurant menu is made up exclusively of gour-

met German dishes. A typical meal might begin with either shrimp and dill or marinated lentils as an appetizer followed by *Kassler Rippchen* (smoked loin pork chops), sauerbraten with potato dumpling, and red cabbage in red wine sauce, or a choice of one of six schnitzels (veal cutlet from milk-fed veal). Our favorite is Zigeuner schnitzel (made with piquant paprika, mushrooms, and sour cream). Old family recipes are used for the dessert—*Sacher Torte mit Schlag*, *Apfelküchen mit Schlag*, and creamy cheese cake. The Golden Ox is a delightful place to enjoy some good food and restful accommodations. No pets. *Room Rates:* Memorial Day through Labor Day, rooms are $18 plus tax; off season, $15 plus tax. Reservations are requested. *Driving Instructions:* Take the Mid-Cape Highway (Route 6) to exit 9, go north to Route 6A, turn right on 6A.

East Orleans, Massachusetts
(including Orleans, South Orleans, and environs)

Orleans was settled in 1693 as a part of Eastham, although the area had many distinguished visitors before then. Leif Erikson is rumored to have landed at Orleans more than nine hundred years ago; Captain Bartholomew Gosnold, who named Cape Cod, anchored here in 1602; and Captain John Smith came ashore here in 1614. The French Cable Museum, built in 1890, once housed the transatlantic cable equipment that linked New York City and France. The cables no longer operate, but they once carried the news of the sinking of the Lusitania and of Lindbergh's landing in Paris. The area has many antique and craft shops. The *Cape Cod Antiques Exposition* is held at the Nauset Regional Middle School in Orleans, usually on the first weekend in August. On *Nauset Beach* the shore and dunes rise to meet orchards and moors. *National Seashore* stretches from Orleans to Provincetown, and the *National Audubon Society* maintains a bird sanctuary in East Orleans.

NAUSET HOUSE INN

Box 446, Beach Road, East Orleans, Cape Cod, MA 02643. 617-255-2195. *Innkeepers:* Lucille and Jack Swartz. Open from April 1 through November 15.

The Nauset House, built around 1800, is an old Cape Cod farmhouse. This small country inn is furnished with antiques and family memorabilia. On cooler evenings the three fireplaces add their warmth to the homey atmosphere. There is an afternoon cocktail hour in the dining room, so that guests can get to know one another. The dining room is reminiscent of an old English pub, with a large fireplace and bar where the inn provides setups and ice for the guests (bring your own spirits). Breakfast is the only meal available—hearty country fare served by the open hearth. The inn has twelve guest rooms, eight with private baths, and one with a fireplace. Nauset Beach is within sight of the inn. An early American antique shop is right on the inn's property. Children over eleven years of age are welcome. No pets permitted. *Room Rates* (1978): Rates range from $15 for a single room with shared bath to $30 for an extra-large double with private bath and sitting room. Breakfast is $2 additional. Reservations are suggested at all times. *Driving Instructions:* Take Route 6 to exit 12; turn right and follow the signs to Nauset Beach. The inn is located a quarter of a mile from the beach.

SHIP'S KNEES INN

Beach Road, East Orleans, MA 02643. 617-255-1312. *Innkeeper:* Dee DeDonato. Open all year (holidays included).

The Ship's Knees Inn is a restored sea captain's house surrounded by lawns and a variety of trees and flowers. The Inn was built more than 150 years ago, with a new section added in 1970. Inside the lantern-lit doorways are nineteen rooms, each individually decorated with antiques and colonial color scheme. Many of the guest rooms have beamed ceilings, quilts, and old four-poster beds. Several rooms

have an ocean view, and the master suite has a working fireplace. In summer months a complimentary continental breakfast is served. The Ship's Knees is just a short walk from the wonderfully secluded Nauset Beach. There is a heated outdoor pool and tennis court on the grounds of the inn, as well as areas for badminton and volleyball. No pets allowed. *Room Rates:* The peak season rooms are from $30 to $40, private bath, and $14 to $32, shared bath. In the off season, rates go from $20 to $26 private bath, and $10 to $18 shared bath. *Driving Instructions:* Take Route 6, exit 12; go to first stoplight, turn right, go two stoplights, turn right again. Follow the signs to Nauset Beach.

Eastham, Massachusetts

First settled in 1644 by settlers from Plymouth, the area had been previously explored by the Frenchman Samuel de Champlain in 1606. Today, Eastham is a quiet community that has gained recent fame as one of the two major entrances to the *Cape Cod National Seashore*. The Salt Pond Visitors Center provides excellent introductions to the National Seashore as well as maps describing hiking, bicycling, and the special summer interpretive programs conducted by National Seashore rangers. Visitors can swim at two area beaches (parking $1)—*Nauset Light Beach* and *Coast Guard Beach*. The *Eastham Schoolhouse Museum* is a one-room schoolhouse built in 1869 that now houses a collection of general Eastham-area memorabilia, early schoolhouse furniture, and other collections of the Eastham Historical Society. The *Grist Mill* is a fully restored mill dating from about 1680. The mill is not actually in operation, for safety reasons.

WHALEWALK

Box 169, Bridge Road, Eastham, Cape Cod, MA 02642. 617-255-0617. *Innkeepers:* Jeanne and Endres Campbell. Open all year. Whalewalk, named for the widow's walk or "whalewalk" atop the inn, is an old Cape Cod home. Built 150 years ago for a sea captain, Whalewalk is a classic example of Georgian architecture. Situated on four acres of fields and meadows, the old inn has a terrace where guests can sit and watch the sun set on the salt marsh. The Campbells wish to retain the original charm of the place and have furnished the

rooms with antiques. There are always fresh flowers in the rooms in summer and lovely bouquets of "Cape Cod weeds" in winter. The first-floor guest rooms have double beds and a fireplace. They each have a private bath. Three of the four upstairs guest rooms share a bath. Guests have the use of the library, living room, game room, and terrace. There are several cottages and apartments on the property. They are equipped with kitchen, sheets, and blankets. Breakfast, including homemade breads, is served to guests in the sun room. The Campbells will gladly recommend nearby inns and restaurants for other meals.

The bay is just down the road, and fresh-water ponds are only a few minutes' drive away. Whalewalk is near Rock Harbor's fleet of charter boats and is handy to all other kinds of fishing. No pets permitted. Children are not permitted in the inn but are welcome in the cottages. *Room Rates:* In summer, rooms are $25 to $33 with private bath, $18 to $20 shared. They are about $5 less in the off season. *Driving Instructions:* Take Route 6 to the rotary in Orleans. Take the Rock Harbor exit, following the arrow to Rock Harbor. Bridge Road is the first right after you pass the Barnstable County Court House.

Harwich and Harwich Port, Massachusetts

Located on the ocean side of Cape Cod, Harwich and nearby Harwich Port offer visitors much to do. There is fresh and saltwater bathing and fishing, as well as shell fishing (permits required; obtainable at the town offices). In the summer there are numerous art exhibitions and band concerts at Brooks Park in Harwich. The *Harwich Historical Society* is located in and maintains the Brooks Academy Building (1844), the site of one of the first navigation schools in this country. The second floor houses scrimshaw, old documents and newspapers, and a fine collection of cranberrying implements. On the grounds of the academy is the old Revolutionary War *Powder House* (1770).

COUNTRY INN

86 Sisson Road, Harwich Port, MA 02646. 617-432-2769. *Innkeepers:* Bernice and Bill Flynn. Open all year.

The Country Inn, with 6½ acres of farmland, is located near the center of Cape Cod on the ocean side. Built in 1773, the main building with its eleven fireplaces was once the farm of the founders of the Jordan Marsh Company in Boston. Through the years, several additions have been made to the inn, including three tennis courts and a swimming pool for guests. There are eight guest rooms in the old inn, six with private baths. Dinner is served in the inn's dining room and features three seafood dishes, filet mignon, and four chicken dishes. Complete meals with soup, salad, entrée, and beverage would average $7.50 to $10.00. The dining room is open to the general public. Children under twelve and pets are not permitted. *Room Rates:* Single rooms are $16; double rooms are $22. Reservations are required in July and August and suggested at other times. *Driving Instructions:* From exit 10 on Route 6 take Route 124 to Route 39 (Sisson Road). The inn is about a mile from Harwich center.

THE LION'S HEAD

186 Belmont Road, West Harwich, Cape Cod, MA. Mailing Address: Box 235, West Harwich, MA 02671. 617-432-0500. *Innkeeper:* Nadine Schmitt. Open from the last week in June through the week following Labor Day.

The Lion's Head is a Cape Cod guest house. It was built in the very early 1800s as a Cape half-house and has been added onto over the years. The old house, once the home of sea captain Thomas Snow, has the original "captain's stairs" with the very high risers, making this an inn for spry adults, definitely not for the very young or the elderly. There are five guest rooms, three with private baths. The rooms are large and airy. Many fine beaches, restaurants, and shops are nearby. Nadine serves breakfast to guests between 8 and 9 A.M. No pets, smokers, or children under twelve permitted. *Room Rates:* Rooms are $8.50 per person in the house. There are two cottages on the property that rent by the week. *Driving Instructions:* One half block from Route 28 in West Harwich.

Hyannis and Hyannis Port, Massachusetts

Hyannis Port gained fame as the summer home of the Kennedy family during its White House years. The entire area is one of the most historic areas on the Cape and has lovely old houses. Visitors often stop at the simple and inspiring *Kennedy Memorial* on Ocean Street in Hyannis, with its lovely view of the harbor. The *Cape Cod Art Association* is here, and there are numerous charter fishing boats that leave daily from the harbor. Golf is available at the two public courses in Hyannis and at the Hyannisport Golf Course. Hyannis Port also has a breakwater dating from 1827.

PARK SQUARE INN AND COTTAGES

156 Main Street, Hyannis MA 02601. 617-775-5611. *Innkeeper:* Pete Johnson. Open all year.

The Park Square Inn is a collection of two old buildings and a number of newer cottages. The main building, formerly a sea captain's house, is of masonry construction and dates from 1790. This building has large, high-ceilinged rooms. The other old home here is the 1710 House, a typical old Cape house with dormers. This house has a full first-floor apartment that may be rented separately, as well as two upstairs bedrooms, each with private bath, which are sometimes rented separately and sometimes rented with the downstairs apartment to accommodate large families. This building is one of the oldest surviving homes in Hyannis. The nine cottages were added within the past twenty years, and all feature pine-paneled walls and are set back from the street among trees and flowers. The cottages vary in size from a tiny place for two to a three-bedroom house.

Although the inn does not offer food, Hyannis has so many fine restaurants that this omission is not a hardship. Pets are not permitted. *Room Rates:* Because of the variety of accommodations it is best to write for exact rates for the type of accommodation desired. As a guide, rooms with private bath range from $26 to $32 per day and cottages range from $26 to $58 per day. These prices are for the high season, and there are lower rates for rooms with shared bath. There are also weekly rates. *Driving Instructions:* Take Route 6 to Route 132. You can write the inn for a map showing the exact location.

Martha's Vineyard, Massachusetts

Martha's Vineyard is a triangular island about 19 miles long and less than 10 miles wide. Named after one of his daughters by Bartholomew Gosnold, who also named Cape Cod, the island was once an active whaling center with ports at Edgartown and Vineyard Haven. Local Indians were often members of the crews on the great sailing vessels that left from these ports, and even Herman Melville once sailed from the Vineyard.

Of the two old whaling ports, Edgartown is the more interesting architecturally, because a fire in 1883 destroyed most of the important buildings in Vineyard Haven. Oak Bluffs is also an interesting village, with its array of gingerbread houses. Visitors to the Vineyard are cautioned to avoid bringing cars to the island, because the volume of summer traffic here is so intense that movement by car is often discouraging. A better plan is to leave cars on the mainland and bring only bicycles. Those who must bring cars are urged to make auto reservations far in advance to avoid disappointment. Auto reservations on the car ferry from Woods Hole to the Vineyard are difficult to get. Holiday weekends are booked as far in advance as February 1. Nonholiday car reservations are booked three or four weeks in advance. Passengers wishing to make auto reservations may call toll free on one of the following numbers. From Massachusetts, call 800-352-7104. From most other northeastern states and those as far south as Washington, DC, call 800-225-3122. If you are in an area not served by these WATS lines, then call 617-540-2022. Reservations are not needed for foot passengers on these or the other two ferries serving the Vineyard.

Among the attractions on the island is the *Thomas Cooke House* in Edgartown. The museum has twelve rooms of antique furniture, scrimshaw, and other artifacts. The Liberty Pole Museum in Vineyard Haven is the oldest surviving building there and was originally a church. Housed here is a wide variety of antique material including china, scrimshaw, musical instruments, and early lighting devices. *Seamen's Bethel* was originally a meetinghouse for seamen visiting the ports of the island. It now houses a collection of historical maritime material. The *Hansel and Gretel Doll Museum* in Oak Bluffs has a large collection of nineteenth-century dolls and their costumes.

BEACH PLUM INN, INC.

Off North Road, Menemsha, Martha's Vineyard, MA 02552. 617-645-9454. *Innkeepers:* Carol and Fred Feiner. Open from mid-June until early September.

The Beach Plum, built in 1898, sits on a hill overlooking the sea and the fishing village of Menemsha. Surrounded by 8 acres of land, the main house contains four attractive guest rooms, dining and living rooms, and a cocktail lounge (guests should bring their own liquor as the town is dry). The inn is well known for its continental and New England cuisine; Fred Feiner is a Cordon Bleu chef. Breakfast and dinner are served to guests, and dinner is also available to the public.

The Feiners also have four guest cottages for rent on the property. Private and public beaches are accessible to guests. Fishing charters, sailboat rentals, and concert and theater tickets can all be arranged for through the inn. No children under ten and no pets permitted. *Room Rates:* Rooms are $78 to $86 a day for two, including breakfast and dinner. *Driving Instructions:* Take the State Road (which is also Menemsha Road) from the ferry slip in Vineyard Haven.

DAGGETT HOUSES

Edgartown, Martha's Vineyard, MA 02539. 617-627-4600. *Innkeepers:* Fred and Lucille Chirgwin. Open all year.

Daggett Houses are a collection of historic houses offering a variety of accommodations on the waterfront in Edgartown. The main house, called Daggett House I, was built in 1750, but it incorporates part of the old tavern run by John Daggett and dating back to the early 1660s. The old tavern room is now called the Old Chimney Room because of its unusual fireplace of beehive construction. The atmosphere of this room is further enhanced by the candlelight doors, a brass flintlock blunderbuss, Betty lamps, and a secret stairway. Breakfast is served in this room, often before an open fire. Accom-

modations are available in Daggett House I, as well as in the Garden Cottage near the water (once a mid-1800s schoolhouse) and in Daggett House II, the former Warren House. The latter is a fine whaling captain's home built in the early 1800s. All rooms have private baths or, in the case of suites, share a common bath. The backyard of the inn is a broad expanse of lawn sloping gently to a bulkheaded sandy beach area. Pets are not permitted. *Room Rates:* Rooms range from $30 to $50 per night, double occupancy depending on season. Full breakfast is included. *Driving Instructions:* From the center of Edgartown, turn left on North Water Street. Go three short blocks to the inn (across from the library).

THE EDGARTOWN INN

North Water Street, Edgartown, Martha's Vineyard, MA 02539. 617-627-4794. *Innkeeper:* Catherine Scapecchi. Open April 1 through November 1.

The Edgartown Inn was originally an old whaling captain's home, built in 1798 for Captain Thomas Worth. A few years later it began a long career as a colonial inn. The Edgartown Inn has played host to many notable guests through the years. Daniel Webster was at first denied admittance because he was dark-skinned and thought to be an Indian. He later returned as a guest, as did Nathaniel Hawthorne. Hawthorne came for a rest but stayed on a year to write *Twice Told Tales.* John F. Kennedy stayed here when he was a Massachusetts senator.

The inn is centrally located in the heart of Edgartown. Minutes away by foot is the white sand beach by the old lighthouse; for real

surf bathing, the South Beach is a short ride by car or bike. Nearby are golf courses, tennis, fishing, and summer theater. The inn's front porch overlooks North Water Street with its picket-fenced old captains' houses. The rooms at the inn are much the same as they were in Captain Worth's time, but tiled baths have been added. Beyond the back patio garden are the "Captain's Quarters," an old barn with guest rooms without private baths for more modest rates. Country breakfasts featuring homemade breads, muffins, and griddle cakes are served in the paneled dining room. The Edgartown will gladly recommend local inns and restaurants for other meals. No pets permitted. *Room Rates* (1978): In summer rooms are $28 to $36; off season, $24 to $32. Reservations are required in summer. *Driving Instructions:* Go to Wood's Hole on Cape Cod, and then take the ferry to Martha's Vineyard.

THE KELLEY HOUSE

Kelley Street, Edgartown, Martha's Vineyard, MA. Mailing Address: Box 37, Edgartown, MA 02539. 617-627-4394. *Innkeeper:* John S. Moffet. Open all year.

The Kelley House was built as an inn in 1742 and is still going strong almost 240 years later. The inn was completely renovated in 1973, and a new wing was added in keeping with the original house. The inn is quite large, with fifty-five guest rooms, and has an attractive colonial air about it both inside and out. The exterior of the Kelley House is painted spanking white with black shutters and is set off by lawns, picket fences, and beautiful gardens. The public rooms are enhanced by cheery fires in the inn's three fireplaces and are decorated with eighteenth- and nineteenth-century antiques. The guest rooms all have been redone and have color television, private baths, and telephones. The dining room serves breakfast, lunch, and dinner to guests and the public. Guests have tennis and outdoor pool privileges nearby. No pets permitted. *Room Rates:* Summer rates range from $45 for a double room in the older building to $65 double in the newer wing, EP; MAP is available at $12.50 extra per person, one week minimum. Rates are $15 to $20 lower in the intermediate and off season. *Driving Instructions:* See under Martha's Vineyard for ferry information. The inn is located in downtown Edgartown, two blocks north of Main Street on the corner of North Water and Kelley streets.

Nantucket Island, Massachusetts

The name Nantucket comes from the Indian word "nanticut," meaning faraway land. Thirty miles off the coast of Cape Cod, it's an island paradise far from the rush and neon of today's world. Four miles wide and fourteen miles long, this is a place for long, rambling walks and bike rides. Primarily a summer resort, the island is lovely any time of year. From the main town itself to the little villages of Madaket, Polpis, Quidnet, and Wauwinet, and the trails through pine groves and over the heathlands, unforgettable scenes unfold at every turn. The beaches are a blinding white. Altar Rock, the highest point at 102 feet, affords a panoramic view of the island's coastline and rolling moors.

Once one of the greatest whaling ports in the world, the town, with its blue-shuttered houses (blue shutters are said to be only for whaling captains and first mates) and winding cobblestone streets, flourished in this proud position from 1740 to 1830. With the decline of whaling, families moved away, and the island stood practically deserted for many years. The island's relative inaccessibility and the whaling depression during America's big surge of building helped preserve the old buildings and towns. It stands today as the best preserved of all New England areas. The *Whaling Museum* in the "candle house" has a completely rigged whale boat, a whale skeleton, and a room full of scrimshaw and other whaling artifacts. The *Jethro Coffin House* (1686) is the oldest house on the island and a National Historic Landmark. These and other historic sites and homes are run by the *Nantucket Historical Association* located in Old Town Building.

The island has an unlimited variety of water sports in a wide choice of waters. The south shore provides ocean bathing in the strong surf. The northern side on the harbor, with its still water and sandy shore, is almost completely landlocked, making it ideal for new sailors and children. In late fall, with most visitors gone, the island takes on a different, quiet beauty—the long uninterrupted stretches of beach, the warm golden colors of the moors, and the peaceful streets and roads offer the visitor a restful vacation in a natural setting.

Because of the island's size and lack of parking facilities, tourists are cautioned to leave cars on the mainland if it is at all possible.

There are several bike-rental places on the island and good bus service. Air service to Nantucket is also available. Those who must bring cars should make reservations far in advance. Foot and bike passengers do not need reservations. The Hyannis Ferry operates in summer only; no cars. On the Woods Hole steamer and car ferry, holiday weekends are booked as far in advance as February. Nonholiday car reservations are booked three to four weeks in advance. Those wishing to make car reservations may call the following toll-free phone numbers: in Massachusetts, 800-352-7104; in northeastern states as far south as Washington, D.C., 800-225-3122. Out of the toll-free area, call 617-540-2022.

FOUR SEASONS GUEST HOUSE

2 Chestnut Street, Nantucket, MA 02554. 617-228-1468. *Innkeeper:* Mrs. Herbert Cabral. Open all year.

The Four Seasons Guest House is a pleasant 1850 residence on a quiet side street near the wharfs, museums, restaurants, and beach buses. The house is located in the heart of the historic district with its picturesque old homes and winding narrow streets. There are nine guest rooms, four with private baths, and an efficiency apartment complete with kitchen that opens onto a patio and backyard area. Pets are not permitted. *Room Rates:* During the summer and holidays, room prices range from $20 to $32. The off-season rates are $16 to $24. The Four Seasons does not serve food, but there are many excellent restaurants nearby. *Driving Instructions:* See Nantucket Island information.

JARED COFFIN HOUSE

29 Broad Street, Nantucket, MA. Mailing address: Box J, Nantucket, MA 02554. 617-228-2400. *Innkeeper:* Philip Whitney Read. Open all year.

The Jared Coffin House recaptures the spirit and feeling of the days of Nantucket's reign as queen of the world's whaling ports. Built in 1845 by Jared Coffin, one of the island's most successful ship owners, the main house is a classic example of Greek Revival architecture. This house and later additions were restored in the 1960s to their original style in both architecture and furnishings. The living room and library are furnished with Chippendale, Sheraton, and American Federal antiques. Reflecting the worldwide voyaging of the Nan-

tucket whalers, a Chinese coffee table and lacquered Japanese cabinet grace the library.

Upstairs in the original house are nine restored guest rooms furnished with antiques and locally woven fabrics. The 1857 Eben Allen Wing has sixteen simply decorated rooms with antiques used wherever possible. The Old House (1700s), located behind the wing, has three bedrooms with canopied beds and examples of crewel embroidery. The Daniel Webster House, across the patio, was built in 1964. It has twelve spacious rooms furnished with a blend of contemporary and colonial reproductions. All have private baths.

Jared Coffin House offers a wide variety of dining for guests and the public. In summer, luncheons are served on the canopied patio. The main dining room, its tables set with Wedgewood china and pistol-handled silverware, features New England and continental cuisine. Fresh seafood and veal dishes are the specialties. The Nantucket Bay scallops are excellent. The taproom has an informal atmosphere, with old pine walls and hand-hewn beams. Year-round entertainment and hearty grilled foods are featured here.

Holidays at the inn are especially wonderful. There is a real old-fashioned New England Thanksgiving. For the twelve days of Christmas the inn is decorated with holly, della robia garlands, and, on the front door, a cranberry wreath. At any time of the year the Jared Coffin House is a delightful place to spend a Nantucket vacation.
Room Rates: Rooms range from $20 to $30 for a single and $40 to $55 for a double. Reservations are required; when making them, be sure to specify if you prefer a room in one of the older buildings.
Driving Instructions: See Nantucket Island information.

MARTIN'S GUEST HOUSE

   61 Centre Street, Nantucket, MA 02554. 617-228-0678. *Innkeeper:* Vivian Halliday. Open all year.

Nantucket Island, its homes, and its twisting streets have changed very little from the old whaling days. One seems to step off the ferry or plane and back into the nineteenth century. What better place to savor the atmosphere than in an old Nantucket home? Martin's Guest House fulfills the requirements. Built in 1805 with additions in the nineteenth and early twentieth centuries, the house sits on a hilly brick-sidewalked street. There is a large lawn and pleasant side porch for relaxing. It is an easy walk to the beaches and downtown with its many shops and restaurants. Martin's has an enormous living room with a working fireplace; Five of the inn's fourteen spacious guest rooms also have fireplaces. No meals are served here, but Nantucket has many excellent restaurants and inns with dining rooms. The place recommended most often for dining is the Jared Coffin House. *Room Rates:* Double rooms with private baths are $38; other rooms are less. Off-season rates are lower. Reservations for July and August should be made before June 15 if possible. *Driving Instructions:* Don't bring your car to Nantucket; most likely you won't need it and parking can be very difficult. Take the steamer from Hyannis or Woods Hole, or take a plane ride to the island.

ROYAL MANOR GUEST HOUSE

   31 Centre Street, Box 1061, Nantucket, MA 02554. 617-228-0600. *Innkeeper:* Leon Macy Royal. Open all year.

The Royal Manor is a large old Nantucket home situated on landscaped grounds in the center of town. Built 130 years ago, the house has four big chimneys, seven fireplaces, and several porches (some enclosed). It is furnished with antiques. The spacious guest rooms have inside wooden shutters, Oriental rugs, and modern comfortable beds. There are nine guest rooms, five with private baths. One special room has its own entrance and facilities as well as a small private porch covered with yellow talisman roses in season (mostly June and September).

This is strictly a guest house, and food is not served, but owner Leon Macy Royal recommends several nearby restaurants, including The Whale and The Mad Hatter, both on Easton Street in town, and the Chanticleer in Siasconset Village 7 miles away. No pets or children under ten are permitted. *Room Rates* (1978): June 15 to September 15, rooms are $10 to $15 per person; $2 less per person in the off season. Reservations are advised. *Driving Instructions:* Take Hyannis or Woods Hole ferry to Nantucket. There is air service to Nantucket also.

SHIPS INN

13 Fair Street, Nantucket, MA 02554. 617-228-0040. *Innkeepers:* Bar and John Krebs. Open from Easter through Thanksgiving. Ships Inn was the home of whaling captain Obed Starbuck between voyages. He built the house in 1812 and named many of the rooms for the ships he sailed. The furnishings in the inn today date back to Captain Starbuck's time, and the charm and atmosphere have

changed little. The inn was also the birthplace of Lucretia Coffin Mott, one of the first women abolitionists. Today the Krebses offer twelve comfortable guest rooms, ten with private baths. Downstairs the living room and dining room are attractively decorated and, on chilly evenings, fires in the two old fireplaces add a cheery warmth. The restaurant, The Captain's Table, features fondues of all kinds including cheese, seafood, beef, and a chocolate dessert fondue for two. The Krebses also serve Nantucket's catch of the day and their specialty, marinated lamb chops. The Dory Bar is just that: a bar made from an old dory. Backgammon, cribbage, and darts are played here, entertaining islanders and tourists alike. The Ships Inn is a very friendly place but no pets are permitted. *Room Rates:* In the peak of the summer season, doubles are $38, singles are $16. Off season, rates are $28 double and $12 single. *Driving Instructions:* Walk or bike; almost anyone at the dock or airport can direct you.

STUMBLE INN GUEST HOUSE

109 Orange Street, Nantucket, MA 02554. 617-228-4482. *Innkeeper:* David L. Place. Open all year.

This six-guest room, wood shingle Nantucket home was built in 1704 by the widow Abigail Howes. Considered an extravagance at the time, the bricks for the foundation came from Holland, and the windows were one pane of glass wider than was typical of the period. The inn retains its old-fashioned charm with wide-board floors, antiques in the rooms, and several places where the beams have been carefully exposed. Modernization now includes the presence of color television in the guest rooms, as well as small refrigerators for late-night snacks. These touches will appeal more to some than they do to us. The living room has a Franklin stove for comfort on cooler days. Mr. Place will be happy to pick up guests at the ferry or airport at no charge with advance notice. Breakfast is served to guests only. Children and pets are welcome, assuming they are well-mannered. *Room Rates:* During the summer season, double rooms are from $33 to $39. Off-season rates are about $4 to $6 less. *Driving Instructions:* See Nantucket Island information.

WEST MOOR INN

Off Cliff Road, Nantucket Island, MA 02554. 617-228-9877. *Innkeeper:* Nanci Walker. Open from May through October.

The West Moor Inn, atop a windswept knoll, is one of the highest houses on the island and one of the few painted ones on an island filled with weathered-shingle homes. Built as a wedding present in 1917, the inn is a fine example of Federal architecture. The wide entry hall with front and rear entrances welcomes guests. There are spacious halls with seating areas, large living and dining rooms, both with working fireplaces, and a glass-enclosed dining area filled with plants. All nine rooms are furnished with antiques, have wide pine-board floors, and give lovely views of the rolling moors and the sea. The inn has spacious grounds and a wonderful secluded beach just 300 yards away. Nanci says pheasant, deer, grouse, and rabbits constantly parade across the lawn. Although the West Moor is secluded, Nantucket center is within an easy stroll. A two-minute walk brings guests to a neighboring riding stable and tennis club. Breakfast and lunch are served to guests at the inn; dinner will be served upon request and for special occasions. Liquor is not served, but it is permitted in the rooms. No pets please. *Room Rates:* Rooms are around $30 for a double; some rooms run higher, especially during peak season. *Driving Instructions:* See Nantucket Island information.

THE WOODBOX INN

29 Fair Street, Nantucket, MA 02554. 617-228-0587. *Innkeepers:* The Tuteins. Open from May to November.

Nantucket's oldest inn, the Woodbox was built in 1709 by a whaling captain named Bunker. An adjoining house was built awhile later, and the houses were joined by cutting through the sides of both. This wonderful old inn is furnished with antiques of the period and has nine guest rooms. The accommodations consist of seven suites and two double rooms, all with private baths. The suites have one or two bedrooms, a living room, and either a sun porch or a small garden. Every suite and double room has at least one working fire-place for a cheery fire on chilly evenings.

The Woodbox has a wonderful dining room with low-beamed ceilings, wide pine boards everywhere, beautiful old chairs, and ta-bles topped with fresh flowers and tall ivory candles in polished period brass candlesticks. Specialties of the inn are fresh native fish off the boats, beef Wellington, farm-fresh vegetables, homemade soups, and hot popovers. The breakfast, "Nantucket's best," includes blueberry, peach, apple, or strawberry pancakes covered with hot maple syrup, or a variety of omelets. Both breakfast and dinner are available to the public. No pets permitted. *Room Rates:* Rooms are $20 to $25 per person, with $3.50 additional for breakfast if desired. *Driving Instructions:* Go along Main Street to Orange Street. Turn left, go two blocks, then turn right on Plumb Lane; go one block to Fair Street and the inn.

Provincetown, Massachusetts

Provincetown has a long history as a summer colony. Before Euro-peans came to this region, members of the Western Cape Cod Indian tribes would summer at Provincetown to hunt and fish while weather permitted. Many historians feel that the Viking explorer Thorvald, brother of Leif Ericson, was the first European explorer to come to this area, in 1004, predating the visit by Gosnold (mentioned in our section on Cape Cod) by almost 600 years. However, the most fa-mous visit of all was when the first Pilgrims set foot from the *May-flower* and landed on what is now Commercial Street in Provincetown. It was while the *Mayflower* was in port in Provincetown that the Mayflower Compact was signed. The *Pilgrim Monument* is a 210-foot-high granite structure erected in 1910 and offering those who climb to its summit a view of the entire Cape.

In its early history, Provincetown was almost entirely supported by the riches of the sea. During those days, the "Cape-style" house came into prominence in this area and quickly spread to other parts of New England. An excellent example of this style of architecture is the *Oldest House*, built in 1746 and open to the public. The *Prov-incetown Heritage Museum* is housed in a Registered National Land-mark building and displays a variety of antiques and artifacts, including fire equipment, fishing gear, and the work of American artists. The harbor at Provincetown is still active and is a fine tourist stop in the late afternoon when the catch is being unloaded. The blessing of the fleet occurs annually on the last weekend in June.

Provincetown has gained more recent fame as a colony for members of the visual and performing arts. The *Provincetown Art Association* shows the works of its members past and present and includes the work of many of the country's most renowned contemporary artists. The *Provincetown Playhouse* is as active today as it was when Eugene O'Neill was a member of its studio workshop. Contemporary plays and revivals of earlier twentieth-century authors' works are performed there by a professional company; the *Eugene O'Neill Museum* is next door.

BRADFORD GARDENS INN

178 Bradford Street, Provincetown, MA 02657. 617-487-1616.
Innkeeper: Jim Logan. Open all year.
If you love the sea and a good country inn, you'll love Provincetown and Bradford Gardens. Built in 1820, Bradford Gardens is a relaxed, informal country inn furnished with antiques and art work. In the old inn are eight rooms, six with working fireplaces, overlooking the garden and, in the winter, the sea. There is the Jenny Lind Room with early spool furnishings and a fireplace, the Yesteryear Room with its brass bed and brass accents, and the Chimney Nook with garden and water views and a fireplace nook.

The Morning Room has a central fireplace and a bay window overlooking the garden. Here guests mingle and enjoy the inn's country breakfasts, the only meal served. No part of town is more than a mile from the inn, so a car is hardly needed. The special parkland bicycle and walking trails are exquisite and, of course, there are miles of beaches for summer swims and winter walks. *Room Rates:* Double rooms are $37 to $60, including breakfasts and firewood; add $5 a day from July 1 through Labor Day. *Driving Instructions:* Follow Route 6 to Provincetown.

SOMERSET HOUSE

378 Commercial Street, Provincetown, MA 02657. 617-487-0383.
Innkeeper: Jon Gerrity. .Open all year.
The Somerset House is one of Provincetown's larger old homes. The

black-shuttered yellow house sits behind a picket-fenced front garden facing the town beach a hundred feet away. The original house was built in 1850 by a successful ship chandler, Stephen Cook. An addition in 1890 doubled the size of the house. Today the Somerset is a guest house offering twelve individually decorated guest rooms and two two-bedroom apartments. The furnishings throughout the house are an eclectic combination of antique and very modern enhanced by a great many plants, flowers, and original paintings and lithographs. Eleven of the guest rooms have private tiled baths, and several rooms have water views of the harbor. The Somerset House serves no food, but the town has a great many unusual (and usual) restaurants, all within a short walking distance. The closest is three blocks away. No pets permitted. Children are welcome only if they are well-behaved. *Room Rates:* Memorial Day and June 15 to September 10, doubles are $24 to $34; singles are $20 to $30. Off-season rates are doubles $16 to $22, singles $12 to $18. *Driving Instructions:* Take Route 6 to Provincetown. Follow Commercial Street (Provincetown's main street) along the water to Pearl Street. Somerset House is on the corner.

WHITE WIND INN

174 Commercial Street, Provincetown, MA 02657. 617-487-1526.
Innkeeper: Sandra Rich. Open March 1 through November.
The White Wind Inn, a gleaming white Victorian mansion, was once

the home of a prosperous shipbuilder. Built in the mid-nineteenth century, the inn is carpeted throughout, has high ceilings, chandeliers, and a blend of antiques and modern conveniences. A complimentary continental breakfast is served in the lounge. There are eleven guest rooms, some with private sundecks. Directly opposite from a quiet stretch of beach, the inn is only a three-minute walk to the center of town with its myriad activities. *Room Rates:* Memorial Day through Labor Day rooms are $16 to $40; off season, they are $12 to $26. Reservations are required. *Driving Instructions:* Take the Mid-Cape Highway to Provincetown. Located on the corner of Commercial and Winthrop Streets.

West Dennis, Massachusetts

West Dennis is on the south shore of the Cape and is part of the Greater Dennis region including Dennis and East Dennis on the north shore and West Dennis, Dennisport, and South Dennis on the south shore. The area was settled in the late 1630s and named after a pastor of the time from Yarmouth. Three of the area's favorite stops are the *Jerico House and Barn Museum* in West Dennis, housing antique furniture and a fine collection of antique tools and household gadgets; the *Scargo Hill Observation Tower* in Dennis, with its fine view of the Bay; and the *Josiah Dennis Manse*, also in Dennis. *The Cape Playhouse* in Dennis, one of the oldest summer theaters in the country (dating from 1926), presents a full summer season of theater and offers guided tours as well.

LIGHTHOUSE INN

Lighthouse Road, West Dennis, MA 02670. 617-398-2244. *Inn-keepers:* Robert and Mary Stone. Open mid-June to mid-September.

The historic Bass River Lighthouse, built in 1850, forms the center sections of the Lighthouse Inn, an old-fashioned Cape Cod resort. Many additions have obscured the old lighthouse, but the lobby and dining room are actually inside it. Situated on 7 acres of lawns and ocean beach, the inn is surrounded by grey- and white-shingled cottages, all with fireplaces (wood is furnished and set up). The inn's dining room specializes in lobster and other local seafood. *Room Rates* (1978): $30 to $45 per person, MAP; $5 less per person in the off season. *Driving Instructions:* Turn right off Route 28 at the Gulf Station in West Dennis.

Yarmouth Port, Massachusetts

The greater Yarmouth area is one of the richest sites of tourist attractions on the Cape. One of the many places of historical interest is the *Colonel John Thatcher House* on Route 6A, with its collection of antiques, some dating from the 1600s, when the Thatcher family raised twenty-one children in this house. The *Winslow-Crocker House* (1780) is also filled with period antiques. Both are open from June through September on Tuesdays, Thursdays, and Sundays from 1 to 5 P.M. The Historical Society of Old Yarmouth is housed in the *Captain Bangs Hallet House* on the Yarmouth Port Common. The Bangs family lived there in the late 1800s and their furnishings are on display here in the summer. The *Aqua Circus* has summer demonstrations by the Acapulco Cliff-Diving Group. There are marine exhibits, a petting zoo, a monkey jungle, and more on display daily from 9:30 A.M. to 9:00 P.M. during the summer and from 10 A.M. to 5 P.M. during the off season. The *Yarmouth Playhouse*, with one of the Cape's fine professional companies, presents performances in the July-to-September season. Call 617-398-9098 for information. *Gray's Beach* is on Cape Cod Bay at the end of Center Street. There can be found picnic tables, a playground, and shade trees, as well as a boardwalk over an extensive salt marsh (Bass Hole).

THE VILLAGE INN

92 Main Street, Yarmouth Port, MA. Mailing address: Box 1, Yarmouth Port, MA 02675. 617-362-3182. *Innkeepers:* Bob and Esther Hickey. Open all year.

The Village Inn is a small family-operated inn housed within what was once the private home of a locally renowned sea captain. Situated in the Yarmouth Port Historic District, the inn has ten lovely guest rooms, of which six have private baths and the other four are really family suites that share baths. There are two comfortable lounges, a spacious porch, and more than an acre of landscaped grounds and gardens shaded by some of Yarmouth Port's famous century-old elms.

Bob and Esther Hickey have made the Village Inn one of the finest on the Cape by their warm and attentive service to their guests and with their comfortable, restful rooms. Indeed, we have been privileged to read many of the letters sent by their overnight guests heaping praise on them for their helpfulness and warmth. Here is an inn where you can expect more than to be shown to your room. Many are the times that the Hickeys have gotten an absentminded guest a tube of toothpaste or an extra toothbrush, lent an author a typewriter, or obtained last-minute reservations at a crowded summer theater or a popular restaurant. No meals are served at the inn, except for the unusually generous breakfast cooked "as you like it" every morning, but many nearby restaurants are highly regarded. *Room Rates:* During the summer months, rates are $14 to $32 per day, double occupancy; in the off season, $12 to $24 per day. *Driving Instructions:* The inn is located on Route 6A in the center of Yarmouth Port.

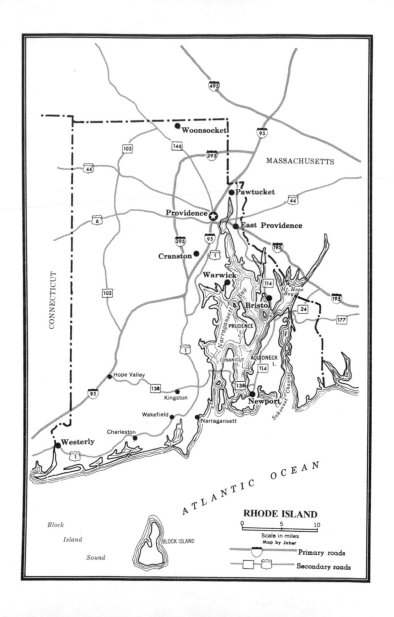

RHODE ISLAND

Scale in miles
0   5   10

Map by Jaber

Primary roads

Secondary roads

Rhode Island

THE NATION'S smallest state has the longest official name—State of Rhode Island and Providence Plantations. Rhode Island is 48 miles long and 37 miles wide, but, with the huge Narragansett Bay almost cutting the state into unequal sections, the tiny state has 400 miles of coastline. In 1635 Roger Williams was banished from the Puritan colony of Massachusetts Bay. He and his followers founded the first white settlement on the Narragansett Bay. Williams named it Providence Plantations in "commemoration of God's providence." The early settlement was known for its political and religious freedom. In 1638 the country's first Baptist congregation was founded. In Newport one can still see both the *Touro Synagogue* (1763), the oldest American Jewish house of worship, and the country's oldest *Quaker Meeting House* (1699). The first U.S. Catholic mass was held in Newport's *Old Colony House*. Farming and the maritime trades thrived here. Its ports were some of the busiest and largest in the colonies. Feisty Rhode Island led the colonies in proclaiming its independence. On land and sea Rhode Islanders were at war with the British long before Lexington and Concord—the most serious incident being the Islanders' burning of HMS *Gaspee* in 1772. In 1793, in Pawtucket's *Slater Mill*, a factory system was begun that heralded the nation's Industrial Revolution.

Rhode Island has been a vacationer's paradise for hundreds of years. It has both freshwater and saltwater sports, pine forests and rolling fields, fifteen state parks, antique and craft shops, and historic villages and towns.

Before you travel to Rhode Island, you should definitely write to the Department of Economic Development, Tourist Division, 1 Weybosset Hill, Providence, RI 02903. The telephone number at the tourist division is 401-277-2601. They will send an excellent packet of information. You should be sure to request three items that are particularly helpful: "This Is Rhode Island;" "Guide to Rhode Island," with its full list of seasonal events of all types, as well as sightseeing attractions; and the State Department of Transportation Road Map.

Block Island, Rhode Island

Block Island is a beautiful little unspoiled piece of land just off the coast of Rhode Island. It is 7 by 3½ miles in size, with 25 miles of coast. There are more freshwater ponds than there are days in a year, all well stocked with fish. The island is on one of the main migratory routes of many birds and is a famous observation point. The *Block Island Historical Society* has an interesting museum in town. The area offers many kinds of outdoor recreational activities, with emphasis on water sports, hiking, and biking. The island can be reached by ferry, private boat, or plane. The ferries run from New London, Connecticut, and Newport, Providence, and Point Judith, Rhode Island. The airport is served by Yankee and New England airlines out of the Westerly, Providence, and New London airports. Charter flights can also be arranged. For information call the nearest airport or ferry terminal.

THE 1661 INN

Block Island, RI 02807. 401-466-2421/2063. *Innkeepers:* Rita, Joan, and Justin Abrams. Open from Memorial Day weekend to Columbus Day.

The setting of the 1661 Inn is truly breathtaking. On top of a small, hill, it overlooks the Atlantic Ocean, the town and harbor (Old Harbor), and two beautiful freshwater ponds with resident swans and ducks. A porch extends around the ocean and harbor side of the inn. Guests can sit and watch the ferries and pleasure boats come and go in the busy harbor. The large white house is surrounded by lawns and wildflower meadows. The name "1661" refers to the year the island was first settled. The inn was built in 1890 in the island's heyday as a fashionable resort. The twenty-one guest rooms are decorated with colonial furniture, braided rugs, green plants, and a

different wallpaper in each room. There is plenty of reading material also. Five of the rooms have private baths.

As an afternoon treat for guests, the Abramses offer complimentary wine and cheese in the lobby around the old hatch-cover table. Both the public and guests are served breakfasts and dinner in the dining room with its wonderful ocean views. Seafood is the specialty here: flounder with a delicious variety of stuffings such as oysters and walnuts or mussels and clams. Meals include fresh garden vegetables grown in the inn's garden, johnnycake, and home-baked breads. The featured dessert is Indian pudding. *Room Rates* (1978): Seasonal rates range from $15.50 to $19.00 per person, including breakfast. From Labor Day to Columbus Day rooms are $8.00 per person (weekdays only) with no food served. The Abramses will pick guests up at the ferry or airport. They also rent out bicycles at the inn. *Driving Instructions:* See **Block Island.**

Newport, Rhode Island

Rhode Island calls itself "the nation's first vacation land." Evidence to support this claim comes from the visit in 1524 of the Italian navigator, Giovanni da Verrazano. While in the employ of the king of France, Verrazano was so enchanted by the beauties of Narragansett Bay that he stayed in the area a full fortnight, thus earning himself the first vacation with pay in the New World.

The problem with visiting Newport is that the area is so filled with tourist attractions that it can be overwhelming. Newport has a most helpful Visitors Center in the midst of the restored downtown area, where maps and suggested tours may be obtained, as well as group tickets to the famous mansions that will save the sightseer several dollars over the individual admission prices. The most popular "cottages" are *The Breakers, The Elms, Marble House, Chateau-sur-Mer, Kingscote, Rosecliff,* and *Belcourt Castle.* Other local attractions include many churches, older houses dating from Revolutionary times, the *Newport Automobile Museum, International Tennis Hall of Fame, HMS Rose, Continental Sloop Providence,* and the *Touro Synagogue,* oldest in the United States. *Cliff Walk* is a pretty, occasionally unnerving trail along the ocean side of many of Newport's mansions. Watch your step, and don't expect to see much of the mansions themselves, as the hedges and vast lawns prevent close scrutiny of most. Cliff Walk should be avoided by families with small children and the elderly.

BELLA VISTA GUEST HOUSE
1 Seaview Avenue, Newport, RI 02840. *Innkeepers:* Alice Simpson and Rosamond Hendel. Open April to November.

Located near Newport's famed Cliff Walk, the Bella Vista boasts neighbors like the Breakers, Belcourt Castle, and Rosecliff. While not on quite that grand a scale, this twenty-room, white-shingled "cottage" was built in the style of an ancient Irish castle. The home was built just before the turn of the century for a governor of Pennsylvania. The Bella Vista overlooks Easton Beach and has eight guest rooms (shared baths), plus a three-bedroom efficiency apartment. The decor here is generally old-fashioned, with an assortment of antiques but new beds in all guest rooms. The large veranda has a lot of white wicker furniture. Bella Vista has a full kitchen on the third floor that is available for light cooking by guests. No meals are served here, but Newport has numerous fine restaurants, most nearby. Pets and small children are not permitted. *Room Rates:* Rooms range from $20 to $35, double occupancy, depending on season. Additional persons in the room, $5. *Driving Instructions:* Starting from the Chamber of Commerce offices in the center of Newport, take Americas Cup Avenue to Memorial Boulevard. Take this uphill seven blocks to Cliff Avenue. Turn right and go two blocks to Seaview Avenue. The Bella Vista is on the corner.

CLIFFSIDE GUEST VILLA

2 Seaview Avenue, Newport, RI 02840. 401-847-1811. *Innkeeper:* Mary Healy. Open from April through mid-September. The Victorian Room, a double with private bath, is available all year.

In 1880, "Villa du Côte" was built by Governor Thomas Swann of Maryland as a summer cottage. Cliffside Villa, overlooking the Atlantic Ocean and Newport's famed Cliff Walk, still retains the character and charm of these earlier times. After a day exploring historic Newport with its famous mansions, antique shops, and museums, or just relaxing on the nearby beach, it is a pleasure to return to Cliffside with its antique-filled rooms and polished wood. The inn does not serve food, but coffee and tea are always available. No children or pets permitted. *Room Rates* (1978): Double rooms are $20 to $30, July through mid-September; $5 less off season. Reservations are required. *Driving Instructions:* Take Memorial Boulevard to Cliff Avenke (near Cliff Walk). Cliffside is on the corner of Cliff and Sea View avenues.

INN AT CASTLE HILL

Ocean Drive, Newport, RI 02840. 401-849-3800. *Innkeeper:* Paul McEnroe. Open all year.

In 1874 Alexander Agassiz, son of the famed scientist Louis Agassiz, built a fine summer home that would serve as base for his studies in marine biology. The fine building served this purpose for many years until the marine institute at Woods Hole replaced its research function. In more recent years it has been a summer cottage for the McEnroe family. The transformation from summer home to the grand inn it is today was done with extraordinary attention to detail by Paul McEnroe. The result is a lovely inn with ten guest rooms that vary in flavor from print wallpaper and white wicker furniture to richly wood-paneled walls. Seven of the ten rooms have private baths, and all are handsomely furnished.

The dining rooms of the inn are noted in the area as among the finest, offering a wide sampling of inventive continental fare augmented by a selection of local seafood. Service is formal and luxurious—appropriate to the Newport setting. Among the offerings are coquilles St. Jacques, escargots bourguignon, veal Zuricher, rainbow trout in pastry, turban of sole with shrimp sauce, and a number of other entrées, including steak, lamb, and duckling for those who prefer more familiar restaurant fare. Complete dinner prices range from $9.75 to $15.00. *Room Rates:* Rates in the inn range from $26.50 to $60.00. There are also rooms in a shingled, motel-type structure and in small beach houses. These lack the feeling of the inn itself. *Driving Instructions:* From downtown Newport, follow all signs to Ocean Drive.

Westerly and environs

Rhode Island's southernmost coast is dotted with little fishing villages and summer vacation cottages. With miles of beaches and enormous salt ponds, the area is a fisherman's paradise. Breach-ways, ideal for fishing and exploring, are huge rock jetties that cut through the beaches, giving boats, fish, and the tide access to the salt ponds. Routes 1 and 1A are excellent sightseeing and antiquing routes, as are the side roads winding past old stone walls and orchards. In Charlestown on Route 1A is the *Fantastic Umbrella Factory,* a collection of craft and antique shops housed in the barns and sheds of an old working farm complete with animals. Another find is *Windswept Farm,* restored old stone barns where several antique dealers are under one roof. The hurricane of 1938 destroyed most of the summer homes that once lined the beaches here. *Watch Hill,* because of its height, survived and is still one of the loveliest towns in Rhode Island. Rose-covered gray-shingled old summer cottages perch high on the rocky hills overlooking the sea and Block Island beyond. At the end of the winding, roller-coaster road lies the village, a miniature resort town with many shops and a harbor with facilities for guest docking. The *Flying Horse Carousel,* America's oldest merry-go-round, built before 1870, still whirls at the edge of town.

There are numerous historical sites in this area of Rhode Island, including many concerning local Indian tribes. The *Indian Church* (1859), and *Royal Indian Burial Ground,* resting place of the Sachems of the Narragansett Tribe, are both located in Charlestown. *Burlingame State Park* with Watchaug Pond offers inland fresh-water recreation the year round.

SHELTER HARBOR INN

Post Road, Shelter Harbor, Westerly, RI 02891. 401-322-8883. *Innkeeper:* Jim Dey. Open all year.

Shelter Harbor Inn is set well back from the road, fronted by a large grassy field. The inn was built as a farmhouse in the early 1800s and was converted to an inn in 1911. In 1978, innkeeper Jim Dey completed the conversion of the farm's barn into the inn annex with ten double rooms with baths, a large living room, and a redwood deck overlooking a secluded wooded area. The eight bedrooms in the main inn consist of two with private baths and six that share baths. The fields around the inn are filled with wild roses and blueberry and Juneberry bushes. In the summer, Jim uses a quaint old lobster boat to ferry guests across Quonochontaug, a large Rhode Island salt pond, to the nearby sandy beach on the other side. Motorboats and small sailboats are available for guests.

Meals are served in the dining room, with its exposed beams, and in the more intimate library. The restaurant is open to the public for dinner, which features traditional New England fare, including such specialties as finnan haddie, Rhode Island's ubiquitous johnnycake, and stuffed flounder. A popular dessert is chocolate pecan pie. Guests are invited to join Mr. Dey on trips to nearby farms to pick vegetables for dinner. Children and pets are permitted. *Room Rates:* Double rooms range from $30 to $40; single rooms, from $15 to $35, including breakfast. *Driving Instructions:* The inn is on Route 1, five miles east of Westerly.

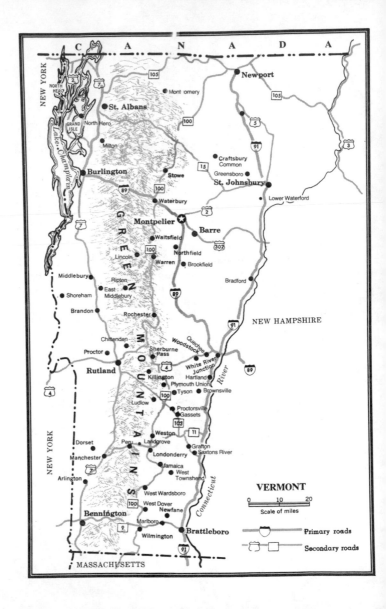

VERMONT

Scale of miles
0   10   20

Primary roads

Secondary roads

Vermont

VERMONT WAS first explored in 1609 by Samuel de Champlain, who voyaged down the lake that was to bear his name. Almost sixty years were to pass before a permanent settlement was made by the French on Isle La Motte in the northern part of Lake Champlain. Later, in 1724, the English established a settlement at Fort Dummer. Soon thereafter, the area destined to become Vermont was the scene of various struggles for its control between the French, settlers from neighboring New Hampshire, and New Yorkers who had claims on it. In response to these controversies, some residents of Vermont formed a small soldiering force called the Green Mountain Boys. Formed first to defend New Hampshire's claim to the land against claims of New Yorkers, the band of fierce fighting men was soon to be called into service of a new cause—the Revolution against the colonial forces of England. After the Revolution, representatives from Vermont met at Windsor and declared themselvs to be a separate republic. Vermont remained separate for fourteen years, with its own customs and mail service, but it was eventually welcomed to the newly formed country in 1791, becoming the fourteenth state.

Although tourism is a leading industry, any visitor is quick to realize that this state, with its great natural resources, is a rich agricultural region and producer of forest products, not the least of which is its famed maple syrup. Vacation planners will be pleased by the high quality of information that is distributed by the state of Vermont. When the state passed its law prohibiting billboards, it felt a responsibility to disseminate the information previously given by signs, as well as general information of use to tourists. The results are seen in the publications sent to any interested vacationer or handed out at the many state-sponsored information booths. Requests for this literature should be directed to the Vermont Department of Commerce, 61 Elm Street, Montpelier, VT 05602. The telephone number is 802-828-3236.

SOUTHERN

Arlington, Vermont

Arlington is 14 miles north of Bennington on Route 7. It is an area known for its summer theaters and art galleries, golfing, antique auctions, and crafts shops, as well as for trout fishing and downhill and cross-country skiing. In the summer, hikers enjoy the famed *Long Trail*, and hunters go after the abundant game found in the area. West Arlington has a covered bridge over the Battenkill River. Norman Rockwell, who lived in Arlington for many years, used some of the local scenes on many of his covers for the *Saturday Evening Post*.

ARLINGTON INN

Arlington, VT 05250. 802-375-6532. *Innkeeper:* Stephen C. Lundy. Open all year except from October 15 to Christmas and during April and May. The dining room is closed Mondays and Tuesdays. The Arlington Inn has been restored and decorated in a sturdy, simple way using period antiques. Its seven very comfortable rooms allow the visitor to feel at home even while on vacation. In addition to the rooms in the inn, a cottage house in the rear has housekeeping facilities. The dining room menu changes daily under the supervision of chef Scott Vineberg and his assistant, George. Typical menus include main dishes like beef Wellington for two, tournedos chasseur, salmon, and veal marsala. *Room Rates* (1978): Rooms are $21 to $30; special suite is $38. Continental breakfast included. *Driving Instructions:* Take Route 7 north of Bennington about 10 miles to Arlington. The inn is on the right-hand side of the road.

WEST MOUNTAIN INN

Arlington, Vermont 05250. 802-375-6516. *Innkeepers:* Clint and Audrey Marantz and Wes and Mary Ann Carlson. Open all year.

At West Mountain, the innkeepers have a dream. They hope in a few years to unite the arts with recreational living by creating an old country inn surrounded by viable, dynamic performing-arts and visual-arts centers. Phase one of this ambitious project has been the total renovation of the West Mountain Inn in Arlington.

Set on 150 acres of rolling hills bordered by state forest land and running down to the Battenkill, Vermont's most famous trout stream, the inn was built in 1920 as the summer estate for a Texas couple. The white clapboard building with its seven-gabled slate roof has an intimate dining room with a fireplace and a fabulous view of the surrounding mountains and the Battenkill.

On the main floor of the inn is the lounge-library, with its wide-ranging selection of reading material, and the Cabaret, a large room open on weekends on a seasonal basis as a showcase for a variety of performers selected from all over the East Coast, including singers, mimes, one-person shows, and improvisational theater groups. Eventually the two barns on the property will be renovated and will house the performing arts center and the visual arts center.

The second floor guest rooms are individually decorated with a blend of authentic antiques and colonial-style furniture. Most rooms have private baths, although some share bath facilities. Each has a view of either the mountains or the Battenkill. There is also a "honeymoon cottage" with full housekeeping facilities and a fireplace. Three suites are available in the Mill House. Rooms may be rented on a weekly basis, a popular arrangement with trout fishermen, in a detached duplex apartment. The inn has a stable with horses and, in winter, ten miles of cross-country skiing on marked trails on the property as well as access to the adjoining state land.

Meals are served from a small, well-thought-out menu. "Diplomatic" is the word that chef Van Turner uses to describe his cuisine. He incorporates the best features of international cookery into the dishes he prepares. Meals are served with home-baked breads and fresh vegetables. Entrées include shrimp Dianne, roast apricot duckling, braised game hen béarnaise, medallions of beef, and New Orleans veal grillades, as well as a number of other freshly prepared items. Full meals with appetizer, soup, entree, and dessert would average $10.50 to $13.00. The inn is open to the public for lunch and dinner and offers guests a continental breakfast. Children are welcome and pets are permitted if special advance arrangements are made. *Room Rates:* Rooms are $18 to $32, double occupancy plus $7 per additional person per room, EP. Rooms are also available on MAP. *Driving Instructions:* The inn is 1 mile west of Arlington on Route 313.

Brandon, Vermont

In addition to being an excellent base for fishermen because of its location on the Nesobe River, the area has good cross-country skiing. It is a short drive to the south to the *Proctor Marble Exhibit*, just outside Rutland, and the *Brandon Brook Recreational Area* is only a few miles to the east of Brandon on Route 73, as is the *Chittenden Brook Recreational Area*. These areas are parts of the U.S. Forest Service system and offer picnicking and fishing. Chittenden Brook has campsites and trailer facilities as well.

CHURCHILL HOUSE INN

Route 73 East, Brandon, VT. Mailing address: RFD #3, Brandon, VT 05733. 802-247-3300. *Innkeepers:* Michael and Marion Shonstrom. Open all year except April 1 to May 15 and November 1 to December 15.

The Churchill House is an impressive three-story farmhouse built in 1871 by the Churchill family from local lumber. Mike and Marion Shonstrom have managed to furnish the house with a large collection of antiques supplemented by a few contemporary furnishings. There are high bedsteads of maple, oak, and cast iron; commodes; and blanket chests, as well as parlor and Franklin stoves in the downstairs sitting room and the book-lined study.

Food here is the product of the hard work of Marion, who loves provincial cooking, be it Vermont-style or with a continental flare. Some of her specialties include pot roast simmered in cranberry and horseradish sauce, roast lamb with yoghurt and barley pilaf, and chicken Provençal. The proprietors grow their own vegetables in the warmer months, and they also bake very fine French bread.

The inn has several special package plans that will appeal to travelers in every season. It offers in the spring, early summer, and fall a special series of fly-fishing programs. Because the inn is located on the Neshobe River and has easy access to local beaver ponds, lakes, and other rivers, it has become a gathering place for fly fishermen. During these periods, the inn offers special fly-fishing clinics, including fly-tying and casting instruction. The inn also offers five-day guided tours using canoes and led by local guide Scott Rideout. Canoe tours stop at other inns in the area.

Bicyclists will enjoy the variety of bicycle tours organized by this inn, which include evening stops at several inns on trips that range in length from two- or three-day tours to a grand tour of seven days and two hundred miles. Besides the Churchill House, nine inns are described in a brochure available from the Schonstroms. Tremendously popular is a similar "hike inn to inn" program that was recently given nationwide coverage in a magazine devoted to backpacking. Write for details.

The Churchill House Inn maintains a complete ski-touring center with twenty-two miles of cross-country trails, as well as a ski shop with rentals, instruction, and guided tours available. The inn participates in a winter program of ski-touring that links several old country inns in a manner similar to the bicycling and hiking programs mentioned above. *Room Rates:* Rooms are $30 to $40 per person, MAP and including gratuities. These rates are based on double occupancy. *Driving Instructions:* Take Route 7 to Brandon, then Route 73 east to the inn.

Brownsville, Vermont (Mount Ascutney)

Mount Ascutney is a small ski area near the Connecticut River in the western part of central Vermont. The mountain is adjacent to the village of Brownsville. The ski area has two chair and three T-bar lifts serving twenty-four trails and four slopes. There are also several miles of marked cross-country ski trails at Mount Ascutney. In the summer, the mountain is a popular gathering spot for climbers.

THE INN AT MOUNT ASCUTNEY

Brook Road, Brownsville, VT 05037. 802-484-5997. *Innkeeper:* Daphne Henderson. Open all year except for two weeks in April and two weeks in November.

The Inn at Mount Ascutney is a 150-year-old country inn with simple rooms. Fireplaces blaze in the living and dining rooms and candles and lamps provide the only light during dinner. Cooking is done on an open hearth in the dining room. The inn has long been famous for its views of Mount Ascutney by day and—thanks to lights for night skiing—by evening. Mrs. Henderson, a graduate of the Cordon Bleu School of Cooking, is an accomplished chef. Nightly she offers a continental menu with seven appetizers including escargots and stuffed mushrooms and seven entrées, including duck à l'orange, fresh salmon with Béarnaise sauce, veal scallopini marsala, and coquilles St. Jacques. Dinner prices are à la carte with entrées averaging $8. Some pets are permitted. *Room Rates:* Single rooms are $17.50, double rooms are $14 per person. Breakfast included. *Driving Instructions:* Take either Route 44 from Windsor to the east or Route 106 to the west. When at Brownsville, take Brook Road to the inn.

Chittenden, Vermont

Chittenden is a small village on the edge of the Green Mountain National Forest. The area is quiet and has several country inns as well as a few larger resorts nearby. Neighboring Rutland and Proctor offer the tourist a number of special attractions, including *Wilson's Castle*, a nineteenth-century mansion; the marble exhibit at the *Vermont Marble Company;* the *Chaffee Art Gallery;* and the *Rutland Historical Society Museum.* Area skiing includes well-organized cross-country skiing at several inns, as well as other trails and downhill skiing at *Apple Hill, Pico,* and *Killington.* Golf is available at the *Proctor-Pittsford Golf Course.*

TULIP TREE INN

Chittenden, VT 05737. 802-483-6213. *Innkeepers:* Barbara and Gerald Liebert. Open all year.

For years the Lieberts had visited New England inns for vacations. Finally, one year, they purchased a rambling, turn-of-the-century country home and used all their skills to renovate and redecorate it in time to welcome their first guests to Christmas at the Tulip Tree. Business has been wonderful ever since at this inn, described by many as being the most fun in Vermont. It is relaxed and happy, giving one the feeling of being a family house guest. There are only ten guest rooms, with six baths. This inn is particularly popular during cross-country skiing season, when it is part of a "ski from inn to inn" plan that connects several popular area inns. A similar "hike inn to inn" program is operated for backpackers in the summer. For further details about both of these programs, write to the Churchill House, RFD #3, Brandon, VT 05733.

Most of the cooking is done by Mrs. Liebert and is representative of several cuisines, all excellent. Thus, many diners lodging elsewhere will make a special effort to eat at the Tulip Tree. Among the favorite dishes are homemade pâté, veal piccata, chicken in phyllo, and an assortment of unusual desserts. No pets permitted. *Room Rates:* Rooms are $26 to $30 per person, MAP plus gratuities. *Driving Instructions:* Take Route 4 east of Rutland or Route 7 north and watch for signs to Chittenden.

Dorset, Vermont

Dorset is a quiet village of great beauty in all seasons and has been a favorite of artists for many years. It was the location of the first marble quarry in the state, now a favorite swimming area. More swimming and boating are available at nearby *Emerald Lake.* The first nine-hole golf course in America was established at the *Dorset Field Club,* which currently offers tennis in addition to golf. One of Vermont's famed summer theaters, the *Dorset Playhouse,* operates here. Four great ski centers, *Bromley, Stratton, Magic Mountain,* and *Snow Valley* are all within easy driving distance. Trout fishing in the Battenkill River and deer hunting in the forests make the area popular with these sports-lovers as well. In 1978, Robert Todd Lincoln's country estate, Hildane, was opened to the public in nearby Manchester.

BARROWS HOUSE

Dorset, VT 05251. 802-867-4455. *Innkeepers:* Charles and Marilyn Schubert. Open all year except November 1 to 15.

Barrows House is actually a collection of buildings in the heart of Dorset. The inn property includes a number of early buildings, all carefully renovated and redecorated by the Schuberts. The buildings offer a variety of types of accommodations, from singles to large families. Each building is named, and the selection includes Barrows House (the main inn), Hemlock House, Truffle House, Carriage House, Birds Nest, and the Stable. Barrows House itself is a two-story, white-clapboard colonial building dating from 1784, with two front sitting rooms (one with fireplace), a formal, candle-lit dining room, and a tavern at the rear that seats about thirty in its dark oak chairs. Ten of the guest rooms are in Barrows House, with the remainder in the other buildings mentioned above. Larger families can stay in Truffle House, where they can share three twin-bedded rooms and a common living room with fireplace. The Stable has rooms with exposed beams and is the most expensive lodging at the inn. Most rooms have wall-to-wall carpeting, and many have coordinated drapes, quilts, and wallpaper, all selected by Marilyn Schubert.

All meals are served under the careful supervision of the young and talented cook, Sissy. First hired as a chambermaid, she quickly made her talent as a chef and supervisor of kitchen help known, and

she is now the driving force behind the inn's recent boom in popularity as a Dorset dining spot. The menu changes daily, with all dinners prix fixe at $10.95, plus tax. Dinners begin with a choice of six appetizers, followed by choice of salad and entrée. Typical appetizers include tomato bouillon, clam chowder, mulligatawny soup, and french fried mushrooms. Entrée selections might include sliced filet of beef Marchand au vin, chicken niçoise, fresh lake trout, veal scallops with mustard cream sauce, roast leg of lamb, or shrimp Kiev. There are several selections of accompanying vegetables, potatoes, or pasta. Dinner includes choice of dessert. An occasional appetizer will bear an additional tariff (oysters on the half shell add $2), but all entrées are available without surcharge.

Recreational facilities at Barrows House are excellent. Many cross-country skiers start right at their door (rentals are available at the inn's cross-country ski shop), and the inn has its own swimming pool, tennis courts, and sauna. There is a gazebo for relaxing at the end of a warm Vermont summer day. Badminton and croquet are popular here in the summer and fall. Golfing at the Dorset Field Club and horseback riding are availalbe in the immediate vicinity. *Room Rates:* Single rooms are $30 to $42, MAP; double rooms are $60 to $72, MAP. Tax and gratuity charges are added. *Driving Instructions:* From Route 7 in Vermont, take Route 30 northeast to Dorset. Route 30 leaves Route 7 just north of Manchester.

DORSET INN

Church and Main Streets, Dorset, VT. Mailing address: Box 8, Dorset, VT 05251. 802-867-5500. *Innkeeper:* Fred G. Russell. Open from late May to late October and from late December to late March.

The Dorset Inn was built in two sections. The first section, dating from 1796, makes it the oldest inn in the state; the second, built in 1850, now houses the living room and dining room. The inn is characterized by quaint, old-fashioned decorations, as well as wide board floors and four-poster beds, antiques, and more recent solid country furniture. Most of the forty-seven rooms have been renovated to include private baths, although seven share baths.

The inn has a swimming pool and is within walking distance of the Dorset Field Club. Cookouts are held every Wednesday evening in the warmer months. The dining room has an intimate feeling with its papered walls and simple curtained windows. Meals are described as "authentic New England menus, prepared to delicious Yankee perfection." The dinner menu is kept small and includes four or five simple selections, such as steak, chicken, or haddock. Appetizer, salad, and dessert are included in the dinner price, which ranges from $5.50 to $7.50, with a surcharge to inn guests on MAP for some of the more expensive items. *Room Rates:* Single rooms are $25 to $34, MAP; rooms with double occupancy are $37 to $48, MAP. A 15 percent surcharge for gratuities is added. *Driving Instructions:* From Route 7, just north of Manchester, take Route 30 into Dorset.

Gassets, Vermont (including Chester)

Gassets is a very small town about five miles north of Chester and eight miles west of Springfield. Chester is a quiet, unspoiled village that is convenient to a number of ski areas, including *Magic Mountain, Timber Ridge,* and *Okemo,* to mention only the closest. Nearby Springfield has several tourist attractions, including the *Eureka School,* the first school built in Vermont (1785). Near the school is one of Vermont's many covered bridges. Springfield also houses the *Springfield Art and Historical Society.* The *Old Stone Village* at Chester is a fine collection of old houses and a church, all built of stone. In town, too, are the Chester Art Guild, the Grist Mill, and the Green Mountain Railroad's Steam Train Terminal.

THE OLDE TOWNE FARM LODGE

Route 10, Gassetts, Vermont. Mailing address: RD # 1, Chester Depot, VT 05144. 802-875-2346. *Innkeepers:* Fred and Jan Baldwin and family. Open all year except Thanksgiving Day.

This large white farmhouse is noted for a handmade spiral staircase that is a real testimony to early craftsmanship. The lodge has nine guest rooms, two with private baths. The remainder share three bathrooms. There are wide-board floors throughout, and the rooms are partially furnished with antiques. The family lounge has a stone floor and stone fireplace. This popular area serves as a cozy relaxing spot for before-dinner drinks (bring your own bottle) and after-dinner relaxation in front of the fire.

The farm was built more than a century ago and was known as the Chester Towne Farm. The indigent of the town were given food and lodging in return for a hard day's work on the farm. The property was sold by the town in the 1950s and was operated as a farm for a while before being converted by its owners into an inn. The inn then changed hands and was more completely renovated in the early 1970s. The Baldwin family purchased the inn in 1977.

The inn has a spring-fed pond for swimming, fishing, and skating. It is heated by a huge wood furnace, and the fragrance of wood smoke greets travelers on their approach to the inn during the winter months. Meals are simple and substantial; they feature such items as breast of chicken with cranberry glaze, roast beef, sirloin steak, lasagne, and Jan Baldwin's special homemade desserts. Pets are not permitted. *Room Rates:* Rooms are $21 to $24 per person, MAP. Rates are half-price for children under thirteen staying in their parents' room. *Driving Instructions:* Take Route 103 north through Chester to Route 10. Turn east on Route 10 and drive ½ mile to the inn.

Grafton, Vermont

Grafton has had the good fortune to be the recipient of extensive restoration funding by the Windham Foundation. The result has been that a number of houses have been purchased by the foundation and restored fully. These are then leased to individuals, with the result that the village is a genuine, functioning Vermont town, one of the most handsome in the state. The fine white-clapboard houses are not marred by any visible power lines, and many gas lamps have been installed to add to the romantic effect. The foremost project of the Foundation has been the extraordinary restoration of the Old Tavern at Grafton, which is open for lodging and fine food. In addition, the *Grafton Historical Society* has a fine collection of Grafton memorabilia including a large collection of historic photographs. There are a number of fine antique shops and other sources of gifts. The *Grafton Village Cheese Company* manufactures Covered Bridge Brand Cheddar Cheese and is open to visitors.

THE OLD TAVERN AT GRAFTON

Grafton, VT 05146. 802-843-2375. *Innkeeper:* Lois Copping. Open all year except Christmas Eve, Christmas Day, and April.

The Old Tavern at Grafton is far and away the most impressive piece of restoration as yet performed by the craftsmen at the disposal of the Windham Foundation. The Old Tavern is an imposing, shuttered, brick-and-clapboard white building distinguished by its seven two-story columns. The main inn, noted for its fine paneling, beautiful pumpkin-pine floors, and extraordinary collection of antiques is joined by a glassed-in breezeway to the original barn, which now serves as the lounge for the guests of the inn. Its exposed beams and ample use of board paneling give the barn a warm feeling. The Old Tavern is our candidate for the most perfectly recreated inn in the northeast. Here no detail has been overlooked. Indeed, this very feeling of perfection, of every panel perfectly painted, of every piece of furniture perfectly placed gives the inn a formality that would not appeal to those who seek the casualness of some Vermont inns. This is no feet-on-a-stool-in-front-of-the-fire inn. Nor does it intend to be. This is an inn that makes few mistakes, an inn in which we would feel sure our parents would be comfortable.

The Old Tavern has thirty-seven guest rooms, all with private bath. Of these, fourteen are in the Old Tavern building described above, and the remainder are in an assemblage of two old houses and a barn directly across the street. Known as The Homestead and The Windham Cottage, this complex also has function rooms that host meetings of business groups from all over New England. Each guest room has a lovely collection of antiques, including canopied or four-poster beds, beautiful rugs, and comfortable furniture.

The inn has a fully developed recreational program, including a natural swimming pond, tennis courts, a croquet court, indoor-games rooms, and bicycles available for rental. There are well-marked hiking trails and nearby horseback-riding and golf. In the winter, guests may get guaranteed reservations at Timber Ridge Ski Area, a special, limited-ticket area that eliminates long waiting in lift lines. Several miles of cross-country ski trails are maintained by the inn, and they can provide snowshoes, sleds, and toboggans for guests. Lunch and dinner are served at the inn for guests and the public, and breakfast is served for guests only. The menu is not a radical one but has nice surprises like cold blueberry soup or cheese-and-bacon pie to augment some of the more standard items.

In its rich history, Woodrow Wilson, Theodore Roosevelt, General Ulysses Grant, Henry David Thoreau, Oliver Wendell Holmes, and Rudyard Kipling have all stayed at the Old Tavern. All in all, this is an extraordinarily well-thought-out inn for those guests who enjoy the ambiance of this very special place. The secret is long since out, so plan to make reservations early. Families with children and pets are placed in one of several guest houses maintained by the Windham Foundation. *Room Rates:* Rooms are $30 to $50 per night, year-round. Please inquire in advance. *Driving Instrkctions:* Take Route I-91 to exit 5, then Route 121 to Grafton.

WOODCHUCK HILL FARM

Middletown Road, Grafton, VT 05146. 802-843-2398. *Innkeepers:* Anne and Frank Gabriel. Open from May to November.

Woodchuck Hill Farm is the oldest house in Grafton, built about 1780. Originally built for the first minister, the inn has been completely restored. During the 1930s, a porch and other additions were built. Located on a hilltop with gorgeous views, the inn is a comfortable, relaxing place where the guests are joined in a family spirit. The living room has a big fireplace with a fire going on cooler days. In the summer, the large porch is a favorite gathering place for guests before dinner. Each evening the Gabriels prepare a single-entrée meal that is served family style with all the guests at a single large table. A recent dinner included Tomato Vintage, a spiced tomato bouillon, home-baked bread and muffins, pickled beets and caponata, salad of homegrown greens, a mixed grill of filet mignon, loin lamb chop, kidney, and tomato served with mushrooms, fresh vegetables, and roast potatoes. Dessert might be homemade apple pie, peach Melba, or a parfait. The evening meal is prix fixe at $10. Although liquor is not served at the inn, setups are furnished with cheese and crackers in the lounge or porch area. Pets and children under eight years are not permitted. *Room Rates:* The four guest rooms (shared baths) are $25 a double and $20 for single accommodations. A fifth bedroom is planned for the near future with private bath, balcony, and entry. *Driving Instructions:* The inn is 2 miles west of the village on Middletown Road.

Hartland, Vermont

Hartland is a small town on the Connecticut River, eight miles north of Windsor. The town has no special sightseeing or recreational facilities but is near the many sights of Windsor, which include the historic *Constitution House,* where the Vermont State Constitution was first framed. The *American Precision Museum* offers a fine collection of machines, tools, and their products. There is golf at the *Windsor Country Club* and skiing at the *Mount Ascutney Ski Area.* A fine covered bridge crosses the Connecticut River here. There are several river-powered mills in this area open to the public.

CADY BROOK FARM
Jenneville Road, Hartland, VT 05048. Mailing Address: RR 1, Box 120, Windsor, VT 05089. 802-436-2486. *Innkeepers:* Ruth and John Sammel. Open all year.

The Cady Brook Farm offers families a chance to stay in a small, remote 1794 Federal-style building that has been renovated recently but retains the feeling of its original period. It was built by an officer who served in the Revolutionary War. The inn was then known as Burkes Stand and was a stop on the stagecoach route between Woodstock and Windsor. Some of its rooms have had the paint removed to reveal original stenciling. There are only four guest rooms, and these all share bath facilities. Meals are served family style and feature simple home cooking. Pets are not permitted. *Room Rates:* For adults, $20 per day or $90 per week, per person, MAP. Rates for children are $15 and $70, respectively. *Driving Instructions:* The inn is off the beaten track and is reached via a dirt road. Guests who make reservations are sent a special map.

Jamaica, Vermont

Jamaica State Park offers swimming and kayaking in the West River, which is the site of many kayak races. The town is quite small and old-fashioned–looking. It is located 4 miles northwest of West Townshend and 14 miles from Newfane.

THREE MOUNTAIN INN
Route 30, Jamaica, VT 05343. 802-874-4140. *Innkeepers:* Elaine and Charles Murray. Open every month but May.

Three Mountain Inn is a small, exquisite inn built in the late 1700s. The white clapboard house with its original twelve-over-twelve windows and big center chimney has been carefully restored by the Murrays, and there is nothing they like better than showing off their handiwork. The inn is a beauty, and they feel everyone should have

a chance to see it. The eight guest rooms are attractively decorated and furnished with antiques. Four of the rooms have private baths and one has a king-size four-poster bed; another, a private balcony overlooking the gardens and pool. A little cottage with kitchen facilities is also available on a weekly basis.

The living room has wide-planked pine walls and floors and the original Dutch oven fireplace with a roaring fire to warm guests on chilly winter days and cool Vermont evenings any season. The library provides plenty of reading material for those long evenings. Dinners are served by candlelight in the dining room. Specialties of Elaine Murray's are a vegetable quiche, a variety of hearty soups, and her desserts. The menu changes frequently and always has a roast and fresh fish of the day. The pub-room lounge offers diners a before- or after-dinner drink. The pub and dining room are open to guests and the public. Breakfasts can be light, continental style with freshly baked muffins, donuts, or rolls and juice; or it can be a hearty country meal of locally smoked bacon or ham, pancakes, and eggs.

The inn has its own swimming pool with a fountain waterfall and border of mountain rocks from one of the three mountains nearby. Cross-country skiing and hiking are within walking distance, and ice-skating and excellent downhill skiing are minutes away. No pets permitted. *Room Rates:* Rooms range from $30 to $45. *Driving Instructions:* Take I-91 to Brattleboro, second exit. Then take Route 30 to Jamaica. The inn is on Route 30, Jamaica's main street.

Killington, Vermont

Killington is located high in the Green Mountains at an elevation of 4,200 feet. The town is 11 miles from Rutland at the junction of Routes 4 and 100. *Killington Ski Resort* is one of the east's largest and offers an incredible number of year-round recreational activities. The *Killington Gondola* has the longest gondola ride in the country, 3½ miles to the top of Killington. The Gondola operates in the summer and fall for sightseers. *Killington Playhouse* and the *Green Mountain Guild* present a variety of summer theater. A complete list of the many attractions at Killington can be obtained by writing Killington Ski Area, Killington Road, Killington, VT 05751, or by calling 802-422-3333.

THE VERMONT INN

Route 4, Killington, VT 05751. 802-773-9847. *Innkeepers:* Judy and Alan Carmasin. Open all year except for three weeks in May. The restaurant is closed Tuesdays.

The Vermont Inn was originally a farmhouse built in the early nineteenth century. The small inn, recently redecorated, has fifteen guest rooms, nine with private baths. The views from the inn of Killington, Pico, and Shrewsbury Peaks are spectacular. It is part of a guided cross-country ski tour that starts at the Tulip Tree Inn in Chittenden. (Write the Tulip Tree for details.) The public rooms have antiques, modern cloth hangings, exposed beams, a wood-burning stove, and plants everywhere. Candlelit dinners are served in the wood-paneled dining room, warmed by a crackling fire in the enormous fieldstone fireplace. All meals are prepared in the inn's kitchen by chef E. Mark Chaput. The New England and continental cuisines are complemented by an extensive wine selection. Pets are not permitted. *Room Rates:* From Thanksgiving to April, rooms are $22 to $28 per person for double occupancy, MAP. Off-season rates are $20 to $26 per room, EP. *Driving Instructions:* Located 6 miles east of Rutland and 4 miles west of Killington, just off Route 4.

Landgrove, Vermont

Landgrove is a tiny town in the Green Mountain National Forest, about 15 miles northeast of Manchester. The town is served by unpaved country roads only. However, it is a short drive to the neighboring towns of Weston, Peru, and Londonderry. Nearby is *Magic Mountain Ski Area*, with its twenty-two trails and three slopes served by a total of five lifts. The immensely popular *Stratton Mountain* has ten lifts that serve 59 miles of trails. This is a huge, year-round resort with hundreds of nonskiing activities, including pools, saunas, indoor tennis, and ice-skating.

NORDIC INN

Route 11, Landgrove VT 05148. 802-824-6444. *Innkeepers:* Filippo Pagano and Inger Johansson. Open from Thanksgiving until April and from July through October.

The Nordic Inn is a converted New England residence built in 1940 and now housing a small inn steeped in Scandinavian tradition. There are four fireplaces in public rooms in the inn, as well as one bedroom with its own fireplace. In 1978, the innkeepers added a new ski shop and did other renovation work using rough-sawn lumber milled from trees cut on their own property. The cross-country ski area now has 14 miles of trails, with 16 more miles planned for the near future. Equipment rentals and instruction are available. Although cross-country skiing is the focus of many guests in the winter, the proximity of several fine downhill areas brings other skiers as well. In addition, the inn is a local center for dart tournaments and has a complete dart shop. The inn is equally popular in the warmer months among those who seek the rural beauty of this area. In all seasons, guests are drawn to the inn to sample Inger's extraordinary dinners with her unmistakable Swedish touch. She is a professional who was head chef for the consul general of Sweden and, later, assistant manager of Corporate Food Services for RCA at Rockefeller Center. The menu is an extensive one, including such popular Scandinavian specialties as smorrebrod, gravad lax med sas, salmon baked on a bed of dill. Continental specialties include sole Veronique, veal à la Oscar, roast baby lamb in herbal mustard sauce, and more. Desserts here are devastating and include mocha crepe, Danish rum pudding, and an almond-custard-filled crepe with raspberry sauce. Entrées are priced from $7.25 to $9.75, with full dinners (appetizer, soup, entrée, and dessert) ranging from $11.00 to $14.50.

Each guest room is decorated differently, many with Scandinavian antiques brought here from the Johansson family farm in Kisa, Sweden. The rooms are named Sweden, Norway, Finland, Denmark, and Vermont. Each is decorated in the colors of the particular country's flag. All are bright and cheerful. If you want the room with the fireplace, ask to stay in "Sweden." The lower level of the inn contains the ski shop and a fully licensed *après*-ski tavern. Pets are not permitted, but children are welcome. *Room Rates:* Rooms are $25.50 to $31.50 per person, MAP, during the winter. In the summer, rates are $9 to $12 per person, EP. *Driving Instructions:* The inn is located between Londonderry and Peru on Route 11.

THE VILLAGE INN

RFD Landgrove, VT 05148. 802-824-6673. *Innkeeper:* D. Jay Snyder. December 1 through April 15 and July 1 - October 15.

The first part of the Village Inn was constructed in 1810 and has had various additions over the years. The most recent was made in 1976. The result is a series of low, interconnected buildings, mostly in clapboard, that has come to serve as a small resort rather than a country inn. On the property are a private tennis court, heated outdoor pool, and a nine-hole pitch-and-putt golf course. Inn guests who enjoy cross-country skiing can use trails that originate there, while downhill skiers have only short drives to Bromley, Stratton, Magic Mountain, Snow Valley, or Okemo. There is a Rafter Room Lounge for guests (bring your own bottle). Guests here can enjoy the combination of rural seclusion and some resort facilities. The guest rooms are large, with curtains, comforters, and an old-fashioned look. Of the twenty rooms available, fourteen have private baths. Dinners at the inn are simple affairs featuring such main courses as roast beef with Bordelaise sauce or chicken Kiev. Desserts include carrot cake, coffee mousse pie, apple knobby cake, and apple crisp. The dining room is open to the public for breakfast and dinner. Lunch is served to guests only (summer). Pets are not permitted. *Room Rates:* In the winter, rooms are $16 to $30 per person, MAP. Summer rates are $18 to $32 per room, EP. *Driving Instructions:* From Manchester, take Route 11 past Bromley ski area and turn left into Peru. At the fork in Peru bear left and continue 4½ miles through the National Forest to the crossroads in Landgrove. Turn left toward Weston; the inn is on the right.

Londonderry, Vermont

Londonderry is located in south central Vermont at the edge of the Green Mountain National Forest. Nearby is *Magic Mountain Ski Area* with its twenty-two trails and three slopes served by a total of five lifts. The immensely popular *Stratton Mountain* has ten lifts that serve 59 miles of trails. This is a huge, year-round resort with hundreds of nonskiing activities, including pools, saunas, indoor tennis, and ice-skating.

THE HIGHLAND HOUSE

Route 100, Londonderry, VT 05148. 802-824-3019. *Innkeepers:* Margaret and Alan Unangst. Open all year.

The Highland House was built in 1840 and has been providing lodging for travelers through southern Vermont for over a hundred years. The seven-guest-room inn is noted for its wide pine-board floors and four-poster beds. There is a small, cozy lounge outfitted with a Franklin stove to dispel the chills of winter. The dining room is an informal, friendly place that offers individually prepared meals from a menu that changes daily and offers a choice of three entrées each evening, as well as homemade soups, breads, and desserts. The evening meal and breakfast are both open to the public as well as guests.

Highland House is a small, informal place. Guests and innkeepers get to know each other in a rural inn filled with a family spirit. Many of the paintings in the inn are by the innkeepers' daughter, Judi. In addition to the inn accommodations, there is a housekeeping cottage that sleeps eight on the property. Pets are not permitted. *Room*

Rates: Rooms are $10 to $15 per person in the inn (shared bath). *Driving Instructions:* The inn is on Route 100 between Londonderry and Weston, almost 2 miles north of Route 11.

Manchester, Vermont

Manchester has long drawn both summer and winter visitors to this mountainous area. Nearby are the Big Bromley and Stratton Mountain ski areas. During the warmer months, there is a spectacular *Equinox Skyline Drive* to the top of Mount Equinox (toll road). Those who fish will certainly enjoy stopping at the *American Museum of Fly Fishing* and also at the headquarters of the Orvis Company, manufacturers of fine fly-fishing equipment. The *Southern Vermont Art Center* has a collection of paintings graphics, and sculpture. Nearby *Emerald Lake State Park* is located to the north of the village on U.S. 7. Also in Manchester is a branch of *Basketville*.

THE 1811 HOUSE

Route 7, Manchester, VT. Mailing address: Box 557, Manchester, VT 05254. 802-362-1811. *Innkeeper*: William P. Childs. Open from June to mid-October and December to mid-April.

This inn was built, as its name implies, in the early 1800s. There have been later additions, in character with the original structure. From 1905 to 1935 it was the private home of Mary Lincoln Isham, granddaughter of Abraham Lincoln. The inn is furnished with some antiques and has six working fireplaces, including four in guest rooms. Wood is provided free of charge during the winter months. All seven guest rooms (including two suites) have private baths. The inn is set on the lovely village green in the village center. No meals are served to guests except breakfast. *Room Rates*: In the summer, single rooms range from $12 to $15, doubles from $18 to $25, and suites from $25 to $35. Winter rates are approximately $3 to $10 higher. Weekly rates are also available. *Driving Instructions*: The inn is on Route 7 in Manchester, a mile south of Manchester Center.

THE INN AT MANCHESTER

Box 452, Main Street, Manchester, VT 05254. 802-362-1793. *Innkeepers*: Harriet and Stan Rosenberg. Open all year.

The inn is a restored and renovated big Vermont home built, at the turn of the century, at the foot of Equinox Mountain in the town of Manchester. The Rosenbergs have furnished it with many antiques. Sitting areas around working fireplaces, well-stocked bookcases, and attractive wallpapered rooms all work to create a warm, comfortable atmosphere. There are two types of accommodations available; pine-paneled dorms with bunks or single beds, and seven more romantic guest rooms, each with coordinated wallpapers, sheets, towels, and carpets. Many of the rooms have fireplaces and big bay windows. The dining room is warmed by a large wood-burning stove and also by the rich colors of the room and its Tiffany-shaded lamps. Meals here are served family style and consist of Vermont home cooking, with special soups, fresh vegetables, and home-baked breads and desserts. Big, hearty breakfasts are also included in the room rate. Liquor is not available, but guests are welcome to bring their own; setups are provided in the lounge areas. *Room Rates*: Rooms are $36 double occupancy, MAP. Lower rates for children and dorm rooms. *Driving Instructions*: The inn is on Route 7 in the town of Manchester, 21 miles north of Bennington.

RELUCTANT PANTHER INN
West Road (just off Route 7), Manchester Village, VT 05254. 802-362-2568. *Innkeepers*: Mr. and Mrs. Stephen Wood Cornell III. Open from Christmas to Easter and from Memorial Day to October 30.

The Reluctant Panther was fashioned out of an imposing clapboard

home built in 1850. The inn has seven guest rooms, several with working fireplaces. The decor in all the rooms is varied but very stylish. Wall-to-wall carpets are the rule.

The two dining rooms (one is a solarium with a glass ceiling) are open to the public and are considered to be among the finest in the area. All dinners are prix fixe, with rates for a complete meal at $10 to $14. The menu includes two cold soups, avgaolemone and gazpacho; two hot soups, carrot-top and green pea; four hors d'oeuvres, including a tiny broiled trout and bacon-wrapped asparagus with Vermont cheddar cheese sauce. There are nine carefully prepared entrées, including *crêpes Rangoon* or *à la Reine,* individual filet of beef Wellington, veal Cordon Bleu, or breast of chicken stuffed with almond and apple dressing. Pets and children are not permitted. *Room Rates*: Rooms are $20 to $35 daily, double occupancy. *Driving Instructions*: The inn is located in the center of Manchester Village, about 20 miles north of Bennington on Route 7.

Marlboro, Vermont

Marlboro is a quiet college town in the southeastern portion of Vermont about 10 miles west of Brattleboro. It is best known for the *Marlboro Music Festival* held each summer under the direction of Rudolf Serkin. Winter visitors to this area are within easy driving of downhill ski areas—*Hogback, Haystack*, and *Mount Snow.*

WHETSTONE INN

Marlboro, VT 05344. 802-254-2500. *Innkeepers*: Mr. and Mrs. Hubert Moore. Open all year.

The Whetstone Inn was built in 1785 and was first used as a tavern in stagecoach days. The public rooms have cheery fires and an ample supply of interesting books, records, and games. The Moores, who have been innkeepers for many years, are most hospitable, and the inn is inviting in all seasons. In winter there is cross-country skiing, sledding, and snowshoeing right on the inn's grounds, and there is downhill skiing a short distance away. Warmer weather finds visitors enjoying hiking or photography or taking part in activities on the campus of Marlboro College, 2 miles away.

The ten guest rooms are large and well appointed. Most have four-poster beds, and five have private baths. Only breakfast is served at the inn. Pets are permitted with advance notice. *Room Rates*: Single rooms are $13, double rooms, $22 to $26. Breakfast included. *Driving Instructions*: Take Route I-91 to exit 2 (Brattleboro) and go 8½ miles west on Route 9, then ½ mile south to the village of Marlboro.

Newfane, Vermont

Newfane is a small town that houses a particularly fine pillared Federal-style *Courthouse* built in 1825. This much-photographed village is within easy drive of the *Townshend State Forest* and a small ski area known as *Maple Valley*, which is in nearby West Dummerston. Also within driving distance are Brattleboro and Marlboro, with its famous summer music festival. Auctions are held in Newfane every Saturday night in the summer.

THE FOUR COLUMNS INN

230 West Street, Newfane, VT 05345. 802-365-7713. *Innkeeper*: René Chardain. Open from late May to November and from late December to April. The restaurant of this inn is closed on Mondays.

The Four Columns Inn houses one of the more distinguished French restaurants in New England. The inn consists of a white clapboard building with its four columns and a red clapboard barn that serves as the restaurant. Here the specialties vary according to season and include salmon a l'oseille, scampi, guinea hen, and pheasant. The restaurant also serves fresh trout and the traditional duck à l'orange, as well as an assortment of dishes prepared in classic French ways. Prices vary according to the seasonal selections and are generally quite expensive. Luncheon is not served in the winter.

The inn has twelve guest rooms featuring spool beds. All rooms have private baths. Pets are permitted. *Room Rates* 1978 : Rooms are $28 to $40. *Driving Instructions*: The inn is 100 yards off Route 30 in the center of Newfane.

OLD NEWFANE INN

Route 30 and the Common, Newfane, VT 05345. 802-365-4427. *Innkeeper*: Eric Weindl. Open from May to October and December to April.

Not far from the Four Columns is a fine old Vermont inn with an impressive menu. Built in 1787, the Old Newfane is filled with early American antiques and retains the wide-board floors, beamed ceilings, and red brick fireplaces characteristic of this period. It was built on Newfane Hill and moved to the present location on the Common in 1825. The extensive and not inexpensive French menu in the dining room lists over a dozen appetizers and even more entrées, including such specialties as medallion de veau aux champignons, frogs' legs Provençale, rack of lamb, duckling à l'orange, and veal Gismonda. The ten papered guest rooms are decorated in traditional old New England style. Eight of the rooms have private baths; the remaining two have a connecting bath. This inn, like the Four Columns, is highly recommended to travelers who wish excellent food

in a somewhat formal atmosphere. No children or pets are permitted. *Room Rates* (1978): Double rooms are $35 to $45. *Driving Instructions*: Take Route 30 to Newfane. The inn is in the center of town.

Peru, Vermont

Peru is a small village that serves as a less hectic base for the enjoyment of *Big Bromley Ski Area* (and its summer alpine slide). Cross-country skiers enjoy nearby *Viking Ski Center, Wild Wings,* and the *Nordic Inn Cross Country Ski Center.* Vacationers seeking other forms of entertainment and sightseeing are encouraged to drive to neighboring Manchester, Manchester Center, and Londonderry. At Londonderry, Route 11 joins Route 100, which meanders through some of Vermont's most beautiful scenery. Hiking along the Appalachian Trail and fishing in the Battenkill River are among some of the warm-weather pleasures available here. Also located in Peru is the *Hapgood Recreational Area*, which offers picnicking, camping, boating, swimming, and hiking. A short drive away is Weston, with its numerous year-round attractions.

JOHNNY SEESAW'S

Route 11, Peru, VT 05152. 802-824-5533. *Innkeepers*: Larry and Anne Ward and Sarah McKim. Open July 4 through foliage season and Thanksgiving through the end of snow season.

The original building of this inn dates from 1926, when it functioned as a dance hall. It has been renovated and made larger since then. At one point, several cottages were added, so that guests now may choose a country inn atmosphere or the greater privacy offered by the cottages, all of which have private baths, fireplaces in the living rooms, and television. The inn has private guest rooms, bunk rooms, a dining room, and the main living room with its round fireplace. Guests frequently gather around the fire in the raised alcove to relax and sing to guitar music. The inn has its own swimming pool and tennis court for summer use.

Dinners at the inn are examples of simple country cooking. Homemade soups, breads, desserts, and pies highlight the meal. Children are often served early to allow their parents to enjoy a more leisurely meal. After dinner, the children may retire to their own

private television room, complete wih pinball machine. *Room Rates*: All rates are per person, MAP. In the cottages, $36; in the inn with private bath, $25 to $33; in the inn with shared bath, $25. Rates for children and in the bunk room are less. *Driving Instructions*: Peru is midway between Manchester and Londonderry on Route 11.

WILEY INN ON BROMLEY MOUNTAIN

Route 11, Peru, VT 05152. 802-824-6600. *Innkeeper*: Grace Tarplin. Open all year except November and April 15 to June 15. The Wiley is a hundred-year-old inn located on Bromley Mountain in the heart of some of Vermont's finest ski areas. The inn is small and cozy and features regional cooking supervised by a former New York caterer with twenty-five years of experience. There are two lounges with fireplaces and twenty guest rooms, eight with baths and twelve that share baths. Summer guests swim in the inn's heated pool and drive to nearby hiking, golf, tennis, and other recreational and sightseeing activities.

Dining is available for both guests and the public at breakfast and dinner. Specialties on the dinner menu include cream of celery soup Louisiana, Oriental chicken breasts, chicken crepes Divan, baked ham-cheese Elégant, Bavarian pot roast, and Cornish hen Marsala. All are accompanied by special baked breads and potato or rice dishes. *Room Rates*: In winter, rooms with private baths are $25 per person, MAP. Rooms with shared baths cost less. Summer rates are somewhat lower. *Driving Instructions*: Take Route 7 to Route 22 and then into Peru.

Plymouth and Plymouth Union, Vermont

Plymouth was the scene of a gold rush many years ago, and over $2 million in gold was taken from the area. Even today, gold is occasionally panned from local rivers. However, Plymouth is best known as the birthplace of President Calvin Coolidge. The *Calvin Coolidge National Historical Restoration* and his family birthplace-homestead is here. It was here that he became the only president to be sworn in by his own father. The *Plymouth Cheese Factory*, run by Coolidge's son, is open to the public; visitors can watch the cheese being made. Skiing is available at the *Round Top Ski Area*, with its two chair lifts. Seven miles away is the *Killington Ski Area* with its famous gondola and the longest ski season in the East. Near the Coolidge homestead is the *Wilder House*, birthplace of Coolidge's mother and now a visitor's center. *Wilder Barn*, in the village, houses a fine museum of farming tools and related farm implements.

SALT ASH INN

Plymouth Union, VT 05056. 802-672-3748. *Innkeepers*: Ginny and Don Kroitzsh. Open in the summer, fall, and winter.

The Salt Ash Inn has had a rich history as, at various times, a stage-coach stop, post office, inn, and general store. Most of the antiques in the building were originally used there. A large circular fireplace warms the lounge, and there is also a small pub. The old post office boxes still remain. You can even see President Coolidge's name on the box where he picked up his mail years ago. The twelve guest rooms are cheerful and retain the flavor of the past. Most have con-

necting baths (two have private baths), and all have wall-to-wall carpeting and quilts on the beds. Food is served family style with home-baked breads and a salad bar. The inn serves both breakfast and dinner to guests and the public at a reasonable $2.50 for breakfast and $5.00 to $6.50 for dinner. No pets please. *Room Rates*: During the peak season (November to April), rooms are $19 to $28, MAP. May to October the rates are $10 to $13 per person, EP. *Driving Instructions*: The inn is at the junction of routes 100 and 100A.

Proctorsville and Ludlow, Vermont

These towns are adjacent to *Okemo Mountain*, with its somewhat more relaxed ski area featuring three double chair lifts and six Poma lifts. There are smaller ski school classes and shorter lift lines than at some of Vermont's major areas. This is one of the most popular areas for family skiing in Vermont. In Ludlow, the *Black River Academy Museum* houses local artifacts. Calvin Coolidge was an 1890 graduate of the Academy. The Okemo Winter Carnival is held in Ludlow in mid-January each year. Visitors may purchase samples of two of Vermont's major food products at the *Crowley Cheese Shop* and the *Green Mountain Sugar House*.

CASTLE INN
Junction of routes 103 and 131, Proctorsville, VT. Mailing address: Box 157, Proctorsville, VT 05153. 802-226-7222. *Innkeepers*: Michael and Sheryl Fratino. Open from mid-May to the end of October and from mid-December to mid-April.

A great variety of country inns dot the countryside in this state, but far and above the most unusual we have run across is the Castle. As its name indicates, guests here are treated to a night at a small, stone castle complete with mahogany and oak paneling, carved plaster ceilings, an oval dining room, sumptuous library, and ten fireplaces scattered throughout the building, many with elaborate carved mantels. Built in 1904 by Allen Fletcher, then a member of the Vermont legislature and later governor, the building was converted to an inn in 1964. The exterior walls are 18-inch-thick gneiss that was quarried from the property on which the inn stands. The gabled ends of the house are carved from redwood and, on the entrance side, the carvings end in four figureheads. Noteworthy inside are the finely detailed carving in the oak and mahogany paneling, the carved pineapple finials on the main staircase, the tile work in the foyer and library fireplace, and the family coat of arms carved into the library and "great hall" paneling.

The inn offers ten guest rooms with a distinct baronial feeling in keeping with the public rooms of the estate. Eight of these rooms have private baths. Breakfast is served to guests, and dinner is available to guests and the general public. The dinner menu lists seven appetizers, three soups, nine entrées, and seven desserts. House specialties include pâté maison, escargots served in mushroom caps, fettucine parmigiano, roast duckling with cherry glaze, baked stuffed filet of sole, shrimp scampi and veal scallopini. Desserts include chocolate mousse, peach Melba, pecan pie, and raisin pie. Michael was formerly the chef at a Mobil four-star restaurant in New Hampshire.

The inn has its own large swimming pool and offers year-round tennis on six outside clay courts, as well as on two under a bubble for winter use. There is a lounge and Knights Pub for before- and after-dinner enjoyment. *Room Rates*: All rates are per person, MAP: Single occupancy, $36; double occupancy, $33; additional persons in a room, $25. Ski packages with Okemo and Round Top are available. *Driving Instructions*: Take Route 103 north through Chester to Proctorsville; the inn is 2 miles south of Ludlow on Route 103.

THE COMBES FAMILY INN

RFD # 1, Ludlow, VT. Mailing address: Box 43 TC, Ludlow, VT 05149. 802-228-8799. *Innkeepers*: Ruth, Bill, and Nancy Combes. Open all year.

As the name indicates, this is a true family inn situated on a quiet country back road in the heart of Vermont's mountain and lakes region. There are 50 aces of rolling meadows and woods to explore and to ski cross-country in winter. Cupcake and Brownie, reported to be the friendliest goats around, share the farm with lots of equally friendly cats, dogs, innkeepers, and guests. The inn itself is a century-old farm house that the Combeses have recently renovated. The dining room has exposed beams and a big bay window overlooking pastures and Okemo Mountain. The lounge area is paneled in Vermont barnboards and is furnished with turn-of-the-century oak. The

living room is warmed by fires in the stone fireplace. There are four guest rooms in the old farmhouse, all with shared baths. Five other guest rooms are in an attached motel unit, each with a private bath. Meals at the inn consist of hearty Vermont-style meals with fresh vegetables, cream soups, turkey, lamb, or pork roasts, and heaps of home-baked breads and desserts. The coffee pot is always on, and guests are welcome to help themselves to Nancy's homemade cakes and cookies.

There is no lack of things to do in any season. Okemo and Round Top Ski Areas are minutes away as are Echo Lake, Lake Rescue, and Lake Pauline for swimming, fishing, and boating. The favorite winter sport at the farm is tobogganing. They have several packed runs and plenty of toboggans for guests' use. No pets permitted. *Room Rates*: In the inn, rooms are $18 to $20, MAP, or $10 to $12, EP. Motel rooms are $26, MAP, or $18, EP. Children under twelve are half price. Holiday rates are slightly higher. *Driving Instructions*: From Ludlow, proceed north on Route 103 about 3 miles. Follow state signs for the inn.

THE GOLDEN STAGE INN

Route 103, Proctorsville, VT. Mailing address: Box 103, Proctorsville, VT 05153. 802-226-7744. *Innkeepers*: Tom and Wende Schaaff. Open all year except April.

Built in 1796, the Golden Stage has been a stagecoach stop and private home for 180 years. The inn was once a link in the underground railroad; much later it was the home of Cornelia Otis Skinner. It has had only six owners in its long history and has been completely

redone by the Schaaffs. The inn is a rambling clapboard building with wraparound porches and attached barn set on 4 acres of rolling lawns and gardens. Summer visitors often lounge on one of the porches and take in the view.

There are eight guest rooms, two with private baths; the others share three baths. The rooms are quite spacious (14 by 14 feet), with comfortable beds, homemade bedspreads, beautiful wide-pine floors, and cheery colonial wallpaper and ruffled curtains. A barnboard-paneled lounge with a copper bar and fireplace, a library, and a large plant-filled living room with another fireplace provide plenty of space for guests to relax. The dining room (open to the public with advance reservations) serves traditional New England dishes and continental cuisine. The menu features homemade soups, crepes, quiches, breads, and fish trucked in fresh from the sea. During the summer and fall, the vegetables come straight from the Schaaffs' own garden. Breakfast and dinner are served. No pets please. *Room Rates*: In winter, rooms are $31 per person, MAP. Summer rates are $35 for a double room, with only breakfast included. There are also special five-day winter ski packages. *Driving Instructions*: Take Route 91 to exit 6, then go north on Route 103, 18 miles to the inn.

Quechee, Vermont

Quechee is a small town that is currently going through a good deal of expansion due to the development efforts of the Quechee Lakes Corporation, which has bought 5500 acres here and is developing about half of them. Quechee is located between the towns of Woodstock and White River Junction on Route 4, approximately six miles from the Connecticut River.

THE QUECHEE INN

Marshland Farm, Clubhouse Road, Quechee, VT. Mailing address: P.O. Box 457, Quechee, VT 05059. 802-295-3133. *Innkeepers*: Michael and Barbara Yaroschuk and Craig Taylor. Open all year.

Colonel Joseph Marsh, the first lieutenant governor of Vermont, built his home, known as Marshland, in 1793, using timber he had transported to uechee from his former home state of Connecticut. The farmhouse and associated barns were used as a private residence until the mid-1970s, when they were restored and converted into an inn.

The renovation of the inn was done with care so as to maintain the original feeling of the guest rooms while providing fully modern private bathrooms for the fourteen guest rooms plus the two-room suite. Furnishings are largely Queen Anne in style, with most rooms featuring wide-board pumpkin-pine floors, braided rugs, old-fashioned print curtains, and comforters on the bed. The lounge in the attached converted coach house has exposed heavy timbers and a brick floor and fireplace. The lounge has a fully licensed bar and is also the scene of the continental breakfast for guests, the only meal served. All and all, the inn has a very homey feel, although some guests might wish that the modern touches of room telephones and television had been omitted. The inn has a newly opened ski shed, which will serve a developing cross-country skiing program utilizing the surrounding pasture and horse-trails. Eventually, the inn's trail system will merge with other systems in the immediate area.

Guests at the inn are given passes for the Quechee Lakes Corporation recreational facilities (a private club). For a nominal fee, inn guests thus have access to boating, racquet ball, squash, skiing, tennis, golf, indoor and outdoor swimming, riding, and the exercise room, all according to season. Pets are not permitted. *Room Rates*: Standard rooms are $36; deluxe rooms are $42. An extra charge for more than two people is $10 per person. *Driving Instructions*: From Route I-91, take I-89 North to Exit 1—Route 4. Take Route 4 West about 1 mile, turn right on Clubhouse Road for 1 mile to the inn.

Saxtons River, Vermont

Saxtons River is a lovely Vermont village located above Putney on Route 121 between Bellows Falls and Grafton. The village has several nice antique shops including *Schoolhouse Antiques*. The woods and trails nearby provide excellent hiking and hunting in the warmer seasons and cross-country skiing in the winter. The attractions in Putney include *Basketville, Santa's Land,* and *Harlow's Sugar House.* The *Old Rockingham Meeting House* in nearby Rockingham dates from 1787 and is open during the summer months.

SAXTONS RIVER INN

Main Street, Saxtons River, VT 05154. 802-869-2110. *Innkeeper:* Averill Campbell Larsen. Open every day April through December. Open Thursday through Sunday during February and March, except open all of Washington's Birthday week. Closed January. The restaurant is always closed on Tuesdays.

The current Saxtons River Inn was built in 1903 as a summer family hotel. After a series of colorful and occasionally eccentric owners, the inn was bought by the Campbell family, who with much help from friends and neighbors revived and restored the inn with obvious loving care. The inn is now run with great energy and talent by Averill Campbell Larsen, who not only cooks all the meals served with great skill but is equally at home with a hammer and saw or a swatch of wallpaper.

The inn has a spacious public dining room, cozy bar with copper top, and several public sitting rooms in addition to twenty individually decorated guest rooms, of which eleven have private bath. Throughout the inn Ms. Larsen has shown tireless care in taking wood to its natural state and augmenting that look with a tasteful, albeit novel selection of wallpapers. Rooms are available in the original hotel building and across the street in the lovely old Colvin House, which also houses the inn's well-stocked store. Baskets, plants, dried arrangements, and kitchen gadgetry, as well as a nice selection of gifts are sold there.

Saxtons River Inn offers lunch and dinner to the public, and it offers a simple but scrumptious breakfast to overnight guests. Dinners are a breath of fresh air in contrast to the pedestrian restaurant fare so common throughout the country today. The menu changes

twice a week and features such special soups as Vermont cheddar cheese, Senegalese, and lentil. Approximately six entrées are offered, including steak au poivre and roast duck for those whose taste buds are not tantalized by such as Sayur Lodeh (Indonesian shrimp and vegetables), crepes Florentine, roulade sole, saltimboca, or chicken breasts Savoyarde. Included with the entrée are salad, vegetables, homemade bread, and coffee. Desserts (at $1.50) may be selected from a sinful collection of confections on display on the inn's former coal-burning cook stove. A complete dinner with soup and dessert as well as the entrée should range from $9.00 to $14.00 per person. The luncheon menu includes large salads, sandwiches, and a selection of imaginative luncheon entrées, including quiche, moussaka, spanakopeta, and crepes. Lit by Tiffany-period stained glass lights, the dining room has deep green walls, colorful tablecloths, and fresh flowers and candlelight. All in all, the Saxtons River Inn is a happy, romantic place. It gives all guests a very helpful information package of what to do in the area. Pets are not permitted. *Room Rates*: Double rooms range from $15 to $35 (one room in the latter price range has its own private porch with wicker furniture). Rates are EP including continental breakfast. *Driving Instructions*: Take Route 121 to 4 miles west of Bellows Falls; then take Route I-91 to exit 5.

Tyson, Vermont (see Proctorsville and Ludlow)

ECHO LAKE INN

Route 100, Tyson, VT. Mailing Address: Box 142, Ludlow, VT 05149. 802-226-8602. *Innkeeper*: Roger Scully. Open all year except for short closings in late fall and spring.

The Echo Lake Inn was first built in 1800 and additions were made in 1869. It has always been either an inn or a hotel. The entire building was fully refurbished in 1971–72, and it is currently decorated and furnished with reproductions of country antiques. The inn has a somewhat formal atmosphere, suitable to a lodging of its size (twenty-one guest rooms). It is situated on Echo Lake and provides guests with a dock full of canoes and rowboats. There is lake swimming at the sandy beach nearby, and guests may use the inn's heated swimming pool. Other facilities include an all-weather tennis court with lights for nighttime play and the inn's own ice-skating rink across the street. Adjacent to the inn is an early cheese factory that has been converted to an antique and gift shop; many of the interesting structural features of this old building have been retained. Pets are permitted in certain special cases only. *Room Rates*: Double rooms with private baths are $27; with connecting bath, $22; with baths in hall, $18. *Driving Instructions*: The inn is 5 miles north of Ludlow on Route 100.

West Dover, Vermont

West Dover is a small village in south-central Vermont noted primarily for its proximity to three ski areas, *Mount Snow, Carinthia,* and *Haystack*. Mount Snow is one of Vemont's most popular ski resorts, and the *Mount Snow Country Club* offers golf, tennis, and horseback riding, among other things, in the summer months. Summer visitors can enjoy the concerts at the *Marlboro Music Festival*, described in our *Country New England Sightseeing and Historical Guide*. Also nearby are the villages of Wilmington, Newfane, and Wardsboro.

THE HANDLE HOUSE

Handle Road, West Dover, VT 05356. 802-464-5449. *Innkeeper*: Winifred Sargent. Open December through April, July and August.

Once a stagecoach stop in Revolutionary days, the Handle House is now a farm-inn with eight guest rooms, all with private baths. The inn has an active summer program for the children of guests including swimming, riding (using the farm stables), archery, sailing, and tennis. Many neighborhood children also participate in the camplike atmosphere. Riding is available for adults as well. In winter, skiing takes over—either downhill at neighboring Mount Snow or Haystack or cross-country, from the doorstep of the inn. Breakfast and dinner are served to guests only. Typical dinner selections might include roast prime ribs of beef or beef Bourguignon. The inn's special programs make it particularly suitable for families with young children. *Room Rates*: Rooms are $22 per person, MAP. *Driving Instructions*: The inn is located near Route 100 north of West Dover. A map is sent to guests when they make their advance reservations.

INN AT SAWMILL FARM

Route 100, West Dover, VT 05356. 802-464-8131. Mailing Address: Box 8, West Dover, VT 05356. *Innkeeper*: Rodney C. Williams. Open all year except November 15 to December 1.

This 1779 property has undergone a renovation that has completely transformed the interior of the buildings into facilities with modern conveniences, while still retaining the old Vermont feeling. The buildings use the original structure with exposed beams and time-softened barnboard in an extremely effective way. Combined with a highly acclaimed kitchen, the reconstruction has made the Inn at Sawmill Farm one of the most respected inns in the state. Many of the guest rooms and suites have fireplaces for added comfort. The inn is filled with brass, copper, and other antiques. There is a pond on the property that provides swimming and trout fishing in the summer and skating in the winter.

The restaurant, with its exposed timbers and old mill tools on display, features an impressive array of dishes. Appetizers include Irish smoked salmon, coquille of lobster, escargots, and their famed Vermont appetizer—asparagus tips wrapped in ham and baked with Vermont cheddar cheese. Dinner entrées include scallopini à l'Anglaise, roast duck au poivre vert, frogs' legs Provençale, and breast of chicken with white wine and black olives. The dessert menu includes chocolate cake, cheese cake, a special chocolate sundae, and homemade pies. Dinners are à la carte, and full dinners would range in price from about $12.50 to $18.50 per person. No pets permitted. *Room Rates* (1978): Double rooms are $80 for two, MAP; fireplace suites, $90 to $100 for two, MAP. *Driving Instructions*: Take Route I-91 to Brattleboro. Then take Route 9 west 21 miles to Wilmington. Take Route 100 north 5 miles to the inn. From the New York Thruway, exit at Troy and follow Route 7 east to Bennington, then take Route 9 to Wilmington and continue as above.

West Townshend, Vermont

West Townshend is located at the edge of the Green Mountain National Forest and is characterized by rolling hills and deep valleys. *Townshend Lake* has swimming, boating, and fishing, and *Townshend State Forest* has facilities for hiking, bird watching, swimming, fishing, and camping. The *Windham Heights Country Club*, 8 miles to the north, has tennis, golf, and swimming available. West Townshend is within 10 to 15 miles of several downhill ski areas, including *Mount Snow, Carinthia, Timber Ridge*, and *Magic Mountain*. There are at least seven ski-touring centers in the general vicinity.

WINDHAM HILL FARM

West Townshend, VT 05359. 802-874-5951. *Innkeepers*: Betty and Jim Seagers. Open from May to October and from December to April.

The road from Windham Road to the inn borders a deeply cleft valley, and the effect is rather like arriving at Shangri-la. The inn has been fashioned out of a 135-year-old farmhouse perched on the edge of a steep hill. There has been one recent addition, by former innkeeper Hugh Folsom, but it was tastefully done in keeping with the original building. The inn is a particularly happy place. The Seagers are joined in their family effort by several of their children and their friends. Their guests, Betty said in a recent visit, are, "for the most part, quite self-sufficient and do not need or participate in organized activities. They're content with back roads, trails, swimming holes, waterfalls, flowers, birds, and wildlife rather than tennis courts and golf courses. They listen to the frogs in our pond rather than canned music from a radio." The effect here is like being a house guest rather than a transient.

Meals are served by candlelight. Summer dinners include food raised in the inn's large organic garden. There is no set menu, so that the freshest in-season foods can be used. The public is welcome at dinner with twenty-four hours advance notice. Dinners are $10 complete.

Each of the inn's guest rooms is decorated in a different way, and all have pleasing views of the woods, valley, or mountains. Several of the rooms seem to perch out into the trees, giving a wonderful relaxing effect. No pets are permitted. *Room Rates*: Rooms are $24 to $27 per person, per day, or $144 to $162 per person, per week. All rates are based on double occupancy and are MAP. Single occupancy rates are higher. *Driving Instructions*: West Townshend is about 21 miles northwest of Brattleboro. In West Townshend, turn up Windham Road, and go one and one-quarter miles to the inn sign on the right.

West Wardsboro, Vermont

West Wardsboro is 5 miles north of Mount Snow and is a winter stopping place for visitors to that famous ski area who do not wish to be in the middle of activities at the ski center or in the busier West Dover. The area has numerous cross-country ski trails. Summer visitors often hike along *The Long Trail*, which passes nearby. Recreational facilities are numerous in all seasons, especially at *Mount Snow*.

THE GREEN MOUNTAIN HOUSE

Route 100, West Wardsboro, VT 05360. 802-896-8491. *Innkeepers*: Bobbe and Ray Price. Open all year.

Located only 5 miles from Mount Snow, the Green Mountain House has been a popular stopping place for visitors to this area since 1825. The original tavern was actually constructed in 1790, and improvements have been made continually. The Prices are both active in YMCA work and have geared their inn to groups of young people, such as the Women's National Cross Country Ski Team, as well as to families and other guests. Originally a popular summer rest stop, the recent explosion of interest in winter sports has made the inn a year-round operation. Cross-country skiing is available on the premises. The Prices like to think of their inn as a home away from home with cheery fires and home-cooked food (for guests only). Pets are permitted. *Room Rates*: Rooms are $12 to $26 per person, MAP. Larger groups of forty or more may book well in advance for special group rates. *Driving Instructions*: The inn is located on Route 100. It is about 5 miles north of the *Mount Snow Ski Area*.

Weston, Vermont

The population of Weston in the mid-1800s was about three times as great as it is today. This is due to the westward movement of many area farmers and the gradual conversion of the farmland into forests. Weston today is a small but thriving community with several tourist attractions, including the *Farrar-Mansur House*, with its collection of local antiques housed in a restored tavern; the *Vermont Guild of Craftsmen*, which is both a museum of old tools and an outlet for contemporary crafts; and the *Vermont Country Store*, one of the state's finest and oldest country stores. During the summer, the *Weston Playhouse* presents a full season of summer theater. The *Weston Bowl Mill* is open daily to the public, with tours of bowl and other woodenware manufacturing processes.

THE INN AT WESTON

Route 100, Box 56, Weston, VT 05161. 802-824-5804. *Innkeepers*: Sue and Stu Douglas. Open June 15 to October 31 and November 15 toApril 1.

The Inn at Weston was described by one visitor as "the friendliest place in New England," and it may well be that. The young innkeepers, Sue and Stu Douglas, have taken an old Vermont farm that was originally a cheese factory and created a homey, inviting inn with a wonderful restaurant featuring home cooking. Built in 1848, the inn has thirteen guest rooms, seven with private baths. Some of the guest rooms are in the recently converted hayloft. Children are welcome here, and there is a game room with television for their

enjoyment. The inn has its original wide-board floors, and the dining room is paneled with old barnboard. Guests can select from a menu that changes daily and reflects Mrs. Douglas's particular talent with both meat and vegetarian dishes (the latter require advance notice). All bread, piecrusts, and pastries are homemade, as are other desserts and soups. The menu reflects ingredients that are fresh and in season. Typical selections include chilled poached salmon, smoked loin of pork, and Russian vegetable pie. All food is served à la carte and is reasonably priced, with most entrées under $7.

Pets are not pemitted. *Room Rates*: Winter rates are $26 to $28 per person, MAP, including breakfast, afternoon tea, and dinner. Summer rates are $28 to $31 double occupancy, EP. *Driving Instructions*: The inn is on Route 100 in the center of Weston.

Wilmington, Vermont

Wilmington is located on scenic Route 100, sometimes known as the "Ski Highway." The village is near several ski areas, including *Haystack* and *Hogback*. Also nearby is *Molly Stark State Park* with its camping, hiking, hunting, and fishing. For further area information, see also the area descriptions for Marlboro and West Dover.

THE HERMITAGE INN

Coldbrook Road, Wilmington, VT 05363. 802-464-3759. *Innkeeper*: Jim McGovern. Open all year.

The Hermitage has been developed from a farmhouse dating back

to the early 1700s. At one time it was the residence of Miss Bertha Eastman, who was the editor of the famed Social Register, the "Blue Book" of society. A number of years have passed since she made the farmhouse her home, and the building and its grounds have since been extensively renovated by its present owner, Jim McGovern.

The reputation of the Hermitage rests primarily upon its cuisine. The restaurant has received much praise from the press and is one of the most frequently recommended by other innkeepers in the area. The inn has four separate intimate dining rooms and a Vermont marble patio dining area facing Haystack Mountain. Among the specialties are an assortment of homemade soups, Wiener schnitzel, frogs' legs Provençale, filet of sole Veronique, shrimps scampi, and chicken amandine. Daily specials often feature local game, such as pheasant or quail. The trout on the menu comes fresh from the Hermitage's trout pond. Desserts include such items as bananas Foster or peach Melba. The inn offers a complete Saturday and Sunday brunch.

Each of the nine guest rooms at the Hermitage is individually decorated and furnished with antiques. All have private baths, and four have working fireplaces. The carriage house has a sauna.

Several years ago the Hermitage established a cross-country skiing center that has well-maintained marked trails laid out on the property's 100 acres. One of the trails connects with Mount Snow's cross-country skiing operation at the country club. The inn offers equipment rentals and cross-country instruction; there is a free shuttle to Mount Snow daily. A wonderful horsedrawn sleigh ride is now available on the premises daily, snow permitting.

The Hermitage was once the site of one of the largest maple-sugaring operations in the state, and Jim McGovern has revived the business in the old sugar house. The maple-sugaring started out as a hobby for Jim, but it is now a full-scale operation, and the sugar is sold under the inn's own label along with its own homemade preserves and jellies. In addition to the maple-sugar business, the inn has a new Wine and Gift Shop next to the main house, with more than 500 labels available.

The inn is a quiet, relaxing place, free from the annoyance of television, radio, and telephones. Visitors enjoy comfortable rooms, excellent cuisine, and a well-stocked wine cellar. *Room Rates*: Double rooms are $35 to $45 with fireplace; opitonal MAP available for $35 more a day for two people. *Driving Instructions*: Take Route 9 to Wilmington. At the traffic light, turn right onto Route 100. Go about 3 miles to Coldbrook Road on your left. The inn is another 3 miles down Coldbrook Road.

Woodstock, Vermont (including South Woodstock)

Woodstock is one of Vermont's most popular towns, with its old homes and shops and oval village green. It has been a favorite summer residence for artists, authors, musicians, and teachers for years. There are excellent golf and tennis available at the *Woodstock Country Club* (their golf course was designed by Robert Trent Jones), as well as horseback riding at the *Green Mountain Horse Association* with its miles of forest trails. The village of Woodstock operates a recreation center with facilities for bowling, billiards, swimming, basketball, and skating, plus community tennis courts and a hockey rink. Sports-lovers enjoy excellent upland bird shooting, deer hunting, and trout fishing in the local brooks, rivers, and lakes. Tourists who are fond of local history will enjoy the *Dana House* operated by the Woodstock Historical Society and *Perkins Academy* in South Woodstock. South Woodstock is also home of the Doscher Country School of Photography, a summer photography workshop in operation for more than thirty years.

KEDRON VALLEY INN

Route 106, South Woodstock, VT 05071. 802-457-1473. Mailing Address: Box 145, South Woodstock, VT 05071. *Innkeepers*: Paul and Barbara Kendall. Open all year.

The Kedron Valley Inn has numerous activities for all members of the family right on the property. It maintains an excellent riding stable with horses and instruction available to guests. The inn also offers guests sleigh or wagon rides. In addition, the Green Mountain Horse Association, adjacent to the inn, has laid out numerous riding trails through the woods. The Kedron Valley also has a nice "swimming hole" that offers, additionally, summer fishing and winter skating (lighted at night). Cross-country skiers are drawn to the inn not only for its own popular trails but also for those of the *Woodstock Touring Center*. There is also a paddle tenis court, so enthusiasts should bring along their paddles.

The Kedron Valley Inn has thirty-five guest rooms, all but four with private baths. The inn offers typical Vermont country inn rooms within the original early nineteenth-century building, as well as eight modern motel-type rooms in a recently constructed log-cabin style building. Two of the inn's rooms have fireplaces and three have parlor stoves. In addition, there are fireplaces in the living room, lobby, dining room, and lounge.

Meals at the inn are open to guests and the public and generally consist of simple, country-style cooking, with such entrées as omelets, baked stuffed shrimp, maple-cured ham, and home-baked breads and desserts. There is a special Sunday brunch with a large selection of items, including eggs Benedict, blueberry pancakes, and quiche Lorraine. Dinner prices range from $7 to $9 complete (some special appetizers or desserts bring the total higher). The complete brunches range from $3.75 to $8.50, with appetizers and alcoholic beverages additional. Pets are permitted. *Room Rates*: Double rooms are $9 to $18 per person. Single rooms and rooms in the motel unit are higher. A service charge is added to bills for meals (not for rooms) in lieu of tipping. *Driving Instructions*: The inn is 5 miles south of Woodstock on Route 106. Woodstock can be reached from routes I-89 (exit 1, west to Woodstock) or I-91 (exit 8, left on Route 131, 8 miles, then right on Route 106, 12 miles).

NORTHERN

Bradford, Vermont

Bradford is a small farming community of 2,000 people located in the Connecticut River valley not too far from Hanover, New Hampshire. Bradford is the scene of an annual *November Wild Game Supper*, which has attracted some national attention. There are numerous country fairs held in the area during the warmer months. Golf, tennis, boating, and canoeing are all available in Bradford. Glider trips are available at the airport in Post Mills, about 10 miles away. Downhill skiing is across the river at the *Dartmouth Skiway* in Lyme, New Hampshire.

MERRY MEADOW FARM AND STABLE

Lower Plain, Bradford, VT 05033. 802-222-4412. *Innkeeper*: Mrs. Betty M. Williams. Open to guests all year, except for July and August, when it is a riding school and summer camp for children. The Merry Meadow Farm and Stable is a working horse farm in the Connecticut River valley consisting of a fourteen-room farmhouse with attached and separate barns and a number of riding rings. The farmhouse has three modern baths and a huge kitchen with beamed ceiling and a wood-burning cook stove. Guests are welcome to participate in daily farm activities, such as feeding the animals, gathering berries, bringing in wood, mending fences, or hitching a pony to a cart. In the winter there is cross-country skiing on the premises and downhill skiing nearby. Special care is taken to ensure that children will be able to enjoy all the facets of farm life. Many city parents rely

on Merry Meadow to have their children spend school holidays at the farm throughout the year.

Meals are home-cooked, of course, and served family style in the sunny farmhouse kitchen. Some of the favorite dishes include stuffed cabbage, beef Stroganoff, fried chicken, and homemade pies and pastries. Much of the produce served comes from the farm garden and the berry patch. The farm consists of more than 200 acres with several miles bordering the Connecticut, so there is plenty of room for guests to roam and explore. *Room Rates*: Rooms are $32 per person, AP (all meals); children under eight $18, AP. These rates include riding privileges but not lessons. *Driving Instructions*: The inn is on Route 5, one and a half miles south of exit 16 on Route I-91.

Brookfield, Vermont

In 1813, a person walking across the frozen pond at Brookfield drowned when he broke through the thin ice. This prompted the village to build, in 1819-20, the first of a series of floating bridges made of wood over barrels. The latest of these was rebuilt in 1978 and is in daily use. This bridge and the adjoining pond form the focus of this scenic village, which was recently placed on the list of designated Vermont Historic Districts, just in time to save the bridge from being paved over. At one time as many as twenty mills obtained their power from a short stretch of the local brook and pond. Most of these exist today only as abandoned foundations. Nearby *Allis State Park* has camping and picnicking facilities, as well as an observation tower.

GREEN TRAILS COUNTRY INN

By the Floating Bridge, Brookfield, VT 05036. 802-276-2012. *Innkeepers*: The Williams family. Open from December through March and May through October.

The Green Trails Country Inn is a complex of buildings put up between 1790 and 1850. It includes the inn with its six guest rooms and a country store, a restored Fork Shop (pitchfork and rake manufacturing place), which is now a restaurant, and a residence occupied by the Williamses, who restored the buildings and now run all the activities there. The inn has rooms furnished in Victorian and early-American style. In addition to these old-fashioned inn rooms, there are four efficiency apartments located in adjoining buildings for guests who wish to live more independently during their stay. Green Trails is located near a floating bridge erected by the village in 1819–20. Many winter guests use the inn as a base for enjoying the excellent cross-country skiing trails that originate there, as well as the downhill areas in central Vermont. Cross-country skiing instruction is available on weekends; at other times, lessons can be arranged by appointment. Summer visitors may swim in Sunset Lake, relax at the private beach owned by the inn, and also enjoy hiking, fishing, and picknicking.

Dining in the Fork Shop Restaurant is open to the public and features a small, interesting menu with such à la carte selections as lobster pie ($6.95), chicken Kiev ($6.50), and Wiener schnitzel ($5.95). The restaurant is decorated with antique forks, rakes, and tools and has a working player piano. No pets permitted. *Room Rates*: A double room with private bath is $30. The efficiency apartments range from $35 to $80 per night. *Driving Instructions*: Bear right at the fork on Route 66; follow Route 14 North for 6 miles to East Brookfield. Follow the sign to Floating Bridge and Green Trails (2 miles up the Brookfield State Highway from Route 14).

Craftsbury Common, Vermont

Craftsbury Common, with its hilltop views of the accompanying countryside, its mountainous backdrops, and its many country gardens, is certainly one of Vermont's most extraordinary sights. This village is most inviting to tourists every season of the year. There is hiking and canoeing in the summer and wonderful cross-country skiing in the winter. The village is 25 miles from Stowe, so it can provide a place to stay for those who wish to ski there but avoid the bustle of that famous area. Craftsbury Common is an absolute gem in the countryside, which has remained unchanged for over a hundred years and yet is in no way primitive.

THE INN ON THE COMMON

Main Street, Craftsbury Common, VT 05827. 802-586-9619.
Innkeepers: Penny and Michael Schmitt.
The Inn on the Common consists of two restored Federal buildings (originally a private house and a cabinet and sleigh shop, respectively), which currently are filled with a mixture of antiques and contemporary furniture. The Schmidts take great pride in their antiques, many of which are heirlooms, and in the extensive art work on the walls. The grounds have an English croquet court, clay tennis court, bocce court, swimming pool, and some of the area's most attractive gardens. Several of the eleven guest rooms have working fireplaces and/or bathrooms with skylights. All rooms share bath facilities. The innkeepers also own a farm in neighboring Greensboro that guests may wish to explore.

Dining is a special occasion at the inn. Children eat at an earlier hour so that adults may enjoy their dinners without interruption. Whenever possible, meals feature vegetables and herbs grown on the inn grounds.

The inn has its own craft shop, free of gimmickry, called the

"Common Market." Winter visitors can enjoy cross-country skiing at the inn or on nearby trails. Ski instruction is available. The inn can arrange for outings in the local countryside in any season. Pets are permitted if special arrangements are made in advance. *Room Rates*: Double rooms are $32 to $37 per person, MAP. Bed and breakfast rates are from $20 to $25 per person, with single-room rates higher. Other plans, including a two-room suite, are available. A 15 percent gratuity charge and applicable taxes are added to the bill. Reservations are a necessity. *Driving Instructions*: Take Route 14 from the Montpelier-Barre area north to the village of Craftsbury Common.

East Middlebury, Vermont (see Middlebury, Vermont)

WAYBURY INN

Route 125, East Middlebury, VT 05740. 802-388-4015. *Innkeepers*: The Greene family. Open all year; closed Tuesdays, except in July and August.

The Waybury Inn was built as a stagecoach stop on one of the major east-west passes through the Green Mountains. It was built in 1810 at the foot of the mountains in the lovely little town of East Middlebury. The inn still takes care of travelers and retains much of its colonial atmosphere. The Waybury has received recognition as a

traditional New England inn from many travel and food-oriented magazines. There are eleven guest rooms; five have private baths and the other six have connecting baths for family groups. The lounge is furnished with antiques and offers a clublike setting. The dining room has big hand-hewn beams and wainscoting of wide weathered pine boards. Guests and public may dine by the fireside on traditional New England fare. In summer, meals are also served on the shaded porch. The dining rooms are open for all meals to guests and the public. The inn permits a few pets; call and check. *Room Rates*: Double occupancy is $16 to $19. *Driving Instructions*: The inn is located on Route 125, 1½ miles from the intersection with Route 7, 4 miles south of Middlebury.

Greensboro, Vermont

Greensboro is a small community in northeastern Vermont most noted for Caspian Lake, a fine fishing and water sports area. The neighboring town of Craftsbury has a number of interesting attractions (see Craftsbury Common).

HIGHLAND LODGE

Craftsbury Road, Greensboro, VT 05841. 802-533-2647. *Innkeepers*: Carol and Dave Smith. Open from Memorial Day weekend to October 15 and from December 22 to April 1.

The Highland is a wide, two-story lake-front inn with a full-length porch. Most of the inn dates from 1926, although one part was a farmhouse for a sheep farm prior to that. Ten nonhousekeeping cottages have been added over the years to the 180-acre property bordering Caspian Lake. The lodge provides a number of activities for guests, including cookouts, swimming in the lake, boating, canoeing, sailing, paddle boating, badminton, and crouet. There is good lake fishing for salmon, lake trout, rainbow trout, and perch. In the winter the lodge offers daily instruction in cross-country skiing, as well as equipment rentals and sales in the ski shop and guided or self-guided tours along their marked trails. The lodge is decorated with some antiques and a variety of sturdy colonial-style furniture from local Vermont furniture manufacturers.

At dinner the menu offers such entrées as top sirloin of beef,

roast turkey, fish filet with shrimp sauce, roast leg of lamb, co au vin, Burgundy beef, and baked pork loin, among others.

No pets permitted. *Room Rates*: In the lodge, rooms are $55 to $70, including gratuities, for two persons, MAP. Cottage rates vary according to occupancy and season. *Driving Instructions*: Take Route 15 to Route 16 (east of Hardwick), where you turn north. Take Route 16 to East Hardwick and follow the signs to Caspian Lake.

Lincoln, Vermont

Lincoln is located on the famed hiking *Long Trail* adjacent to the *Green Mountain National Forest* in central Vermont, northeast of Middlebury. The New Haven River with its lovely waterfalls passes through the village. The town of Lincoln has two tourist-oriented special weekends, both called Hill Country Holidays. One is the first weekend in Febrkary and features ski races, and the other is the first weekend in August, with tennis tournaments and a flea market, among other things. Nearby Middlebury offers more formal tourist attractions.

THE LONG RUN

Lincoln Gap Road, Lincoln Center, VT. Mailing Address: RFD 1, Box 114, Bristol, VT 05443. 802-453-3233. *Innkeeper*: Gen Burke. Open all year except April and November.

The Long Run is a lovely, gabled village inn in the mountain town

of Lincoln. Overlooking the New Haven River, the inn was a lumberjack hotel in the 1800s. Constructed in 1799 and expanded later to twenty rooms, the inn has two dining rooms, a fireplace lounge, and a large "rocking chair" porch. It is part of an inn-to-inn cross-country skiing package during the winter and a similar "hike inn-to-inn" package in the summer (average daily per person charges for the packages are $30, including transportation and lunch).

The inn is a popular place for enjoying cross-country skiing in the winter and is quite near large downhill ski areas. In summer months there is swimming in the river in front of the inn, hiking (the famous Long Trail is nearby), and bicycling. Horseback riding trips that go inn to inn also stop here. For details, write the inn or Country Roads Horse Trekking, Box 16, Middlebury, VT 05753.

The Long Run offers simple country meals with homemade bread, cakes, soups, garden salads in season, beef Burgundy, and roast turkey among the items served. Apple pancakes with maple syrup, sausage, and bacon is a favorite special at the inn. Liquor is not served, but guests are welcome to bring their own. Candles and oil lamps add a warm, homey touch to the informal atmosphere of the inn and the dining room. *Room rates*: The six guest rooms share three baths, and the charge is about $25 per person, MAP. *Driving Instruction*: Take Route 17 east to Bristol. In Bristol, turn right at the second stone bridge outside the village (Lincoln Gap Road). Go 5 miles to Lincoln Center and the inn.

Lower Waterford, Vermont

Lower Waterford, the center of the maple syrup industry, is one of the most photographed and painted villages in Vermont. The white houses of the village look across the Connecticut River to a marvelous view of the White Mountains in the distance. Route 18 crosses the river here and provides the traveler with access to the New Hampshire mountains via Littleton, New Hapshire. Nearby St. Johnsbury is a larger Vermont town, with a population of approximately 8,500 and a number of interesting tourist attractions. These include the *Fairbanks Museum of Natural History* and the *St. Johnsbury Athenaeum*. There is also a *Maple Museum* with syrup production in season, a year-round exhibit about the industry, and tours of the maple-sugar factory.

THE RABBIT HILL INN

Pucker Street, Lower Waterford, VT 05848. 802-748-9766. *Innkeepers*: Nancy and Ed Ludwig. Open all year.

The four large, hand-hewn Doric columns that support the front porch of the Rabbit Hill give it a somewhat imposing look that is quickly forgotten within the relaxed atmosphere of the inn. The property consists of a main inn built in 1827 and enlarged about fifteen years later to its present size. It has always served as an inn, except for a short period when it was used as a private home. In its early days, the inn served the active logging community in the area, and the floors still bear the marks of the spiked boots of the drovers and lumberjacks who stopped there. The "Briar Patch," a smaller building put up in 1795, currently houses a gift shop below and some old-fashioned guest rooms above. In the mid-1850s, a third building was constructed consisting of a ballroom with a carriage house and woodsheds below.The ballroom has been subdivided into a number of motel-type rooms.

Guests who stay in this inviting inn can choose their accommodations according to their preference for more contemporary or old-fashioned surroundings. Fireplaces and Franklin stoves are also found in the common rooms. For the guests' enjoyment there are cross-country skiing on the property, spectacular views of New Hampshire's White Mountains, and a large nearby lake for swimming, boating, and fishing.

Two connecting dining rooms serve an interesting variety of seafood, meat, and poultry dishes with names like Barre Pike beefsteak, Vermont Drovers Journey End steak, veal Waterford, and breast of chicken Burlington. A complete dinner of appetizer, soup, entrée,

and dessert, served with "cheese tasty, relish tray, salad, potato, vegetable, and hot, homemade bread," should average $9 to $11. The inn serves breakfast and dinner to both guests and the public and will prepare box lunches for guests on request. Pets and children are permitted. *Room rates*: Double motel-type rooms are $24 (1855 wing). Old-fashioned rooms in the inn and annex range from $28 to $34, the latter with fireplace. There is a two-bedroom suite with fireplace for $38. Fall foliage rates are $4 additional per room. *Driving Instructions*: The inn is located on Route 18 about 7 miles north of Littleton, New Hampshire, or the same distance south of Route 2.

Middlebury, Vermont

Middlebury is best known for Middlebury College and its lovely New England campus. The town of 7,000 is more than a college town. One of its most importat attractions is the *State Craft Center at Frog Hollow*, where hundreds of Vermont artisans (on a rotating basis) have workshops, display galleries, and salesrooms. The town has many fine antique shops, and *Van Raalte* has an outlet store there with low prices on men's and women's clothing. Skiers can enjoy both alpine and cross-country skiing at the *Middlebury College Snow Bowl*, about 10 miles outside of town. The John "Red" Kelly

Trail is a 3.5 kilometer trail around the college golf course. It is lighted for night skiing. Boating and sailing is available on *Lake Dunmore* and golf at *Middlebury College Golf Course*. The *Sheldon Museum* and the *Morgan Horse Farm* are open during the warmer months. The college sponsors a winter carnival in February, and there are two country fairs nearby in the summer: the *Bristol County Agricultural Fair* and the *Addison County Farm and Field Days*.

THE MIDDLEBURY INN

17 Pleasant Street, Middlebury, VT. Mailing address: Box 631, Middlebury, VT 07753. 802-388-4961. *Innkeepers*: Frank and Jane Emanuel. Open all year.

The Middlebury Inn, overlooking the village green, consists of a large, attractive brick building first constructed in 1827, a brick annex, and a motel unit behind the main inn. The Middlebury is a fine example of a dignified town inn with a special tone set by the nearby college. As new innkeepers, the Emanuels have undertaken the task of a major facelift for the old inn, with the help of a grant from Vermont's Division of Historic Preservation. The outside of the building and the public rooms on the ground floor have all been freshened up. The building was painted and reroofed, and the lobbies, lounges, and dining room were all redecorated and wallpapered. The two floors above the lobby offer about fifty guest rooms of assorted sizes and shapes (most with private or connecting baths). Most of these guest rooms have been carefully redone, including such details as wallpapering the sprinkler pipes to "jazz" them up.

The lower level of the hotel (below the lobby) is in the process

of restoration. Gift shops will be housed here and should be in operation early in 1979. The Morgan Room Cocktail Lounge and the inn's dining room are open to both guests and the public for breakfast, lunch, and dinner. *Room Rates*: Double rooms are $28 to $48; suites are from $40, E.P. On certain college weekends the inn is booked well in advance and only package rates are available. Be sure to call ahead of time. *Driving Instructions*: The inn is located on U.S. 7 in the town of Middlebury.

Milton, Vermont

Milton is located north of Burlington and adjacent to *Arrowhead Mountain Lake*. The village is about 5 miles from the *Sand Bar Wildlife Area* and a short drive from the Champlain Islands, including South Hero, Grand Isle, North Hero, the Alburgs, and Isle La Motte. Recreational opportunities include trail riding, fishing, swimming, and boating in Lake Champlain, and weekly auctions during the summer months in Milton. There are also the attractions of Burlington and the *Shelburne Museum* to the south.

THE WRIGHT PLACE
   Westford Road, Milton, VT 05468. 802-893-4900. *Innkeepers*: Patrick and Lori Wright. Open all year.
The Wright Place is not an old country inn; rather it is a new, three-story log cabin surrounded by a small farm complete with farm animals. It offers guests the warm family atmosphere of a farm vacation along with the conveniences made possible by contemporary construction. The farm provides a variety of recreational activities for all ages. For children, there are pony rides, a sandbox, sledding and skating in winter, a brook for wading in summer, and, when needed, a baby-sitter. For adults, there are horses and trails, cross-country skiing, fishing or ice-fishing.

   The lodge is small and accommodates guests in only four rooms, which share a bath. Meals are served to guests only and feature dinners with home-raised, country-cured ham, Yankee pot roast, chili soup, hot muffins and breads, pies, cakes, and jams. No pets permitted. *Room Rates*: Adults, $19 per day or $90 per week; children, $11 per day or $30 to $60 per week, AP. Riding is included.

Babies free. *Driving Instructions*: Take Route 7 to the blinking light in Milton and turn east. The lodge is 1⅓ miles on the right.

Montgomery, Vermont (including Montgomery Center)

Montgomery is a peaceful, small Vermont town situated near the Canadian border. Lovely mountains, back roads, and little covered bridges spanning trout streams abound. In winter the area offers a great many skiing choices: *Jay Peak Ski Area*, four Canadian mountains, and cross-country ski touring everywhere. The famous *Vermont Long Trail*, for skiing and hiking, passes through here. The Montgomery Recreation Center provides tennis and ice hockey. The Montgomery Historical Society sponsors many events throughout the year. In the milder seasons there are church suppers, flea markets, and auctions.

BLACK LANTERN INN

Route 118, Montgomery Village, VT 05470. 802-326-4507. *Innkeepers*: Rita and Allan Kalsmith. Open all year.

The Black Lantern Inn was built as a stagecoach stop at the turn of the nineteenth century. The old brick building is located fewer than 10 miles from the Canadian border and minutes from the big Jay Peak Ski Area to the east. The inn has eleven guest rooms, nine with private baths, each individkally decorated with antiques. There is a

television room, and a cozy sitting room warmed by an open wood-burning stove. A dining room and a taproom are open to guests and the public and are quite popular with skiers from Jay. The bar has exposed beams and a casual atmosphere. The candlelit dining room offers a continental menu featuring such entrées as lamb Marguerite, veal tarragon, and fresh seafood, all served with salads, fresh vegetables, and homemade breads and desserts.

In winter the area offers a variety of skiing choices in addition to Jay Peak. Cross-country skiing is excellent right out the door of the inn, and for downhill skiers there are four nearby Canadian ski mountains. Spring and summer bring numerous recreational activities, including fishing in many nearby streams and swimming in the old swimming hole. No pets permitted. *Room Rates*: In winter, rooms are $20 to $24 per person, MAP. Off season, they are $20 to $24, EP. *Driving Instructions*: Take Route 100 north to Route 118 in Eden. Follow Route 118 through Montgomery Center to Montgomery Village.

North Hero, Vermont (the Champlain Islands)

This area was originally very sparsely settled because of its inaccessibility in the middle of Lake Champlain. However, the area gained some prominence when 64-acre lots were deeded to Ethan Allen and the Green Mountain Boys as rewards for services performed during the Revolution. Now the Champlain Islands are mostly summer colonies and serve as logical stopping points for the exploration of the Lake Champlain–Burlington area. In nearby South Hero is the *Hyde Log Cabin*, thought to be the oldest log cabin in the country.

NORTH HERO HOUSE

North Hero, VT 05474. 802-372-8237. *Innkeepers*: Roger and Caroline Sorg. Open from late June through Labor Day.

The North Hero House is actually a complex of buildings dating from the 1800s. The main building is a gracious old inn, built in 1890, that has been completely renovated to contain guest rooms with private baths, dining rooms, a craft shop, and the Green Mountain Lounge. Cove House is the old storekeeper's house, dating back to the early 1800s. Contained within it are six unique guest rooms with private baths and screened porches. Two additional buildings contain a total of ten more rooms. There are also family accommodations in the old cobbler's shop, which contains a bath, bedroom, sitting room with original fireplace, and screened porch. Rooms are decorated with sturdy contemporary country-style furniture and attractive walllpaper or paneling. The waterfront area provides excellent swimming, as well as a carefully preserved steamship dock. Motor boating, canoeing, sailing, and fishing for bass, walleye, and northern pike are among the many water sports available to guests at North Hero House. The dining room serves abundant meals from a different menu every evening. A restaurant specialty is freshly caught lake fish, and the inn serves many vegetables raised in its own garden.

Dinner guests are welcome to select a wine from the wine cellar personally, before their meal. The inn thoughtfully provides dining in the greenhouse for nonsmokers. Thursday evening meals center around a lakefront lobster cookout, weather permitting.

Pets are not permitted. *Room Rates*: Double rooms range from $16 to $30, with single rooms slightly less. *Driving Instructions*: The Champlain Islands are reached by ferry from Plattsburg, New York, or by bridge northwest of Burlington. On the islands, follow Route 2 to North Hero.

Ripton, Vermont

Ripton is a small community about 8 miles southeast of Middlebury. Located just down the road from the center of the village is the Bread Loaf Mountain Campus of Middlebury College, site of a famous annual writer's conference, and the Robert Frost Cabin, summer home of the late poet laureate.

CHIPMAN INN

Route 125, Ripton, VT. Mailing address: Box 37, Ripton, VT 05766. 802-388-2390. *Innkeeper*: Joan Bullock. Open all year except mid-April to mid-May.

This small, fully restored 1828 farmhouse offers guests overnight accommodations in ten bedrooms, of which six have private baths. The public rooms include a living room–library; the Tavern Room, with its Dutch-ovened fireplace and bar-lounge; the Robert Frost Room, often the scene of a late-evening cheese fondue before the fireplace; and the inn dining room, which serves dinner to both

guests and the public. Guests are offered a family style five-course meal with the emphasis on country cooking. The public is offered a "pot-of-the-day" meal featuring kettle cooking, such as a hearty stew, soup, or chili dinner. Included with these popular winter meals are salad and homemade breads. This inn is part of the hike-ski inn-to-inn activities that have been made so popular by the program's organizers at the Churchill House Inn in Brandon (which see). Chipman Inn was the first home built in Ripton by Daniel Chipman. At one point he improved the local road and then charged tolls for its use. *Room Rates*: Rooms are $23 to $25 per room, double occupancy; $12 extra per person for meals. *Driving Instructions*: Take Route 125 to the inn.

Shoreham, Vermont

Shoreham is a small (population 250) village in the northwestern portion of the state, not far from Middlebury.

THE SHOREHAM INN

Shoreham, VT 05770. 802-897-5081. *Innkeepers*: Cleo and Fred Alter. Open all year.

The Shoreham is a small, informal family-run inn that dates back to 1800. Unlike many inns in Vermont, the Shoreham has always been an inn serving this tiny community. As you enter, you are greeted by the old stairway leading to the guest rooms above. The balustrade is actually from an old church in Shoreham. The dining room and especially the guest rooms are furnished with comfortable "country auction" antiques. The five guest rooms share two baths. The dining room with its exposed beams is currently used only for guest breakfasts, often served by a nice fire in the fireplace. Cleo and Fred strive to emphasize the informal, family atmosphere here—guests share tables for breakfast and often make quick friendships. Adjacent to the inn is the Shoreham General Store, also run by the Alters. This store is more than a hundred years old, although a recent fire resulted in a major rebuilding effort. Cleo has stocked the shelves with a nice selection of local Vermont crafts, including quilts and other items from a nearby Amish community. The store also offers simple lunches for travelers, who often choose to eat them on picnic tables provided by the inn and located on a small green across the street. In August, the inn sponsors a street dance and bring-your-own-supper affair that has gained local popularity and is attended by guests at the inn, many of whom make reservations year after year. Incidentally, the inn was undergoing some minor renovation work when we last inquired. This did not seem to bother the guests in residence, but it would be wise to inquire, if it might disturb you. This inn is popular with Middlebury College parents, who often stay here while visiting their children at school. For this reason, graduation weekends are booked several years in advance. *Room Rates*: Rooms are $15, single; $20, double—including breakfast. *Driving Instructions*: The inn is on Route 74 West, 22 miles north of Fair Haven and 12 miles southwest of Middlebury.

Stowe, Vermont

Stowe has gained fame as the East's most highly organized ski town. With more than sixty area lodges and motels, the town is jammed with skiers all season. *Mount Mansfield* has twenty-nine slopes and trails served by complete base facilities. Also in Stowe is the *Trapp Family Ski Touring Center*, credited with being the major force in the early establishment of cross-country skiing in America. In the warmer months, the gondola at Mount Mansfield offers scenic rides to the top of the mountain, and there is area golf and tennis. The *Mount Mansfield Summer Playhouse* presents a summer slate of plays. Historically minded tourists will enjoy visits to the *Bloody Brook School House* and the *Stowe Historical Society Museum*. The village of Stowe is literally crammed with shops of all sorts guaranteed to supply gifts, crafts, antiques, and clothing for all ages.

EDSON HILL MANOR

R.R. 1, Stowe, VT 05672. 802-253-7371. *Innkeeper*: Elizabeth Turner. Open mid-June to the end of October and mid-December to early April.

This handsome brick manor was built as a luxurious private ski lodge in 1939. No expense was spared, as evidenced by use of Delft tiles on some of the inn's many fireplaces and wonderful big beams in the main living room. Much of the inn's interior is paneled in pine, and

most of the guestrooms have working fireplaces. The furnishings are a comfortable mixture of antiques and functional furniture. The sixteen guest rooms are in two newer additions to the manor, the Wing, added in 1952, and the Annex, built in 1957. The Edson Hill Manor sits on 400 acres of woods and pasture. Below the inn is a secluded swimming pool, terrace, and lawns. As a popular cross-country ski center in winter, the inn has many beautiful trails with spectacular views. There is a cross-country ski school at the inn, with certified instruction and a complete ski shop. Downhill skiing is available at the popular Mount Mansfield nearby. In the summer, the inn offers a complete riding program with trail riding and excellent instruction in the British method, by British instructors. Instruction is also available in side-saddle riding. The inn dining room is open to the public at most times of the year (except for lunch during the summer months). The emphasis here is on well-cooked, hearty New England fare served family style. The inn will be glad to pack trail lunches for cross-country skiers. Pets are not permitted. *Room Rates*: Winter—$32 to $52 per person per day, MAP. Summer—$18 to $38 per person, including full breakfast. There are several special package plans for skiers or summer visitors, and discounts are occasionally available. *Driving Instructions*: From Stowe, take Route 108N (the Mountain Road) for 3½ miles to the Buccaneer Motel. Immediately after the motel on the right, take the right fork and go 1.7 miles, following the signs to the Manor.

Waitsfield and The Valley, Vermont

The Valley is the area surrounding the four north-central villages of Waitsfield, Fayston, Moretown, and Warren. The Valley itself is surrounded by three of Vermont's more famous ski areas—*Glen Ellen, Mad River,* and *Sugarbush.* It is an area of both rolling hillside farmland and breathtaking mountains. Sugarbush, located in the village of Warren, is a superb ski area with a gondola tramway and six other ski lifts. On Columbus Day weekend, Sugarbush holds an *Octoberfest* with a flea market and a sidewalk art sale. Sugarbush also has indoor tennis, pools, saunas, movies, skating and ski touring. Summer activities include golf and tennis tournaments and soaring meets. Warren is also known for its Fourth of July celebration. Waitsfield is the home of the Glen Ellen and Mad River ski areas, with five and four lifts, respectively. The *Bundy Art Gallery* in Waitsfield has collections of contemporary painting and sculpture. The village is filled with antique and crafts shops and also has a covered bridge. The abundance of skiers in the winter has brought myriad contemporary and traditional restaurants to this region, featuring almost all international cuisines as well as traditional Vermont country cooking.

KNOLL FARM COUNTRY INN

Bragg Hill Road, RFD, Waitsfield, VT 05673. 802-496-3939. *Innkeepers*: Bill and Ann Day Heinzerling. Open all year except April and November.

The Knoll Farm Inn, on 150 acres of hillside pasture and woods, is a converted farmhouse with five guest rooms, a large family kitchen with an old wood stove, dining room, study, and living room. The farm has a red barn and a smaller barn-shop. The barn is used to hold the thirty tons of hay needed to maintain the farm's twenty animals. This was a working farm in the 1800s and was converted to a combination farm and inn in 1937. The farm continues to produce its own meats, vegetables, fruits, eggs, butter, and breads. Dinners feature these ingredients in hearty meals including pot roasts, pork roasts, stews, bacon, sausage, apple desserts, jams and jellies. The Heinzerlings serve what may be the biggest breakfast in any Vermont inn, using their own fresh ingredients and featuring blueberry pancakes with Vermont (what else?) maple syrup on Sunday mornings.

The inn has its own pond with a dock and a rowboat in the

summer and good skating in the winter. Ann is an accomplished naturalist, known in the area for her nature talks and slide shows; she is happy to guide the inn's guests on various nature walks. Riding horses and horsemanship clinics are available. The inn has a collection of old buggies and sleighs, which are used for rides. Guests are welcome to help with any chores, from milking to mending fences. For those who wish, there is tennis, golf, white-water canoeing, polo and rugby, all nearby. In truth, however, most guests prefer to hike, swim, and ski cross-country.

Beyond all this there is a special feeling here that is difficult to communicate. Innkeepers and guests all eat together, meet and talk together, and gradually a special relationship of friendship evolves. In Ann's words, "As you walk on our hill in any season, in solitude or companionship, you will find renewal and inner re-creation. The vital activities of the farm become meaningful to the basic life they represent. You will find your own creative mode of living which will be inspired by the natural beauty of our environment and peaceful simplicity of our country life." If this appeals to you, reserve early. The inn is always booked for the summer months about one year in advance. Children under six and pets are not permitted. *Room Rates*: Rooms are $22 to $25 per person, MAP. Weekly rates from $125 to $140. Family group rates available. *Driving Instructions*: The farm is a half mile up the hill (Bragg Hill Road) from the junction of routes 100 and 17.

MILLBROOK LODGE

Route 17, Fayston, VT. Mailing address: RFD Box 44, Waitsfield, VT 05673. 802-496-2405. *Innkeepers*: Bud and Lynn Baker. Open all year.

The Millbrook Lodge is a renovated 1847 farmhouse with six guest rooms. The Bakers cater to young people and families in a friendly, informal atmosphere. The inn, furnished with antiques, has a comfortable living room with a fireplace and a sitting room with an antique Glenwood parlor stove. The Millbrook is part of a "hike-inn-to-inn" and "bike-inn-to-inn" program in the spring, summer, and fall. The Bakers serve country-style meals, including fresh-baked breads, pies, and cakes, to their guests only. Vegetarian meals are prepared upon advance request. No pets please. *Room Rates*: Rates vary from $10 per person for a bunk room to $16 per person for a family room, double occupancy, with private bath. The Bakers also have several package plans. Cross-country and downhill ski and snowshoe rentals are available. *Driving Instructions*: Take Route 100 to Waitsfield and then Route 17 West ⅛ of a mile to the inn.

MOUNTAIN VIEW INN

Route 17, Waitsfield, VT. Mailing address: RFD Box 48A, Waitsfield, VT 05673. 802-96-2426. *Innkeepers*: Fred and Suzy Spencer. Open all year.

Built in the early 1800s as a farmhouse, the Mountain View became one of Mad River's first ski lodges in the 1940s. The Mountain View today is an attractive New England inn, furnished with many heirloom antiques and plenty of green plants. In the living room, which always has a cozy fire during chilly weather, guests can play the piano or sip mulled cider. The four guest rooms also have antiques, and the beds are covered with handmade quilts.

Hearty home-cooked meals are served family style around a large old harvest table in the dining room. In addition to the food, guests are treated to spectacular mountain views from the table. Meals are available to the public with advance reservation. Liquor is not served, but guests may bring their own. No pets are permitted. *Room Rates*: Rooms are $25 per person, MAP. There is a bunkroom that accommodates four for $22 each, MAP. *Driving Instructions*: At the junction of Route 100 and Route 17 near Waitsfield, take Route 17 west for 2 miles.

TUCKER HILL LODGE

Route 17, Waitsfield, VT 05673. 802-496-3983. *Innkeepers*: Zeke and Emily Church. Open all year.

Tucker Hill Lodge was built in 1948 by the Martin family, although many who first come to the lodge are under the impression that it is more than a hundred years old. Located on 145 acres on a wooded hillside away from the road, the lodge is popular in all seasons. The living room has a large fieldstone fireplace, and additional fireplaces grace the dining room and lounge. Zeke and Emily are from North Carolina, and they pride themselves on the inn's "southern hospitality that has been transplanted to Vermont."

The dining room at the lodge offers a nice selection of unusual dishes from a menu that changes nightly. Among the inn's specialties is roast loin of pork with mustard sauce, chicken breasts Florentine, southern fried steak, roast stuffed leg of lamb, tile fish with champagne sauce, and bluefish with aioli sauce (a Greek lemon-based sauce). A favorite dessert is the Churches' secret-recipe pecan pie, which uses pecans they import from an undisclosed source in the South. Chef Ron Clark, incidentally, learned his trade in New Orleans, a notable bastion of fine international cookery.

The inn has twenty guest rooms, of which eleven have private baths. This inn is particularly popular with skiers who come for the

15 miles of mountainous cross-country trails offered by the Tucker Hill Ski Touring Center or the fine downhill skiing at Mad River, Glen Ellen and Sugarbush, all nearby. During the warmer months there is tennis on the inn's clay courts, golf at a neighboring eighteen-hole course, and plenty of hiking, biking, and horseback riding in the area. *Room Rates*: From Thanksgiving through Easter, rooms are $22.50 to $28.50 per person, MAP. The rest of the year rates drop to $18 to $24 per person. *Driving Instructions*: The inn is 1½ miles from the junction of routes 100 and 17 in Waitsfield.

New Hampshire

IN 1623, following several earlier exploratory parties, Samuel Thomson and his followers formed the first permanent white settlement in the future state at what is now Dover, New Hampshire. Early grants for the property of the state were given to a Captain John Mason in 1629. The earliest real property settlements were in the Portsmouth area, because the harsh weather of the inland sections, as well as continuing difficulties with the Indian tribes, made living and travel there difficult.

In its infancy, New Hampshire was first part of Massachusetts, later a royal province of England, and finally part of Massachusetts again, in time to join the growing feeling of discontent with the colonial rule of England. During the Revolution, one of New Hampshire's military leaders, General John Stark, joined his forces with those of the Green Mountain Boys to meet the advancing British troops of General Burgoyne and rout them in a decisive battle outside Bennington, Vermont. This battle was the turning point for Burgoyne, who finally surrendered at Saratoga.

Today New Hampshire is famous not only for tourism but for thriving industrial communities as well. It is generally divided into six major centers for tourism. These include the Seacoast Region, around Portsmouth; the White Mountain Region, the area of the tallest mountains in the East; the Lakes Region with the great Lake Winnipesaukee, as well as Squam Lake, Lake Winnisquam, and many smaller lakes; the Dartmouth–Lake Sunapee Region to the west of the Winnipesaukee area; the Monadnock Region, named for its famous mountain; and the Merrimack Valley Region, which includes the Merrimack River and the three largest cities in the state—Concord, Manchester, and Nashua.

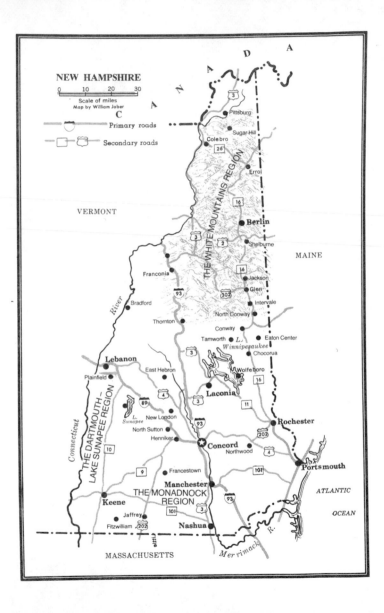

NEW HAMPSHIRE

0   10   20   30
Scale of miles
Map by William Jaber

○── Primary roads

□── Secondary roads

CANADA

VERMONT

MAINE

THE WHITE MOUNTAINS REGION

Pittsburg

Sugar Hill

Colebro

Errol

Berlin

Shelburne

Franconia

Jackson

Glen

Intervale

Bradford

North Conway

Thornton

Conway

Tamworth

Eaton Center

L. Winnipesaukee

Chocorua

Lebanon

East Hebron

Wolfeboro

Plainfield

THE DARTMOUTH – LAKE SUNAPEE REGION

L. Sunapee

New London

Laconia

North Sutton

Henniker

Concord

Rochester

Northwood

Connecticut

Francestown

Manchester

THE MONADNOCK REGION

Portsmouth

ATLANTIC

OCEAN

Keene

Jaffrey

Fitzwilliam

Nashua

Merrimack R.

MASSACHUSETTS

Vacationers can get help in planning their trip to this state by writing to the State Division of Economic Development, State House Annex, Box 856, Concord, NH 03301. The telephone number is 603-271-2666.

SOUTHERN

Fitzwilliam, New Hampshire (see The Monadnock Region)

FITZWILLIAM INN

Route 119, Fitzwilliam, NH 03447. 603-585-9000. *Innkeepers*: Barbara and Charles Wallace. Open all year.

The Fitzwilliam Inn first opened its doors in 1796 and has continually provided lodging and food to travelers in the southwestern Monadnock Region. In fact, some of the original furniture is still in use in parts of the inn. The inn is located at the end of the village green in a small, unspoiled village. There are twenty-two rooms, seven with private baths. The pub is rustic, and the restaurant serves old-fashioned country-style food in the New England tradition. The inn has its own swimming pool for use in the summer, and many guests climb nearby Mount Monadnock. Winter visitors frequently ski on several nearby cross-country ski trails. The mantel over the sitting room fireplace has painted on it a cryptic message that captures the

attention of all who visit the inn and was recently featured in a six-minute segment of the *Today* show on NBC-TV. Pets and children are permitted. *Room Rates:* Single rooms are $10 to $16; double rooms are $14 to $20. *Driving Instructions:* The inn is on the common just past the junction of routes 12 and 119.

Francestown, New Hampshire (and nearby Antrim)

Francestown has gained worldwide recognition because of its Crotched Mountain Rehabilitation Center. The immediate area has two downhill ski centers and one cross-country skiing center. *Crotched Mountain Ski Area* and *Bobcat Ski Area* are to the northwest of the village of Francestown on Route 47. The ski-touring center is at Crotched Mountain. Neighboring Hillsboro is the site of the *Franklin Pierce Homestead* and offers golf at the *Angus Lea Golf Course*, as well as many recreational opportunities at *Fox State Forest*. Antrim, located between the villages of Hillsborough and Francestown on Route 202, is a small village on the Contoocook River.

THE INN AT CROTCHED MOUNTAIN

Mountain Road, Francestown, NH 03043. 603-588-6840. *Innkeepers:* Rose and John Perry. Open Memorial Day weekend through October 31 and Thanksgiving to the end of the skiing season.

marilyn S. Pratt '74

Originally built as a farmhouse by James Wilson in 1822, the inn served as a stopping point on the underground railway—slaves were hidden in a secret tunnel that connected the cellar to the Boston Post Road. During its first century, the inn was used as both a farm and a boarding house. Purchased by Sidney Winslow in 1929, the property was named "Hob and Nob Farm" and became one of New England's most spectacular farms, with prize-winning sheep, champion horses, Angora goats, and numerous other farm animals. In the mid-1930s, a tragic fire destroyed most of the farm. The Winslows rebuilt it in its present state. John and Rose Perry purchased the property in June 1976.

The ivy-covered inn sits on the northern side of Crotched Mountain with a spectacular 40-mile view of the Piscataquog Valley. The inn is a relaxing place with cozy fireplaces including working ones in three of the ten guest rooms. Dinner and breakfast are available to guests and public alike. The inn offers guests two clay tennis courts and a mountainside pool. Nearby there are fishing in mountain streams and ponds, hiking and mountain-climbing, three golf courses, and, of course, skiing. *Room Rates*: Singles range from $15 to $18, doubles from $20 to $25. Rates are higher in winter. *Driving Instructions*: In Francestown, turn off Route 47 onto Mountain Road. The inn is a mile up the road.

Henniker, New Hampshire

Henniker, founded in 1768, is a small New England village with a population of about 2,200. It is the home of New England College, a private liberal arts school. The town is situated along the Contoocook River, with many lakes and ponds nearby. An old covered bridge crosses the river in Henniker. The town has many antique shops, and numerous auctions are held throughout the summer and fall.

The river and lakes provide fishing year-round, as well as canoeing and swimming. Pat's Peak has excellent alpine skiing, and the local Pole and Pedal Shop maintains 45 miles of marked cross-country trails. It's a short, scenic drive to Concord with its many summer theaters and state parks.

COLBY HILL INN

West Main Street, Henniker, NH 03242. 603-428-3281. *Inn-keepers*: The Glover family. Open all year.

Colby Hill Inn is an attractive white country house, built around 1800. Once a working farm with five acres remaining, the many barns, sheds, and old stone walls offer a glimpse of the farm life of a hundred years ago. The inn has eight spacious guest rooms, all comfortably furnished with antiques, four with private baths. Looking out the many-paned windows one is treated to open vistas of the surrounding hills and mountains. Guests can waken to the smell of freshly baked bread coming from the farm kitchen. The Glovers' menu features traditional New England fare using locally produced ingredients when available, including vegetables fresh from the farm garden. The inn serves breakfast to guests only, but is open to the public for dinner. Homemade soups and desserts are specialties of the house. There is a selection of wines, spirits, and lagers available with dinner.

Year-round and seasonal activities abound here, from canoeing and fly fishing in the many ponds and lakes in summer to white-water canoeing and ice-fishing in other seasons. And, of course, there is skiing—downhill at nearby areas plus 45 miles of local cross-country trails maintained by Pole and Pedal. Children over six years old are welcome. No pets permitted. *Room Rates*: Single rooms are $18 to $23; double rooms, $23 to $26; guest room with adjoining sitting room, $28. Reservations are advised. *Driving Instructions*: Take the Henniker-Bradford exit off routes 9 and 202. Take Route 114 south to town center. Turn right on Main Street about half a mile to The Oaks. The inn is on the right, just off West Main.

Jaffrey (see The Monadnock Region)

MONADNOCK INN

Main Street, Jaffrey Center, NH. Mailing address: Box 167, Jaffrey Center, NH 03454. 603-532-7001. *Innkeepers*: The Roberts family. Open all year.

The Monadnock was built in the early 1800s; in the 1870s, Mrs. Sarah Lawrence began taking in summer visitors. She named the place "Fairview" and later "The Monadnock." The Monadnock has

changed hands many times since then but has been operating as an inn ever since (with a short rest in the early 1900s). The Roberts family took charge several years ago, and now the inn contains a comfortable mixture of early American, colonial, and Victorian furniture, a large living room with a fireplace, and an old-fashioned lounge and bar warmed in winter by a wood stove. Of the thirteen guest rooms, seven have private baths. Lunch and dinner are served to the public and guests; breakfasts are continental style for guests only. On Sunday there is a wonderful brunch from 8:00 to 11:30 A.M. The dinner menu at the inn has a refreshing variety of choices at very reasonable prices. Dinners, including homemade soups, breads, and fresh vegetables, range from $6.50 for a creamy chicken en crôte to $9.50 for filet mignon. There is also a good selection of wines. No pets please. *Room Rates*: Rooms range from $14 single with shared bath to $21 double with private bath. The rates are slightly higher in the leaf season. *Driving Instructions*: Take Route 124 to Jaffrey Center. The inn is on Main Street.

WOODBOUND INN AND LAKE COTTAGES

Jaffrey, NH 03452. 603-532-8341. *Innkeepers*: The Brummer family. Open from mid-May to mid-October and from December 26 to mid-March.

The Woodbound Inn and Cottages is a small resort on the lake front at Lake Contoocook. The resort is centered in a large white clapboard main building that dates, in part, from 1823. There are a number of pine-paneled cottages and a lodge annex that furnish additional housing for a total of ninety-eight guests. The inn should appeal most to families and older visitors. On the grounds are a nine-hole golf course, a half-acre trout pond, and a tennis court, as well as a ski slope with a rope tow and a barn where square dances are held. The inn rents both cross-country and downhill skiing equipment and offers instructions in both forms of skiing. Cross-country ski trails start at the inn. *Room Rates*: Rates are AP and include the use of all inn facilities. Rates for double rooms in the main building or lodge annex range from $28 for a room with shared bath to $36 for a room with fireplace and private bath. Cottages are about the same price, with specific rentals depending on the number of people in the party. *Driving Instructions*: The inn is 2 miles from routes 119 and 202 in southwestern New Hampshire.

The Monadnock Region (including Antrim, Fitzwilliam, Hancock, Hillsboro, Jaffrey, Keene, Milford, Peterborough, Sharon, Troy, and Westmoreland, New Hampshire)

This is an active maple sugaring area with a good deal of industrial development in the immediate vicinity of Keene. This part of New Hampshire includes a number of family-style ski areas, including *Crotched Mountain* and *Onset* outside Bennington, Big Bear near the Massachusetts line in Brookline, New Hampshire, *Pinnacle Mountain* near East Sullivan, Temple Mountain outside Peterborough, the *Fitzwilliam Ski Area* in Fitzwilliam, and *Pat's Peak* near Henniker.

Mount Monadnock, south of Troy, is one of the state's most popular peaks for viewing or climbing. There are a number of state parks in the confines of the Monadnock region, including *Rhododendron State Park* near Mount Monadnock, *Miller State Park* near Peterborough, *Silver Lake State Park* south of Milford, *Greenfield State Park* in Greenfield, and *Monadnock State Park* outside Jaffrey.

Sightseeing might include a visit to the *Cathedral in the Pines* in Rindge, to the *Friendly Farm*, a farm of interest to children and others wishing to see farm animals up close and pet them; or to the

Old Fort No. 4 in Charlestown with its collection of seven fort buildings. The *Sharon Arts Center* on Route 123 has a large gallery, and *Steamtown USA* has the world's largest collection of steam locomotives and equipment. This region, incidentally, has seven covered bridges and more than eleven museums and historical buildings that are open to the public.

Northwood, New Hampshire

Northwood is a small town located about midway between Concord and Portsmouth and the same distance from the southernmost tip of Lake Winnipesaukee. The immediate area contains five lakes of some size—Jenness Pond, Northwood Lake, Bow Lake, Pleasant Pond, and Long Pond. The Blue Hills Range is nearby, with Catamount Mountain and Blue Job Mountain dominating the group. Two state parks are located here—*Bear Brook* and *Pawtuckaway*. *Rochester Country Club* has an eighteen-hole golf course.

THE RESORT AT LAKE SHORE FARM

Jenness Pond Road, Northwood, NH 03261. 603-942-5921; 942-5521. *Innkeepers*: Ellis and Eloise Ring. Open all year.

In April 1848, Reuben Watson wrote to his new wife HuldahJane "I hav ben to work upon our new house. I hav got the frame up. . . . I think you will like it." Thus began the construction of Lake Shore Farm. Today the farm, greatly enlarged, welcomes guests under the

direction of members of the fifth generation of descendants of Reuben and HuldahJane.

Over the years the farmhouse grew and evolved, with porches being added, closed in, and built over. In 1964 a modern annex was built near the main building to provide more rooms with private baths. Finally, a building was constructed to join the annex to the main house and provide more guest rooms and a large game room with fireplace and lounge. Recently constructed tennis courts add to the resort atmosphere. The inn is surrounded by sweeping lawns—once pastures—that slope gently toward Jenness Pond, where there is a sandy beach for swimming. The inn also provides boats and canoes for relaxation or a try at fishing. Meals at the farm are hearty country fare based on the abundance of fresh produce and dairy products that are available from the surrounding agricultural community. *Room Rates*: The inn operates on the American Plan, but 1979 rates were not available at the time of publication. *Driving Instructions*: Take Route 4 east of Concord past Route 28 to Route 107 north at Heritage Hardware. Follow Route 107 and turn off at the signs for Lake Shore Farm.

CENTRAL

Bradford, New Hampshire (see The Dartmouth-Lake Sunapee Region)

THE BRADFORD INN

Main Street, Bradford, NH 03221. 603-938-5309. *Innkeepers*: Tom and Woody Best. Open all year.

There has been an inn at the Bradford's Main Street location for two hundred years, although the Bradford Inn dates from the early 1890s. The Bests bought the old Bradford Hotel in 1976 and have been gradually remaking it into a true country inn, with twelve guest rooms. The rooms are simply but comfortably furnished, and three of them have private baths. The inn itself is decorated with antiques and Woody and Tom's memorabilia, collected over the years. The sitting room and lounge fireplaces burn cheerily on chilly fall days and throughout the winter months.

The Bests describe their inn as a "place for rustic romantics who relish the casual luxury of sleeping in country comfort, dining on home-cooked specialties, and reaping the daily rewards of New England life." Meals are prepared by Tom, who offers a dinner selection of six basic entrées, including beef in wine, lobster Newburg, a vegetarian plate, and steaks. The buns, breads, muffins, and desserts are all made from scratch in the inn's kitchen. Dinner and breakfast are available to the public also, but be sure to make reservations for dinner. Liquor is served in the lounge. No pets please. *Room Rates*: Rooms are $20 to $25. *Driving Instructions*:Take Route I-89, exit 9, then Route 103 to Bradford. The inn is located near the junction of routes 114 and 103.

Chocorua, New Hampshire (see Tamworth, New Hampshire)

STAFFORD'S-IN-THE-FIELD

Route 113, Chocorua, NH 03817. 603-323-7766. *Innkeepers*: Ramona and Fred Stafford. Open every day from Memorial Day to November, then open holiday weeks; from December 26 to April 1, open weekends only.

At the end of a picturesque country lane sits Stafford's-in-the-Field overlooking fields, forests, and a babbling brook. Built about 1778, the Federalist house had several additions made between the years

of 1880 and 1905. The inn and its eight guest rooms are furnished with comfortable antiques. There are four guest cottages on the property as well as a big old barn, Stafford's Barn, known for its good acoustics for string quartets and summer square dances. Guests eat family style at large tables in the dining room. Ramona is the chef, preparing many international dishes. For breakfast, guests might have blueberry-apple pancakes with the Staffords' own maple syrup, green chili omelets, eggs Benedict, and freshly baked currant muffins and warm breads. A dinner might include soup au Pistou and roast tenderloin with a Madeira sauce, followed by a rich dessert such as maple mousse or Brazilian orange cake.

To work off these meals, guests can square dance, swim in the old swimming hole in summer, or hike the long winding road that leads to Lake Chocorua with its view of Mount Chocorua. In the winter there is cross-country skiing on the property or at other nearby touring centers, plus a wide choice of alpine ski areas in the surrounding mountains. Children are welcome in summer only. No pets permitted. *Room Rates*: Double rooms are $32 to $35 per person, double occupancy, MAP. *Driving instructions*: The inn is on Route 113, a mile west of the intersection of routes 113 and 16.

The Dartmouth-Lake Sunapee Region (including Bradford, Canaan, Georges Mills, Hanover, Lyme, New London, Newbury, Sunapee, and Webster, New Hampshire)

The Lake Sunapee area is rich in history as well as in its more easily recognized recreational opportunities. The area includes Dartmouth College, in Hanover, *Old Fort No. 4* (a replica of an old stockade) in Charlestown, *Webster Meeting House Museum* in Webster, and the *Saint Gaudens National Historic Site* in Cornish, among other attractions. There are eight state parks and recreational areas within the confines of these towns, including *Mount Sunapee State Park* with its spacious beach and enclosed gondola ride to the top of a 2,700-foot peak. Almost every recreation available in the state is here with the exception of a major downhill skiing center. Golf is available at the area's nine golf courses, and swimming is possible at hundreds of locations. In addition, there is boating, fishing, hunting, hiking, horseback riding, tennis, and picnicking. Numerous country fairs are held each summer and fall, and country auctions and antique hunting along back roads offer pleasant pastimes. Theater lovers enjoy year-round theater at the *Hopkins Center* at Dartmouth and the summer theater presented by the New London Players in that town.

East Hebron, New Hampshire

East Hebron is located on the shores of Newfound Lake a few miles south of Plymouth, New Hampshire, and a short drive from the White Mountain National Forest. *Wellington State Park*, across the lake from East Hebron, has swimming at one of the state's finest inland beaches, facilities for picnicking, and hiking. It is a short drive to the *Polar Caves* in Plymouth, where there are tours of the glacial caves as well as a maple sugar house, a waterfowl exhibit, and a nature trail.

HILLSIDE INN

Route 3A, Newfound Lake, East Hebron, NH 03232. 603-744-2413. *Innkeepers*: Peter and Veronica Zereas. Open almost all year.

The Hillside is a huge, rambling inn with porches, decks, and gables jutting out in a most interesting manner. The inn has evolved slowly from its first building, which was constructed in 1760, until the latest, finished in 1972. The result is a typical New Hampshire lake-front inn with accessory buildings nearby. The place combines the feeling of an antique-filled country inn with some of the pleasures of a small resort. Among the latter are the tennis courts, the beach, the game room, shuffleboard, croquet, and Ping-Pong. The main inn features four separate living rooms that are filled with antiques, two grand pianos, and four fireplaces. In addition, there are large cottages that have two or three bedrooms, tub and shower, and fireplaces in their living rooms. These cottages do not have housekeeping facilities and are, with one exception, closed during the winter months. The inn has a small, comfortable lounge overlooking the lake. It is a popular gathering spot for before- and after-dinner drinks.

The inn serves both breakfast and dinner to guests and the public. The dinner menu features veal, steak, and roast beef. Recreational activities include swimming, sailing, fishing, and tennis in the warmer months and skiing at several nearby areas in the winter. No pets permitted except in the family cottages. *Room Rates*: Rooms range from $20 to $38 per couple, EP, depending on time of year. American Plan is available at an additional $14 per person per day. *Driving Instructions*:North on Route I-93 to exit 23, then 7 miles west on Route 104 to Bristol. Go north on 3A 8 miles to the inn.

Eaton Center, New Hampshire

Eaton Center is a small town south of Conway and near the edge of the *White Mountain National Forest*. The nearest ski area is *Mount Cranmore* in North Conway with its two skimobile tramways, three double chair lifts, and one Poma lift. For further information on the general region to the north of Eaton Center, see the White Mountains Region.

ROCKHOUSE MOUNTAIN FARM-INN

Eaton Center, NH 03832. 603-447-2880. *Innkeepers*: The Edge
family. Open mid-June until November 1.

The farm is located on the side of Rockhouse Mountain overlooking
Crystal Lake, where the farm has its own private beach with boats.
Operated for thirty-two years by the Edge family, the inn is designed
for families who wish a complete farm vacation with horseback riding,
barbeques, and even milking cows and feeding calves and piglets.
There are 350 acres of field and mountain for peaceful hikes.

The farmhouse was built in 1904 on the granite foundation of the
original farmhouse that had burned that year. Both the farmhouse
and the barn have comfortable guest rooms. The living room in the
farmhouse is filled with Edge family antiques and special family pos-
sessions. Breakfast and dinner are provided. The inn's specialities
are unusual vegetable casseroles and delicious freshly baked breads
and desserts. No pets are permitted. *Room Rates*: Rooms are about
$20 to $24 per person, MAP. Bunk rooms for teenagers are less.
Weekly rates are available. *Driving Instructions*: From Conway, take
Route 153 south as far as Crystal Lake; turn right; take the first right
beyond the post office and continue uphill a half mile.

New London, New Hampshire

New London is the home of Colby-Sawyer College and a summer theater known as the *New London Barn Players*. The village center is a short distance from Lake Sunapee, and skiers in this area use either *King Ridge* in New London or *Mount Sunapee* farther south. Ski touring in the winter and golf and tennis in the summer are featured at the *Lake Sunapee Country Club*.

PLEASANT LAKE INN

North Pleasant Street, New London, NH. Mailing address: Box 1030, New London, NH 03257. 603-526-6271. *Innkeepers*: The Jaggard family. Open all year, except for short vacations in April and November.

Located on the shores of Pleasant Lake, this inn was originally built as a farmhouse. Although the earliest parts of the inn date from 1770, the main portions of the inn were constructed in 1868. In the days when the property was a farm, the beautiful countryside surrounding the lake was shared by the farmers with the Penobscot Indians, with whom the families had friendly relations. The conversion to an inn was done by a Civil War veteran who operated it first as a summer and fall inn. As winter sports became increasingly popular to the economy of the state, so did year-round operation increase at New Hampshire inns, including this one.

The inn has twelve guest rooms that share several baths (no more than two rooms to any bath), and much of the inn is furnished in

country antiques. The Jaggards (two brothers and their families) go out of their way to have each guest feel as if he is visiting the Jaggard home. Days start with a large country breakfast, and many guests join the family for late afternoon tea. Dinners may be selected from a menu that offers such daily specials as chicken Pleasant Lake and shrimp au Rolf, as well as a printed menu that includes prime ribs of beef, crab imperial, and Black Forest pork chops, among others. Typical prices for a complete meal, including appetizer, entrée, dessert, and beverage, range from $8 to $11. Pets are not permitted. *Room Rates*: $17 for a single room and $21 to $25 for a double. *Driving Instructions*: Take Route 11 to New London, turn onto North Pleasant Street at the Shell Station and go 1½ miles to the bottom of the hill at the lake.

North Sutton, New Hampshire

North Sutton is located on the shores of *Lake Kezar*, a popular swimming, boating, and fishing spot. Golf is available to the public at the *Mount Kearsage Inn and Country Club* and the *Maple Leaf Golf Course*. Skiing is available at *King Ridge Ski Area* in nearby New London. It is only a short drive to *Sunapee Lake*, the largest lake in the Dartmouth–Lake Sunapee Region.

FOLLANSBEE INN
   North Sutton, NH 03260. 603-927-4221. *Innkeepers*: Larry and
   Joan Wadman. Open all year.
Like so many New Hampshire inns, the Follansbee has grown over the years to accommodate an increasing number of overnight guests. The lake-front inn was originally a two-story farmhouse built in the early 1800s but receiving an additional two stories in 1928–30. The result is an imposing structure with twenty-three guest rooms and full lounge and dining facilities. The innkeepers shed earlier careers in the states of Delaware and New Jersey and came to the inn filled with enthusiasm for their new family venture. Three months were spent in a thorough renovation of the old inn, and the Follansbee reopened its doors in mid-1978. The Wadman family's furniture is now ensconced in the lounge, along with articles collected on their world travels.

The new innkeepers had the foresight to hire a fine young chef to prepare the meals offered by a menu whose refreshing number of unusual dishes breaks the steak-ribs-chicken doldrums of so many commercial kitchens today. Among his special offerings are veal Oskar, sautéed frogs' legs, baked stuffed trout Montbarry, shrimp Fra Diavolo, and a large selection of the more familiar steaks, chops, and seafood, all done with interesting accompanying sauces. Entrées, all served with salad, vegetable, and potato or rice, range in price from $5.95 to $11.50, with extra charges for appetizer, soup, and dessert. *Room Rates*: Rooms range in price from $16 to $24. Eleven of the twenty-three guest rooms have private baths. *Driving Instructions*: The inn is 4 miles south of New London on Route 114.

Plainfield, New Hampshire (including Windsor, Vermont)

Plainfield is a small village near the Connecticut River south of Lebanon and Hanover. Because it is so near the famed *Windsor Covered Bridge* (the longest in Vermont), it is appropriate to include sightseeing activities in that area as well.

On the New Hampshire side of the river, the most important attraction in the immediate area is *Saint-Gaudens National Historic Site*. Augustus Saint-Gaudens lived and worked here for several years, and some of the buildings are open to the public. The newly established *Maxfield Parrish Museum and Views and Vistas Trail* is located at The Oaks on Route 12A, 2 miles from the Saint-Gaudens site.

Windsor was the birthplace of the Vermont constitution. *Constitution House* is open in the warmer months and contains memorabilia of early New England. The *American Precision Museum* has an interesting collection of hand and machine tools. Nearby *Mount Ascutney* is a popular family ski area.

THE OAKS

Route 12A, Plainfield, New Hampshire 03781. Mailing address: R.R. #2, Windsor, VT 05089. 603-675-5360. *Innkeeper*: Maurice Gilbert. Open all year.

Dating from 1898, The Oaks was conceived and built by the American illustrator and artist, Maxfield Parrish. This is a true baronial estate, part of the greater Cornish Art Colony, which at one time had 450 resident painters, sculptors, writers, and actors. The inn has only six guest rooms, but each is quite impressive. The master bedroom suite, for example, has a marble shower, sitting room, and a 20-mile view. The smallest bedroom is decorated with Delft tile. The common rooms of the inn include the Parchment Room, used for small gatherings; the Acorn Room, a small dining room with low beams, brass and copper ornaments, and a fireplace; and the cocktail lounge, with its view of Mount Ascutney. Perhaps most spectacular is the Oak Room, once the music salon and now the main dining room of the inn. Paneled in oak with massive beams, it has a 14-foot-wide fireplace and Palladian windows that look out on Mount Ascutney and the Connecticut River.

The restaurant at The Oaks has received a great deal of acclaim. The menu is simple, with a choice of four appetizers, a soup of the day, and seven entrées, which currently include quiche Lorraine, chicken amandine, capon Cordon Bleu, crab Mornay, seafood Constantine, brochette de boeuf, and feast of Old King Cole (sirloin steak surrounded by mushrooms stuffed with shrimp). Dinner prices range from $6.95 to $12.95. On weekends there is live piano and cello music in the Oak Room. Pets are permitted by prior arrangement only. *Room rates*: Room prices are from $26.95 to $52.95, depending on room and season. *Driving Instructions*: Take Route I-89 to Lebanon, exit 20. Then take Route 12A south 9 miles to The Oaks. Or take I-91 to Route 12A, then go north to the inn.

Tamworth, New Hampshire (see also The Dartmouth–Lake Sunapee Region)

The town of Tamworth was established in 1766. Logging is and has been important to the area since before the Revolution, when masts for the king's ships were hauled down "Old Mast Road" by ox cart. Most of the villages in the area have remained relatively untouched for the past hundred years.

Today it is a quiet section of the state known to tourists primarily for hiking and mountain climbing, including the relatively easy and popular *Mount Chocorua*. No special equipment is required for completing this hike although many visitors camp out near the summit. *The Barnstormers Theater* in Tamworth is the oldest summer theater in the state and is directed by the son of President Grover Cleveland, who had a summer home there. Auctions are held frequently in the warmer months next to the Tamworth Inn. There are dog-sled races in the area in January and a number of cross-country skiing trails nearby. *The Hemenway State Forest* is just north of Tamworth, and the *White Lake State Park* is in Tamworth itself and offers swimming, fishing, hiking, picnicking, and camping. In summer months there is square dancing at *Stafford's Barn* in Chocorua. A country fair is held annually in Sandwich each Columbus Day. Sandwich is also the home of the original building set up by the *League of New Hampshire Craftsmen*.

TAMWORTH INN

Main Street, Tamworth, NH 03886. 603-323-7721. *Innkeepers*: Bill and Sue McCarthy and Doug and Linda Conway. Open all year, but call in advance to make sure.

The Tamworth was first constructed in 1830, with additions made from 1870 through 1900; it has been an inn since 1888. The inn has a pub room with entertainment on weekends. The pub and the living room both have working fireplaces and many antiques. It has its own pool, and there is excellent trout fishing nearby. This is an area of few crowds and warm hospitality. During the summer months, the

local theater draws interested spectators from other parts of the state.

Meals are chosen from a simple menu consisting of eight entrées, including scallops Tamworth, roast turkey, and steak au poivre. Entrée prices range from $4.95 to $9.70, with additional charges for appetizer, soup, and dessert. *Room Rates*: Double rooms are $15 to $27. There are a variety of ski package plans and special plans that are MAP as well. *Driving Instructions*: Take Route I-93 to exit 23, Route 104 East to Route 3, Route 3 a short distance to Route 25, and then drive northeast to Whittier and Route 113, which runs north to Tamworth.

NORTHERN

Franconia, New Hampshire

Franconia is one of the White Mountains' most famous towns. Perhaps best known is the *Old Man of the Mountains*, the famous rock profile seen from just south of the village. The *Cannon Mountain Ski Area* has a tramway that takes you to the top of the 4,200-foot peak in all seasons. The *League of New Hampshire Craftsmen* has an outlet in town. Another favorite is the *Flume*, the rock gorge to the south of the village. For further information on this area, see the White Mountains Region.

FRANCONIA INN

Route 116, Easton Road, Franconia, NH 03580. 603-823-5542. *Manager*: Dwight Blakeslee. Open December 15 to April 15 and May 29 to October 15.

For many years, there was a farm on the property that now houses the Franconia Inn. In the mid-1860s, the farm started to take boarders. By the early 1900s, the farmhouse had been converted to a full tourist home and was being run as McKensie's. In 1934, however, a tremendous fire destroyed the original inn. Rebuilding started soon after, and the current structure was finished the following year. The inn ran successfully for many years, but then it closed. It was finally purchased and totally refurbished by Wade and Rachel Perry with the help of the Blakeslees.

The inn has twenty-nine rooms with solid, comfortable furnishings. Some of the rooms have wood paneling, and some are painted. Almost all have either private or connecting baths. Recreational facilities include a swimming pool, a nearby swimming "hole" in a quiet bend of the stream, outdoor clay tennis courts, and 65 miles of cross-country ski trails, forty of which are continually groomed. Meals are served in a spacious dining room, from a menu that changes daily. Each menu features five appetizers, three soups and about seven to ten entrées. Dinner prices range from $8 to $12 for a complete meal. Typical dinner choices include fried pork tenderloin, Hungarian goulash, veal cutlet aux champignons, skewered lamb, and stuffed fresh Boston scrod. Christmas dinner has included baked suckling pig as one of six entrée choices. Children are welcome, but pets are not permitted. *Room Rates*: As a general rule, double rooms are from $34 to $40 per person, MAP. There are, however, a variety of rate structures and special packages. *Driving Instructions*: Franconia is in the northwestern section of the White Mountain National Forest. The village of Franconia may be reached by local routes 116 and 117. Consult a map for exact instructions.

LOVETT'S BY LAFAYETTE BROOK

Profile Road, Franconia, NH 03580. 603-823-7761. *Innkeeper*: Charles Lovett, Jr. Open December 24 to April 1 and June 30 to October 9.

Lovett's is a semiresort centered around a 184-year-old main inn and surrounded by several contemporary self-contained duplex units located in the pine woods around the property. The inn has much to appeal to its adult clientele; however, there are numerous activities for children including Ping-Pong, pinball, and bumper pool. The main inn houses a comfortable bar, a sun-porch game room, a sitting room, and the dining room. Furnishings are generally colonial-style reproductions mixed with more contemporary pieces. The inn has its own swimming pool and ample grounds that offer numerous views of the nearby White Mountains. Accommodations are varied and include both simple and spacious rooms in the inn, motel rooms, and others in the Igloo Chalet, the Yellow House, and Stony Hill. *Room Rates*: Rates are complex because of the variety of accommodations. As a general guide, double rooms range in price from $20 to $38. MAP rates are also available. *Driving Instructions*: The inn is 2.5 miles south of Franconia on Route 18.

Glen, New Hampshire (see The White Mountains Region)

BERNERHOF INN

Route 302, Glen, NH 03838. 603-383-4414. *Innkeepers*: Ted and Sharon Wroblewski. Open Christmas to April 15 and Memorial Day to Thanksgiving.

The Bernerhof Inn was built in the early 1890s by a local businessman to serve travelers on their way to the Mount Washington Hotel.

Since then it has been in continuous service as a hostelry, although ownership has changed several times. Its current name was coined about 1956, when new owners of Swiss background chose a name that means House of Berne. The inn is finished with a number of antiques; an intimate dining room and the oak-paneled Zumstien Room (lounge) contain Swiss and other Europen artifacts. The inn offers eight guest rooms that share bath facilities. Dinner is distinctly European, with such specialties as delice de Gruyère, escargots Bourguignon, Wiener schnitzel, piccata Bernerhof, fondue (cheese and beef) and Hungarian goulash among the more than twenty selections. Lunch and breakfast are also served at most times of the year. Call first. *Room Rates*: Rooms are $19.50 per person, MAP, with several package plans available for longer stays. *Driving Instructions*: The inn is 6 miles north of North Conway (1 mile north of the intersection of routes 302 and 16).

Intervale, New Hampshire (see The White Mountains Region)

HOLIDAY INN

Route 16A, Intervale, NH 03845. 603-356-9772. *Innkeepers*: Lois and Bob Gregory. Open from May 30 through fall foliage (late

October), then from December 26 through the skiing season (late March).

Holiday Inn—no relation to the big chain—has been in continuous operation since the 1800s. Situated in the heart of Mount Washington Valley, with spacious grounds, mountain views, and a heated swimming pool, this small inn is a comfortable place. The rooms are furnished in the style of an old New Hampshire home, with working fireplaces, flowered wallpaper, spindle beds, and crisp white curtains. Home-cooked meals are served family style and are available to guests and the public.

Holiday Inn has something for everyone: swimming and canoeing in the summer, hang gliding for the more adventurous, skating on the inn's lighted rink, cross-country skiing from the front door in winter. There are ten guest rooms, each with private bath. *Room Rates*: Rooms are $21 to $24 per person, MAP, with package plans and mid-week discounts available. Rooms are less with just breakfast, double occupancy. *Driving Instructions*: Take Route 16 out of the north end of North Conway; go 1½ miles on Route 16A.

THE NEW ENGLAND INN

Intervale, NH 03845. 603-356-5541. *Innkeepers*: Jerry and Betty Davis. Open all year. The dining room is open from June to October 31 and from December 22 to March.

The New England Inn matured slowly over the last 170 years. It

began its life as the Bloodgood Farm, taking in road-weary travelers en route from Boston to Montreal. It provided them with a good bed, substantial meals, and a place for their horses. By the mid-1800s, the travelers were replaced at the farm by artists and other summer visitors. The White Mountain School of Art developed nearby, and even today the inn has paintings swapped for room and board. It has been modernized over the years, and most of the farm buildings have been converted into additional residences, but the modernization is not intrusive within the buildings. The farm grounds now offer a number of sports facilities, including several excellent clay tennis courts (most of the big name tennis pros who play at the Volvo Tennis Tournament practice here during that week), a four-hole golf course, and swimming and wading pools. The buildings themselves have colonial decorations, making use of antiques wherever possible. The front parlors have fireplaces, and there is a lounge in the ski barn. This is not a small establishment. The complex consists of the main inn, Hampshire House, five duplex cottages, four single cottages, a motel unit, and the sports facilities already mentioned.

The inn serves a full country breakfast and a complete dinner every day. The dinner menu changes daily but often contains a dozen entrée choices including lobster, steak, roasts, and fresh fish. All dinners include appetizer, soup, entrée, salad, and dessert and are priced from about $6.25 to $11.50. One of the dessert specialties is frozen lemon pie. Pets are permitted only in the cottages. *Room Rates*: Rates vary according to room selection and season. Rooms generally range from $22 to $38 per person, MAP, with mid-week rates and special package plans available. *Driving Instructions*: The inn is on Route 16A, 3½ miles north of North Conway.

Jackson, New Hampshire (see The White Mountains Region)

CHRISTMAS FARM INN

Route 16 B, Jackson, NH 03846. 603-383-4313. *Innkeepers*: Sydna and Bill Zeiff. Open May to mid-October and mid-December to April 1.

Christmas Farm Inn offers a variety of lodgings for skiers and other lovers of the good country life. The Main Inn, built in 1786, has comfortable colonial guest rooms and dining and living rooms with fireplaces. The other guest quarters include a log cabin, a 1771 salt box, and a converted maple-sugaring house. All in all, there are twenty-two, of which all but two have private baths. The rooms have spectacular views of Attitash and eleven other surrounding peaks and carry out the Christmas theme by bearing names like "Mr. and Mrs. Claus," "Noel," "Dancer," and "Three Wise Men." The dining room features hearty skiers' breakfasts, as well as homemade stews, soups, and freshly baked breads and pastries. The evening menu includes

the choice of three entrees. The dining room is open to the public for all three meals.

For the cross-country skiers, some of Jackson's nearly 80 miles of trails begin right at the inn. All trail fees are provided, as well as a waxing room and trail lunches. There is also a free shuttle to nearby areas. Pets are not encouraged. *Room Rates*: Rooms are $18 to $35 per person, MAP. The inn also offers numerous packages for all seasons and amounts of time. *Driving Instructions*: Take Route 16 north, through North Conway and over the covered bridge into Jackson Village (16A). Follow the signs to the inn.

THORN HILL LODGE AND CHALETS

Thorn Hill Road, Jackson, NH 03846. 603-383-4242. *Innkeepers*: Jacques and Carol Gagnon. Open from December to April and June to November.

The Thorn Hill Lodge is an 1895 inn with a distinct Victorian feeling. The main building was recently augmented by four chalet buildings—three individual units and one with seven bedrooms. Thus, guests can choose between two distinct styles.

The main building contains a large living room with a well-stocked library. The papered walls, gold rugs, and a fireplace give a warm feeling to this room with its large picture windows overlooking the Presidential Range. There are two dining rooms adjacent to the lounge. One is a dining porch with striking views of the mountains; the other has a country feeling in a Victorian setting. The nineteen guest rooms all have either private or connecting baths. The inn maintains a waxing room in the basement for the many skiers who come here to enjoy the inn's access to three cross-country trails offering nearly 80 miles of fine skiing on trails maintained by the Jackson Ski Touring Foundation. There is a large swimming pool for summer guests. The inn also offers special art workshops during July, September, and weekends in October.

Meals have a distinct New England flavor, with daily specials including turkey, broiled sirloin, prime ribs of beef, or Yankee pot roast. There are also five regular dishes to choose from, including a vegetarian special of the day. Complete dinners with appetizer, entrée, and beverage range in price from $6.50 to $10.00. In the summer the inn maintains its own large vegetable garden, which supplies fresh produce for the salads and vegetable dishes. Children are always welcome and pets may be brought with guests using the chalets only. *Room Rates*: Rates are either $27 to $30 per person, MAP, or $26 to $38 per room, double occupancy, EP. *Driving Instructions*: Take Route 16 North through North Conway and over the covered bridge into Jackson Village (16A). The inn is 300 yards from Jackson Village (follow signs).

THE WILDCAT INN AND TAVERN

Main St., Jackson Village, NH. Mailing address: Box 159, Jackson, NH 03846. 603-383-4245. *Innkeepers*: Marty and Pam Sweeney. Open all year.

The Wildcat is a nineteenth-century informal inn featuring antique furnishings. The lounge in the Tavern has two fireplaces and a number of sleigh seats and couches that create a relaxing atmosphere further enhanced by the performances by folk singers on weekends and Monday evenings. There is also a fireplace in the reading room and an old parlor stove in the dining room. Winter guests are often drawn to the Wildcat by the *Jackson Touring Foundation* cross-country skiing trails and by the exciting skiing at *Tuckerman's Ravine* and *Wildcat Mountain*. The inn has an enclosed, heated porch that is popular in all seasons for relaxing and enjoying the sunsets over the mountains. The inn offers accommodations for forty guests in private guest rooms or in small bunk rooms. Seven of the eighteen rooms have private baths. There is a recreation room with television and games. The village skating rink is just across the street, and there is a riding stable around the corner from the inn.

The inn has made an effort to create a menu with a real flair, to attract a dining clientele interested in food rather than frozen, prepackaged portion control. Among the inn's specialties are Bulgoggi, a Korean dish of thin sliced beef, marinated in soy sauce, sesame oil, and a blend of seasonings; char-broiled beef, served on a bed of rice; sole Melissa, wrapped around asparagus spears, baked in wine, and covered with melted Swiss cheese; shashlik, the popular Russian skewered lamb; Wildcat chicken, a boneless breast stuffed with ham and cheese, wrapped in puff paste, and served with mustard sauce. There is also a vegetable loaf, lasagna, and their Tavern Steak. The inn prides itself on its strict adherence to the principle of food cooked to order. Many vegetable offerings are cooked in a wok, to retain their ultimate freshness. Rolls and desserts are freshly made at the inn. Dinner prices range from $5 to $10 for the entrées. Pets are not permitted. *Room Rates*: Rooms are $24 to $28, plus a 15 percent charge for gratuities and a 6 percent state tax. *Driving Instructions*: Jackson is on Route 16 about 12 miles north of Conway.

North Conway and Conway, New Hampshire

North Conway is the home of *Mount Cranmore Ski Area*. Full downhill and cross-country ski services are available here, and many visitors come just to ride the trestle-track tramway known as the Skimobile. If your sporting love is hang gliding, you can take lessons or watch the birdmen at the hang-gliding school operated by *Sky People, Inc. Eastern Mountain Sports* in the village is one of the country's largest purveyors of sports equipment, with the emphasis on outdoor sports. In the summer, the *Mount Washington Valley Theater* presents a full season of contemporary drama and comedies. The *Conway Scenic Railway* is one of the state's most popular tourist attractions and operates from early May through late October.

CRANMORE MOUNTAIN LODGE

Kearsage Road, North Conway, NH. Mailng address: P.O. Box 1194, North Conway, NH 03860. 603-356-2044. *Innkeepers*: Bob and Dawn Brauel. Open all year.

Bob and Dawn Brauel, the inn's youthful innkeepers, have come to innkeeping as a retreat from the more hectic lifestyle of earlier careers as a certified public accountant and a social worker, respectively. Their contentment in their new profession is evident in their enthusiasm for their work.

Cranmore Mountain Lodge was built in several sections, the earliest of which dates from the mid-1800s. First a farmhouse, the early building was converted to an inn in the late 1800s by the addition of an octagonal wing. Later additions have included a main dining room, added in the 1930s, and very recent tennis courts, swimming pool, basketball court, and an outdoor Jacuzzi bath. At one time, the lodge was run by Babe Ruth's daughter. The Babe was a frequent guest, using the inn as his hunting and fishing retreat. His room was furnished with lovely oak twin beds, and it continues to be the favorite room of many guests.

The main inn has eleven comfortable guest rooms with varied bed arrangements that can accommodate small or large families. There are also dorm facilities with bunk bedding in the old barn. These are used most frequently for larger groups of skiers during the winter months. The main floor of the inn has a sitting room with fireplace, a television and game room, and a dining room serving home-cooked single-entrée meals (to guests only). The inn has an alpine ski shop. Pets are not permitted. *Room Rates*: Rates are $7 to $10 per person, room only; $9 to $12 per person, bed and breakfast; $13 to $16 per person, MAP. *Driving Instructions*: At the traffic light on Route 16 in North Conway, turn east on Kearsage Street, which dead-ends into Kearsage Road. The lodge is a mile to the north.

DARBY FIELD INN

Bald Hill, Conway, New Hampshire 03818. 603-447-2181. *Innkeepers*: Tommie Stivers and Paul Jaeger. Open May 1 through the last weekend in October, and December 15 through the last weekend in March.

A thousand feet above Mount Washington's valley sits the Darby Field Inn. Perched on top of Bald Hill in the White Mountains, the inn commands a magnificent view of the famous mountain, and the beautiful surrounding peaks and valley. The inn was named for the intrepid adventurer Darby Field, the first white man to climb Mount

Washington, the highest mountain in the northeast. Local Indians, in 1642, felt that spirits lived on top of the mountain, making it taboo, and that anyone climbing it would never return. As innkeeper Tommie Stivers, points out, it is so cold up there all year that most of those who tried may have frozen to death! Yet old Darby climbed it and survived to tell the tale. His name lives on today at the inn. Each of the eleven guest rooms is decorated uniquely with a variety of calicos and gingham checks. Nine have private baths, and all have four-poster beds and views of the valley. Some of the rooms are more formal than others, but each has its own charm. Downstairs, guests have the use of the inn's lounge, with its enormous stone fireplace, and the combination library and sitting room, where they will find a large collection of good books and magazines.

The pub and the dining room at the Darby Field are open to the public in the evenings but only to guests for breakfast. The dining room has a view of Mount Washington and the candlelight dinners feature fresh seafood, veal, and—the specialty—rack of lamb. The breads, salad dressings, and desserts are made fresh daily in the inn's kitchen. Children and "civilized" pets are permitted. *Room Rates*: With private bath, $28-$32, EP; shared bath, $24. December to March there is also a modified American plan at $24 to $30 per person. *Driving Instructions*: Off Route 16, a mile south of Conway, turn onto Bald Hill Road. A mile up the road, turn right at the sign of the Darby Field Inn. Follow this road almost a mile to the inn.

NERELEDGE INN

River Road, North Conway, NH. Mailing address: Box 432, North Conway, NH 03860. 603-356-2831. *Innkeepers:*Marti and Steve Gourley. Open all year, except Easter to mid-June.

The Nereledge Inn, built in 1787, has two parlors (one with a fireplace), a dining room, and eleven guest rooms that share three baths. The dining room has a panoramic view of the Saco River, Intervale, and the White Horse and Cathedral ledges. Many of the rooms contain antiques or attractive reproductions.

The inn is known locally for its hearty breakfasts, which always include home-fried potatoes and hot apple pie and are a real buy. Dinners are also a bargain. A 16-ounce broiled sirloin steak is $7.95; other items include shrimp, pork chops, scallops, roast beef, liver and onions, and spaghetti or lasagna. In addition to the regular menu, there is a daily special—usually a roast dish priced from $3.95 to $4.95. Dinner and breakfast are open to the public as well as to guests. No pets permitted. *Room Rates*: Double rooms are $16.50 per person, MAP; $11.00 per person, bed and breakfast; $9.00 per person, EP. Single rooms are slightly higher. Skiing package plans are available. *Driving Instructions*: The inn is 300 feet from Route 16 on River Road in North Conway.

THE SCOTTISH LION

Route 16, North Conway, NH. Mailing address: Box 560, North Conway, NH 03680. 603-356-2482. *Innkeepers*: Jack and Judy Hurley. Open all year except two weeks in April and two weeks in either November or December.

The Scottish Lion was built in 1877, the third building and second inn on the site. After a long period as a private home and a shorter time as a restaurant, Jack and Judy Hurley bought the house and established the Scottish Lion Inn. Steeped in Scottish traditions, the inn is a fine, hospitable place. The furnishings and feeling of the inn transport the guest to the British Isles.

The Black Watch Pub gives as Scottish a feeling as it can on this side of the Atlantic, with its military paintings by Ernest O. Brown. Scotch lovers rejoice; there is a choice of more than two dozen brands. Diners may eat in any of three dining rooms, including the St. Andrews Room, which has a fire burning in the fireplace during the winter months. In the summer, guests are welcome to dine on the

Flower Deck outdoors. Meals here offer a sampling of such favorites as Scottish oatcakes, rumbledethumps (a blend of cabbage, potatoes and cheese), Scotch eggs, finnan haddie, salmon steak Scotch style, and Scottish steak and mushroom pie. For the most part, however, the menu is a traditional American selection of seafood, poultry, and meat entrées, with a smattering of continental influence. Complete dinners range from $7.25 to $15.00. There is a fully stocked Scottish gift shop featuring crystal, stoneware, sweaters, clothing, and Scottish foods. A mail order catalog is available. Pets are not permitted. *Room Rates*: The eight rooms share several baths. Rooms are $12.50 per person, including a full breakfast. *Driving Instructions*: The inn is a mile north of the village of North Conway, on Route 16.

Pittsburg, New Hampshire (including Colebrook and the Connecticut Lakes Region)

Pittsburg is the fishing and hunting headquarters for this area. In 1832, during a border dispute between Canada and the United States, an independent nation was declared here called the Indian Stream Territory. In the area there are the three Connecticut lakes plus man-made Lake Francis. The 45th Parallel passes nearby, marking the spot equidistant from the Equator and the North Pole.

To the south, Colebrook is situated in the shadow of Mount Monadnock. Set in a great logging area, the town now has a modern shopping center and a small airport. The area also provides golf on three courses, hunting, fishing, and canoeing. In addition, it is a photographer's and artist's paradise. The *Wilderness Ski Area* at Dixville Notch has both downhill and cross-country skiing.

THE GLEN LODGE

First Connecticut Lake, Pittsburg, NH 03592. 603-538-6500. *Innkeeper*: Betty H. Falton. Open from May 15 to early October. The main lodge here was built in 1900 as a private lake-shore lodge and retreat. It soon became a fishing resort. In 1947, ten cottages were added that variously accommodate two to eight persons. Staying here is rather like visiting a private wilderness estate. The cottages have rustic log exteriors and wood paneling inside. The main lodge also has a rustic feeling, with its working fireplaces and sturdy pine furniture. Both lake and stream fishing are available, and the catch might include landlocked salmon, lake trout, rainbow trout, brown trout, and squaretails. The staff will be happy to arrange fishing trips in more remote waters for the adventurous.

The dining room serves three meals daily to both guests and public, with home-baked breads, pies, and cakes, as well as a salad bar. There is a weekly buffet, and cookouts are optional at lunch. The lodge is a relaxing place without organized social activity. Its great appeal is to lovers of sports and nature, and to those who just want to be away from the more organized tourist scene. Pets are permitted. *Room Rates* (1978): Rooms are $24 to $32. *Driving Instructions*: Take Route 93 or 95 to Route 3 in Lancaster. Then go north through Pittsburg village 10 miles. The lodge is a mile off the highway on a private road. Call up for detailed instructions.

Shelburne, New Hampshire

Most visitors to the Shelburne-Gorham area are drawn there for the mountains and the scenery. In the winter, there are numerous cross-country skiing trails, and it is a relatively short drive to Sunday River and Wildcat ski areas. For further information on this area, see the White Mountains Region.

PHILBROOK FARM INN

North Road, Shelburne, NH 03581. 603-466-3831. *Innkeepers*: Nancy Philbrook and Constance P. Leger. Open from May 1 to October 31 and from December 26 to April 30.

The Philbrook Farm Inn is a typical New Hampshire building that, like so many others, has expanded gradually over the generations. The first section was built in 1934 and the Philbrook family has lived here since 1861. The Philbrooks have always been proud of their relaxed and homey atmosphere: an inn "filled with peace, quiet and contentment in a world turned upside down." The Philbrook survives as the only inn in an area that used to abound with inns. Some of the guests are now the fourth and fifth generation from their families to visit Philbrook Farm.

The inn is furnished with family antiques, and with paintings done by guests, old maps of the area, and Currier and Ives prints. There are several fireplaces, including ones in the two living rooms and the dining room with its knotty pine paneling. The playroom has table tennis, pool, and a collection of old farm tools and kitchen things, as well as its own fireplace. Meals are served family style from a menu that changes daily. Much of the food served in the summer months is raised in the inn garden. Meals generally include a fresh, homemade soup followed by a roast meat or poultry, vegetables, potato, and dessert. On Saturday nights there is a New England baked bean supper, and Sunday morning breakfast traditionally consists of fishballs and cornbread.

The nineteen guest rooms are in the inn's main building and the Lodge, the Little House, Undercliff, the Casino, and Birch Cliff. Most of the last are rented by families or larger groups. Pets are permitted in the summer cottages only. *Room Rates*: Double rooms, per person, MAP, range from $18 to $20. Single rooms, MAP, are $23 to $30. *Driving Instructions*: The inn is 1½ miles off Route 2. Look for the direction sign, turn, cross the railroad tracks and bridge, then turn right at the crossroads and drive for ½ mile.

Sugar Hill, New Hampshire (see also The White Mountains Region)

Sugar Hill is quite near all the attractions of the White Mountains region. The town has several antique and gift shops, including The Sugar Hill Sampler, Colonial Cottage Antiques, Harman's Country Store, the Hildrex Maple Sugar Farm, and Miss Lynn and Miss Monahan's, and there are many antique shops in the surrounding countryside. There are country auctions by the dozen in the warm months—several each week. Golf and cross-country skiing are available at the *Sunset Hill House*. Sugar Hill Historic Museum is in the town.

THE HOMESTEAD

Sugar Hill, NH 03585. 603-823-5564. *Innkeeper*: Esther T. Serafini. Open from Memorial Day to November 1, Thanksgiving weekend, and from the Christmas holidays through April 15.

The Homestead has been in Esther Serafini's family since the Teffts, her grandparents, first opened the old farmhouse to guests in 1880. The original house was built, using hand-hewn beams, in 1802 by Sugar Hill's first settler. Many of the beautiful handmade antiques at the Homestead today were brought here in ox-drawn carts by the first settlers. Mrs. Serafini's grandparents enlarged the farmhouse to its present size in 1898. In 1917, the inn property was expanded again with the addition of the Chalet, built entirely of stones gathered in the surrounding meadows and logs hauled here in horse-drawn sleds.

The Homestead offers seventeen guest rooms—ten in the inn itself, and seven in the other three buildings on the property. The

Family Cottage and the Early Family Home are both small farmhouses containing charming rooms with private baths. They have porches and verandas with views of rolling meadows and the White Mountains. The Chalet can be rented as a unit. It has a 44-foot living room with a cathedral ceiling and an unusual brick-and-fieldstone fireplace. From the balcony porch one can see three mountain ranges. The Chalet also has a kitchen, a dining room, and two bedrooms. It is decorated with unusual antiques, and handmade threshing equipment is displayed on its walls.

All the rooms in the inn are filled with antiques and family memorabilia. The entire place is just plain "old fashioned comfortable." The inn has two floors for occupancy, each with five guest rooms and two hall bathrooms. Mrs. Serafini points out that although the rooms are chock full of antique dressers, lamps, and beds, the mattresses are definitely *not* antique. There are many up-to-date little comforts here, but in no way do they detract from the character and charm of the old inn.

Downstairs the hand-hewn ceiling beams are exposed to view. There can be found an entrance hall, a reading room, a Victorian parlor with a fireplace, and the pine-paneled dining room. The cupboards in the dining room are filled with Mrs. Serafini's extensive and beautiful glass and china collection. Dinners are hearty and a real New England farm treat. Everything is homemade here, from the relishes and conserves to the pies, parfaits, and sauces, and there are no steam tables. Breakfasts are the kind your grandmother would make you. The public may eat here for dinner but only with a reservation. Gentlemen must wear jackets. Guests are not encouraged to bring pets or young children to the inn. *Room Rates*: Singles range from $28 to $38; doubles, $30 to $40. The rates are all per person, MAP. *Driving Instructions*: Sugar Hill is off I-93 (exit 38 coming north or exit 39 coming south).

Thornton, New Hampshire (including Campton) (see The White Mountains Region)

AMITY HOUSE

Route 49, Thornton, NH. Mailing Address: RFD 1, Campton, NH 03223. 603-726-9881. *Innkeepers*:Peter and Carolyn Wolfe. Open from July 1 to October 30 and Thanksgiving to April 1.

Amity House is a friendly little country inn, offering five guest rooms with shared baths and three small bunk rooms that appeal most to winter skiers and summer hikers who are attracted to the Waterville Valley area. Children have fun exploring the woods, river, swimming hole, and the working farm nearby. The inn itself is a renovated farmhouse with a fieldstone fireplace, braided rugs, wide-board floors in the dining room and bedrooms, a few antiques, and lots of books and paintings. In the summer, the Wolfes put fresh flowers in every room. They work hard to cultivate their flower beds and a small organic garden. Combined with the friendly spirit and informal atmosphere is a touch of elegance here and there. Guests dine by candlelight and are invited to bring their own wine. The menu changes daily and usually includes a choice of at least two entrées. A recent dinner menu offered fresh mushroom soup, fettucine Alfredo, broiled fresh salmon steak, or sauté de veau au calvados, salad, homemade bread, and a fresh fruit tart. The full dinner price was either $10 (for the salmon) or $11 (for the veal). No pets permitted. *Room Rates*: Double rooms are $17 to $19 per person; bunk rooms are $14 per person, both MAP. *Driving Instructions*: Take exit 28 off Route I-93, bear right toward Waterville Valley to Goose Hollow (about 4 miles). The inn is on the left at the intersection.

The White Mountains Region
(including Campton, Conway, Franconia, Glen, Gorham, Intervale, Jackson, Jefferson, Lincoln, Littleton, North Conway, Twin Mountain, and Woodstock, New Hampshire)

This region of New Hampshire probably has more tourist attractions than any comparable area in New England. Among the many popular sights are the *Attitash Alpine Slide* in Bartlet; the spectacular *Gondola Rides* at Wildcat Mountain, Loon Mountain, and Cannon Mountain; the *Conway Scenic Railroad* with its old-time train ride; *Storyland* at Glen, with its castle and storybook adventures and people; the brand new *Heritage-New Hampshire* adjacent to Storyland; and the *Polar Caves*, New Hampshire's natural wonder left over from the days of glaciers. There is also *Santa's Village* outside Jefferson, *Six Gun City* in Jefferson, and the *Flume* at Franconia Notch.

The White Mountain National Forest has 730,000 acres of mountains and deep forest with numerous camp grounds, hiking trails, and ski areas, including *Wildcat, Loon, Waterville Valley, Attitash, Cannon Mountain, Black Mountain, Bretton Woods, Tyrol*, and *Mount Cranmore*. In addition, there are more than fifteen ski-touring centers, and the area is the home of the Appalachian Mountain Club, which operates numerous mountain huts for hikers and skiers. The rivers provide excellent canoeing, although several are rated as difficult and must be approached with caution. Most of the ski areas are surrounded by numerous shops and restaurants. The *League of New Hampshire Craftsmen* operates branch outlets in Franconia and North Conway.

No visit to this region would be complete without a trip to the top of Mount Washington via either the *Mount Washington Auto Road* (in warm months; a toll is charged) or the *Mount Washington Cog Railway*.

Maine

MAINE is no stranger to visitors. Inhabited by a number of American Indian tribes for thousands of years, the first European visitors to the area were probably explorers connected to the early Norwegian explorations headed by Leif Ericson around the year 1000. Some five hundred years later, Giovanni da Verrazano, the great Italian navigator, landed here and there along the Maine coastline. But in 1604 Sieur de Monts made the first settlement north of St. Augustine, Florida, on Neutral Island, at the mouth of the St. Croix River; the settlement moved to Nova Scotia after one winter.

Much of Maine was originally owned by Massachusetts, though the more northern portions were claimed by France. The French claim was contested in a number of bloody French and Indian wars until 1760, when the final surrender and treaty turned over the control of the land area that is now Maine to Massachusetts. The timber riches of this vast area provoked continuing disputes over the exact location of the Canadian border. These disputes were finally settled by the War of 1812 and later border treaties. Finally, Maine seceded from Massachusetts in 1819 and was granted statehood the following year. Gradually, new industries were added to those of timber and fur, primarily fishing, lobstering, quarrying, farming, and ship building. All these industries today remain major sources of revenue in Maine. For many years, however, another important industry has been tourism.

Most visitors to Maine never really comprehend the magnitude of this state. To grasp Maine's size more fully, it is necessary to realize that all five other New England states could almost fit into the state of Maine. Furthermore, much of the East Coast's lumber, a large percentage of its annual potato crop, its blueberries, and

MAINE

Scale of miles

Map by Jober

Primary roads

Secondary roads

nearly all of its lobsters are produced in Maine. This is the land of thousands of lakes, millions of acres of forest, and more than 2,000 miles of ocean and tidal coastline. Maine was, until recently, known to tourists almost exclusively for its coastal features. Gradually, however, interest has grown in the interior regions with their extensive fishing, hunting, and lakeside recreation. The advent of Maine skiing, both downhill and cross-country, has brought thousands of winter sports' enthusiasts to the state. Snowmobiling here is not only a sport but also a practical means of transportation for many. This year-round attractiveness is gradually being reflected by Maine's inns, which are staying open longer and longer.

Visitors to Maine can get excellent advance vacation-planning help from two sources within the state. The Maine Publicity Bureau is a privately funded promotional organization that will be happy to mail potential visitors an excellent packet of information. Its address is Maine Publicity Bureau, 1 Gateway Circle, Portland, ME 04101. Its phone number is 207-773-7266. The Maine State Chamber of Commerce also provides excellent information. Write to it at 477 Congress Street, Portland, ME 04111. In addition, many areas have roadside information booths to help travelers. Some of these are open in the summer months only.

COASTAL

Blue Hill, Maine (see also Deer Isle)

Blue Hill is an old town with white clapboard homes set at the base of Blue Hill, a 900-foot hill topped with a fire tower and affording a spectacular view of the bay and its islands, and of a beautiful cove. The town has many craft shops, including two well-known potteries, *Roantrees* and *Rackliffe*. The *Kneisel Hall Music School*'s Chamber Players give concerts every Wednesday and Saturday night and Sunday afternoon throughout the summer. The school was founded by violinist Franz Kneisel. The *Blue Hill Country Club* has a nine-hole golf course open to the public. In South Blue Hill one can see the reversing tidal falls. *Acadia National Park* is extraordinarily beautiful in all seasons. Deer Isle, Isle au Haut, and Bar Harbor can all be reached by day trips from Blue Hill.

BLUE HILL INN

Blue Hill, ME 04614. 207-374-2844. *Innkeepers*: Jean and Fred Wakelin. Open all year.

The Blue Hill was built in 1830 and has been serving guests as an inn since 1840. The lovely old building is brick ended, with white clapboard sides and many chimneys. Large shade trees surround the inn. The bright, cheery rooms are cooled in the summer by ocean breezes and are warm and cozy in winter. All nine guest rooms have private baths. Colonial wallpapers, crisp white curtains, and many-paned windows add a country charm to the old inn.

The Wakelins serve a different menu each day, including a continental or full country breakfast and a home-cooked dinner with their own special chowders, soups, breads, and desserts. The public is invited by reservation only. Guests may bring their own liquor, since there is no liquor license at the inn. Blue Hill Country Club extends privileges of tennis, golf, and its beach to guests of the inn. No pets please. *Room Rates*: From June 1 through October 31, rooms are $24 single occupancy and $30 double. In the off season, rooms are $18 single and $24 double. *Driving Instructions*: Take the Maine Turnpike (I-95) to Augusta. Take Route 3 past Bucksport, then turn right onto Route 15 and proceed to Blue Hill.

Boothbay Harbor, Maine

Boothbay Harbor is a jewel along the rockbound coast of Maine. The Boothbay Harbor area was first visited by Captain John Smith, who landed on Monhegan Island, a short distance from the harbor area, in the year 1616. Today it is a very active harbor with many fishing boats, and is the home of the *Windjammer Days* parade of old schooners in mid-July. Visitors exploring this village are encouraged to visit the *Boothbay Railway Museum* to ride on the country's only steam-operated, two-foot-gauge railroad and to see the museum's many other fine collections of transportation memorabilia. Also in Boothbay Harbor is *Hyde House*, home of the Boothbay Region Historical Society, and the *Grand Banks Schooner Museum*. More than forty cruise and fishing expeditions now leave from Boothbay Harbor at different times.

CLIPPER INN

94 Commercial Street, Boothbay Harbor, ME 04538. 207-633-5152. *Innkeeper*: Fredrick J. Hughes. Open all year.

The Clipper, a small waterfront inn, has thirty-four rooms with private baths, as well as a restaurant with a view of the harbor and a roaring fire on cool days. Guests at the inn are automatically enrolled in the Boothbay Harbor YMCA, which has excellent recreational facilities, including tennis, handball, racquet ball, and pool. Of special interest, according to innkeeper Fred Hughes, is the fact that the inn seems to be haunted "by the ghost of a young bride whose husband disappeared on her wedding night. One small third floor of the inn has been shut off completely because of this. There is no longer a staircase leading to it—the only access is through the walls." All this adds to the romantic atmosphere of the inn. The only meal offered is dinner (for the public as well as guests). During the winter months, they specialize in cooking such food as steaks, kebabs, and trout over the log fire in the bar. *Room Rates*: Double rooms start at $26 in the summer and at $22 in the off seasons. There is a "Getaway Anyday" package available from October 1 to June 1 at $19.50 per person, per day, MAP. *Driving Instructions*: From Wiscassett (on U.S. 1), take Route 27 south to Boothbay Harbor.

THE THISTLE INN

53 Oak Street, Boothbay Harbor, ME 04538. 207-633-3541. *Innkeeper*: Leonie Greenwood-Adams. Open all year.

This street-front inn in the center of the village is both a popular tourist attraction and a favorite haunt of the local fishermen and lobstermen. This is undoubtedly due to the immense popularity of the innkeeper, Leonie Greenwood-Adams, who has described herself as a "surly proprietress." She has, in fact, created an extremely friendly inn where a strong Scottish influence prevails in a 145-year-old former home of a sea captain. Lunch and dinner are served in the restaurant and the menu includes scallops flambé ($7.95), T'Donalds Scottish lobster pie ($8.50), and a house steak with mushroom and lobster sauce ($12.00) among the many meat and seafood offerings. There is a popular dory bar, which is often the loudest place in town, especially when all the lobster boats are in at the same time. The inn has ten rooms, only one with a private bath. Rooms are decorated with New England furniture dating from the late 1800s. Pets are permitted. *Room Rates*: Rooms are $9.45 to $18.90 during the summer season; $8.40 to $14.70 from Labor Day to June 1. *Driving Instructions*: Take U.S. 1 to Route 27 South to Boothbay Harbor.

Brooksville and West Brooksville, Maine (see Blue Hill and Deer Isle)

DAVID'S FOLLY

Route 176, West Brooksville, ME. Mailing Address: R.R. #2, Brooksville, ME 04617. 207-326-8834. *Innkeepers*: The Cutler family. Open from mid-June to October 1.

The inn consists of a white main building connected by a converted woodshed to an old barn. There is a huge living room with two bay windows, a library for relaxing, and, in the barn, a recreation room and lounge. The Cutlers purchased the farm in 1939 and restored it to its original beauty.

The dining room serves farm-fresh food family style, with every-

thing made from scratch. Some of the daily specials include fresh fish on Tuesdays, a cookout on Wednesdays (weather permitting), boiled lobster on Fridays, and a roast of lamb, beef, or turkey on Sundays. The inn sometimes serves a real New England boiled dinner as well as other New England specialties—Indian pudding, coffee jelly, johnnycake, and homemade pickles. The kitchen's black iron stove is still used to bake the traditional Saturday-night baked beans, raisin brown bread, and blueberry pie.

David's Folly is a saltwater farm. The fields slope gently to the inn's private cove, where guests can swim, fish, dig for clams, and row out to the nearby islands to explore. The guest rooms are spread out between the main house, the converted woodshed, the barn, and a separate cabin. Some rooms have private baths and some share baths. *Room Rates*: Prospective rates were not available at time of publication, but a rate increase is expected. Rooms were $28 to $30 per person, AP, in 1978. Weekly rates are available. The cabin is rented only on a weekly basis. *Driving Instructions*: From Bucksport, take Route 15 to North Bucksport, where you turn left onto Route 199 to Penobscot. Take a right onto Route 175 and follow this to North Brooksville, where you turn right on Route 176. The inn is 4 miles ahead in West Brooksville.

OAKLAND HOUSE

Herrick Road, Brooksville, ME. Mailing address: Sargentville, ME 04673. 207-359-8521. *Innkeeper*: James Littlefield. Open from June 20 to September 10 with full facilities, and for six weeks before and after these dates without the dining room.

Nestled between Lake Winnewaug and Penobscot Bay, the Oakland House was built as a private residence prior to 1776. Additions were made in 1889 so as to create a house with rooms for rent. The inn was originally a resting place for travelers who arrived by steamships that landed at Herrick's Landing. Over the years, a number of cottages have been built, so at the present time a guest can choose the more old-fashioned rooms in Oakland House itself or the privacy of one of the ten family cottages. In addition, there is an Annex that has a living room with fireplace, three guest rooms and bath on the first floor, and four guest rooms and a bath on the upper floor. There is also a detached building called Shore Oaks with ten large guest rooms (two with fireplaces).

Meals are served in the main house and feature lobster, clams, crabmeat, and fresh fish dishes, plus homemade pastries, desserts, and rolls. Weekly features are the lobster picnic on the beach every Thursday evening and the Sunday buffet, which always includes a lobster dish.

The inn could be described as a low-key resort. Activities are not pushed on guests, but there is much to do here. It is unusual in that it has access both to saltwater bathing from its own private beach and to freshwater bathing on the shore of Lake Winnewaug. The inn provides rowboats for both types of water at no extra charge. Sailboats may be rented nearby for longer visits and moored at Oakland House. Pets are permitted. *Room Rates*: June 20 to September 10, rooms are $115.50 to $217 per person per week, AP. During off season, the cottages are available for rental for $125 per cottage per week, without meals. *Driving Instructions*: Take Route 15 South approximately 12 miles from Blue Hill to the inn's sign on the right. (If you come to a large green suspension bridge, you have passed the turn by ¾ mile.)

Camden, Maine

This classic harbor town in midcoast Maine is set on the slopes of the Camden Hills, which descend into the harbor. Visitors to this area may use Camden as a base to explore the midcoast region, whose attractions include *Camden Hills State Park*, the *Old Conway House and Museum*, numerous scenic cruises on Penobscot Bay, and the famed *Windjammer Cruises* along coastal Maine, many departing from this port. This village has easy access along Route 1 to the nearby towns of Lincolnville to the north and Rockport and Rockland to the south. Winter visitors will enjoy using the skiing facilities of the *Camden Snow Bowl* and *Ragged Mountain*. Golfers have use of the *Goose River Golf Course* and the *Rockland Golf Club* in nearby Rockland. Camden also provides a scenic base for those who wish to attend the immensely popular *Maine Seafood Festival*, held in Rockland during the first weekend in August each year. A short trip inland will bring visitors to our favorite country fair, in Union, usually held the third weekend in August.

CAMDEN HARBOUR INN

83 Bayview Street, Camden, ME 04843. 207-236-4200. *Innkeepers*: Jim and Loureen Gilbert. Open all year.

The Camden Harbour Inn has eighteen rooms in a sturdy-looking Victorian (1892) building with an enclosed wraparound porch. Eight of these rooms share baths, while the other ten have private baths—all with the original claw-foot tubs. Comfort here is old-fashioned, without such modern distractions as television or room telephones. The inn's kitchen specializes in steaks, chops, prime-rib roasts, and fresh seafood picked up daily from local suppliers. It features lobster dinners in season. Children and pets are welcome. *Room Rates*: From June 1 to November 1, rooms range from singles with shared baths for $21 to doubles with private baths for $38, including full country-style breakfasts. Off season, when no breakfast is included, the rates are $14 single and $28 double. *Driving Instructions*: Take U.S. 1 to the center of Camden. From the only four-way intersection in town, turn down Bayview Street and follow the harbor three blocks to the inn.

WHITEHALL INN

52 High Street, Camden, ME 04843. 207-236-3391. *Innkeepers*: Jean and Ed Dewing. Open from late May to mid-October.

The Whitehall Inn occupies a commanding position in the center of the lovely town of Camden. Edna St. Vincent Millay was sixteen years old when she first recited her poetry at the inn, and there is a special room filled with Millay memorabilia there. The building has grown out from underneath the original sea captain's house that was built in 1834 and forms the nucleus of the buildings. The inn has thirty-eight rooms today and possesses a quiet elegance in keeping with its history. Antiques have been used throughout in a pleasing way and add to the feeling that one is a guest in a large but comfortable country home. Coastal Maine is an inviting place for peace and quiet surrounded by the panorama of coastal sea-life. The Whitehall is a fine place to enjoy just that.

Meals at the inn feature typical New England food with homemade breads, muffins, pastries, and cakes (frequently with Maine's own famous blueberries), New England chowders, and fresh seafood at the head of a long list of specialties. The innkeepers pride themselves on using local ingredients purchased from the many farmers and fishermen in the Camden area, whenever possible. Pets are not permitted. *Room Rates*: In 1978, rooms were $26 to $34 per person, MAP, depending on the number of people in the room and on bath location. Double rooms, EP, were $30 to $38 during peak season, and less in the early summer and during September and October. *Driving Instructions*: Take Route 1 North to Warren, Maine. Then take Route 90 to the center of Camden. From northern Maine, take Route 1 South to Camden.

Castine, Maine

Castine lies at the tip of a peninsula that projects into Penobscot Bay south of Bucksport and east of Blue Hill. Castine was a port of entry for about two hundred years and a shipbuilding town. Because of its strategic location, it has been the site of several fortifications, including *Fort George*, which survives as an earthworks. *Wilson Museum* on Perkins Street has a wide-ranging collection of material varying from prehistoric artifacts to nineteenth-century farm, carpenter and kitchen tools. There are three restored smaller early buildings on the museum grounds.

THE PENTAGÖET INN
Main and Perkins Streets, Castine, ME 04421. 207-326-8616. *Innkeepers*: Marilyn Michaels and Julie Radford. Open from April 15 to October 15.

The Pentagöet was built in 1894 to be an inn. The inn is clearly Victorian but in a happily informal way. Much of the furniture here

is restored oak and fun. Eleanor Roosevelt stayed at the inn in 1936, and a number of contemporary writers have stayed there, some to remain in Castine as permanent residents. The inn has fourteen guest rooms, of which nine share four baths and the remainder have private baths. No meals other than a fine breakfast and afternoon teas are served. There are, however, many good restaurants in the Castine area. *Room Rates*: Double rooms with bath are $28, with half-bath are $26, and with shared bath are $22. Single rooms are $5 to $7 less. Breakfast is included in all rates. *Driving instructions*:Two miles north of Bucksport on Route 1, take a right on Route 175 South. This turns into Route 166, which leads directly to Main Street, Castine.

Damariscotta and Newcastle, Maine

These towns, often referred to as the "twin cities of Maine," are located near the head of the Damariscotta River at the peninsulas that terminate at Boothbay Harbor, Christmas Cove, and Pemaquid Point. The towns retain many of the original colonial homes in a setting that has come to include modern shopping and other commercial enterprises. There is a public bathing area at the *Pemaquid Beach Park* and a *Fisherman's Museum* at Lighthouse Park. The area has excellent freshwater fishing for trout, pickerel, perch, small-mouthed bass, and landlocked salmon. Charter boats leave for ocean fishing from several sites in the twin towns as well as farther down the peninsula at Boothbay Harbor. The lighthouse at *Lighthouse Park* is frequently photographed and painted. The state park at Pemaquid Beach includes *Fort William and Henry* and the *Round Tower* (1692) as well as the *Pemaquid Restoration*, which is an active archaeological digging site where visitors can see the foundations of several historic buildings recently uncovered.

THE BRANNON-BUNKER INN

Route 129, Damariscotta, ME. Mailing address: H.C.R. 64, Damariscotta, ME 04543. 207-563-5941. *Innkeepers*: Dave and Char Bunker. Open June through Columbus Day.

The Brannon-Bunker Inn is situated on the Damariscotta River. A favorite pastime of guests is to go down to the river at low tide and watch the seals cavort and sun themselves on the rocks. There are about two dozen of them, and they put on a fine show. The inn is actually a late 1800s barn connected to the Bunkers' 1820 Cape-style house. The barn was once a rather notorious dance hall in the 1920s. It now contains four guest rooms, a lounge with a piano, a large fieldstone fireplace, and a dining area where guests are served a complimentary breakfast of fruits in season, juice, coffee or tea, and homemade muffins and coffee cake. The Bunkers also provide hors d'oeuvres and setups in the lounge at cocktail hour (guests supply their own liquor). All the rooms in the inn are furnished with antiques. In addition to the rooms in the inn, there is a two-bedroom apartment in a nearby building on the property. Meals are not provided, but the Bunkers will recommend local restaurants. Guests are

welcome to use the kitchen or outdoor grill for cooking lobsters, but they must clean up afterward. The Bunkers will supply the necessary pots. This is a relaxed, comfortable, rural Maine vacation inn. *Room Rates*: In summer, the rooms range from $17 for a single with shared bath, to $35 for the two-bedroom apartment. In fall, the rooms are each $5 less. *Driving Instructions*: Take Route 1 through the town of Damariscotta to Route 129. Take Route 129 to the inn (approximately four minutes from town).

Deer Isle, Maine

Deer Isle is a jewel of an island in Penobscot Bay, not too far from Bar Harbor, *Acadia National Park*, and the village of Blue Hill. Deer Isle was first settled in 1763, while Maine was still part of the Massachusetts Colony. Early occupations included farming, ice cutting, and stone quarrying, but lobstering was and still is the major industry here. Another important industry is tourism. The island was linked to the mainland by bridge in 1938. The Deer Isle–Stonington Historical Society operates a historic house and museum called Aunt Salome Sellers. Here visitors can see collections of local artifacts and an Indian collection.

PILGRIM'S INN

Main Street, Deer Isle, ME 04627. 207-348-6615. *Innkeepers*: George and Eleanor Pavloff. Open from April 1 to December 1. In 1793, Ignatius Haskell built one of the most impressive homes on Deer Isle. The owner of a thriving sawmill, Haskell was a framer of the constitution of the state of Maine. Now listed on the National Register of Historic Places, Pilgrim's Inn has a true colonial flavor with its pumpkin-pine wide-board floors, soft colonial tones on the walls, paneled parlor, and numerous working fireplaces. Guests can sit in the common room and gaze out over the millpond nearby. Before-dinner cocktails and hors d'oeuvres are also served in this room. The inn has eight guest rooms, all with wood stoves, and with electric bedwarmers beneath the sheets, and all but one with semi-private baths.

Dining room meals are enhanced by a specialty of the inn's open-hearth cooking. Whenever possible, roasts and fowl are cooked in a hearth oven in front of a 7½-foot fireplace. Dinners do not follow a set menu but are selected according to the freshest ingredients available. A typical recent dinner included avocados stuffed with shrimp, poisson à l'Orientale (marinated in ginger, orange, and soy sauce, and then broiled), vegetables from the inn garden, rice pilaf, home-made French bread, garden salad, blueberry pie, coffee, and cheese. Dinner reservations are accepted from the general public with advance notice, and the meal is prix fixe.

The inn has a rowboat and bicycles available to guests, as well as horseshoes, croquet, badminton, and an interesting library. *Room Rates:* Rooms are $38 per person, per day, MAP, or $250 per person, per week, MAP. Tax and gratuities not included. *Driving Instructions:* Take Route 1 north of Bucksport and turn south on Route 15 to Deer Isle Village. There, turn right on Main Street (the Sunset Road) and drive one block to the inn on the left side of the road.

Dennysville and surrounding Washington County

Washington County is the last frontier on the East Coast of the United States. A county of tremendous size, its area is larger than the combined states of Rhode Island and Delaware. It has over 1.5 million acres and includes 133,000 acres of lakes left by the action of three successive glaciers. This is a sportsman's paradise as well as a welcome retreat from the crowds of more southerly Maine. The county produces the largest crop of blueberries annually in the world. There are two cities of note: Calais, pronounced locally as Cal-luss, and Machias, pronounced Mach-EYE-us. Calais is on the Canadian border and has a special bond of friendship with its Canadian sister city, St. Stephen. Calais imports all its drinking water from across the border, and fires in either city are answered by fire-fighting forces from both. The *St. Croix Historical Society* has its headquarters here.

The *Thomas Ruggles House* in Columbia Falls has carved flutings and beadings and a fine flying staircase. The house, preserved in its original form, is open daily to the public from June through mid-October.

Machias is the shire town of the county and is noted for its fine white houses lining the Machias River, which opens into a salt bay via a series of rugged ledges. Machias was the scene of the first naval battle in the Revolutionary War. The *Burnham Tavern* survives from this period and is maintained by the DAR.

Dennysville and West Pembroke are small neighboring towns filled with New England white clapboard homes. The Dennys River is a popular swimming, boating, and salmon fishing spot. West Pembroke is the location of a famous reversing falls.

LINCOLN HOUSE COUNTRY INN

Dennysville, ME 04628. 207-726-3953. *Innkeepers:* Mary Carol and Jerry Haggerty. Open all year, by reservation.

At the end of the Revolutionary War, Benjamin Lincoln accepted the sword of surrender from General Cornwallis. He then was permitted by General Washington to purchase 10,000 acres of land in northern Maine (at the time, part of Massachusetts). In 1787, Mr. Lincoln built a fine country house of fifteen rooms on the property.

The inn has had a rich history in its 190 years. Indians often received lodging in the summer kitchen of the inn, and John James Audubon was a guest there on his way to Newfoundland. Audubon was so pleased with his two-week stay at the Lincolns' home that he named a sparrow the Lincoln Sparrow.

In late 1976, the Haggertys purchased the old home and began to return it carefully to its former splendor. The process has been a

slow one, because Jerry Haggerty, a restorer of antiques, is a perfectionist and insists on restoring rather than renovating.

The result is a simple elegance, which has been re-created in a fine country home. There are two dining rooms, a main kitchen and a summer one, and six comfortable guest rooms. From several guest rooms you can see the river below, with its family of nesting eagles. In the winter, it is currently the only inn open in Washington County. North Atlantic salmon fishing, choice birding, nature trails, tennis, boating, canoeing, and river swimming are all within walking distance of the inn.

Mary Carol Haggerty takes great care in supervising the cooking at the inn. Dinners—served to the guests and, with advance reservations, to the public—feature the choice of two or three fine entrées, such as stuffed scallops or roast sirloin, poached salmon or leg of lamb. She always offers a choice of soup, such as brandied pumpkin or she-crab, and a choice of dessert that might include apple crisp, cheesecake, or homemade pie. The entrée includes homemade bread, salad, and vegetables. Dinner prices vary according to the entrée, from $8 to $10 complete. Folks have been known to drive all the way from Ellsworth, just for Mary Carol's dinner.

Recently Jerry went into the woods and found a 4,000-pound elm log, hewed it in half, moved it to their newly refurbished woodshed, and refinished the top into the grandest bar in Washington County. The result is the new bar, "The Woodshed, A Village Pub." A wood stove keeps the bar open all winter long.

The Haggertys are gradually expanding a plan to offer fine antiques for sale at the inn. Carefully restored pieces are placed in the inn itself, where they can do service until they are admired by a guest and purchased. In this way, antique lovers can see a limited selection of pieces in a functional setting. Children and very small pets are permitted. *Room Rates:* Single rooms are $20. Double rooms are $25 to $35. *Driving Instructions:* The inn is within sight of the intersection of routes 1 and 86.

Georgetown Island, Maine

Georgetown Island is one of many islands and peninsulas that extend from the mainland in southern Maine. Just south of the Bath area, the island is noted for *Reid State Park*, the land for which was donated by the builder of the Grey Havens Inn. The area has several fine beaches, picturesque sights of the local lobstering industry, and an Audubon sanctuary. The Georgetown Fire Department auction in July is a popular local event. It is only a short drive to the *Bath Marine Museum* and several other historical attractions in the area.

GREY HAVENS INN

Reid Park Road, Georgetown, ME. Mailing address: Box 2, Five Islands, ME 04546. 207-371-2616. *Innkeepers:* A. Hardcastle, Jr., and Hilda Hardcastle. Open Memorial Day through Columbus Day.

At Grey Havens you can lie in your turret guest room and have a 180-degree panoramic view of the ocean. The inn is on an island that feels remote but is accessible by road and a short drive from Bath. Indeed, four of the rooms are in the inn's twin turrets and six of the seventeen rooms have been renovated to have private baths. The inn was built by Walter Reid in 1901 and has been carpeted, insulated, and replumbed and rewired. There is electric heat throughout to take away the evening chill. The inn has 260 feet of deepwater anchorage and its own dock. It is within rowing distance of an island nature preserve, and an Audubon sanctuary is just down the road. The inn's lounge has a big rock fireplace and a 12-foot picture window that was hauled to the inn by barge from Rockland. At the time (1904), it was the largest piece of glass in the state. The inn is noted for its huge wraparound porch, where guests can relax and even have breakfast if they wish. The dining room features a homey selection of down-east cooking, including corn and cheddar chowder, pumpkin chowder, fresh broiled and baked seafood, roast beef hash, and codfish balls with homemade ketchup, each accompanied by home-baked breads and followed by fresh desserts.

Pets are generally permitted, as well as children over twelve. *Room/Rates:* Double rooms are $25 to $45, including complete continental breakfast. Prices reduced by 20 percent in the early and late part of the season. *Driving Instructions:* Just east of Bath, take Route 127 South. Drive 10½ miles to Reid Park Road, on the right. The inn is ¼ mile down this road, on the left.

Islesboro, Maine

Islesboro is a secluded island in the middle of Penobscot Bay, 3 miles off the coast at Lincolnville Beach, north of Camden. It is largely a summer community of substantial homes, with few activities and little provision for a tourist population. Because access is by a ferry that follows a limited daily schedule, island road traffic is kept to a minimum. There are few shops other than those that serve the island's summer residents. This is a lovely island to visit if you are lucky enough to be a guest at a home here or in one of its few inns. The island ferry dock and public boat launching area serve boaters who wish to gain access to *Warren Island State Park*, which is accessible only to campers who arrive by boat. This area provides the only camping on Islesboro. Day visitors are encouraged to take a leisurely drive around the island to enjoy the spectacular scenery and to explore or relax on the beaches.

ISLESBORO INN

Islesboro, ME 04848. 207-734-2221. *Innkeeper:* Doris T. Anderson. Open from mid-June to mid-October.

The Islesboro Inn describes itself as a converted "summer cottage." The magnitude of this understatement can be determined when the reader learns that this "cottage" has twelve working fireplaces. Indeed, seven of these are located in guest rooms and the remaining ones in various public rooms that boast spectacular views of Penobscot Bay. Even the ride to the island is a treat aboard the *Governor Muskie*, a 24-car, 125-passenger ferry that leaves from the small harbor at Lincolnville. As you watch the mainland slip away, you are easily convinced that a time of great relaxation is ahead. The inn has a lovely terrace often used for luncheon as well as cocktails before dinner. There are six guest moorings for yachts reserved next door at the nine-hole golf course that is open to the public. The inn also has a clay-surfaced tennis court. Life at the inn is purposely slow and relaxing, and the separation of the island from the mainland means that guests are more likely to be contented with sailing, bicycling, bird-watching, berry picking, or beachcoming. However, day trips to the mainland and nearby Lincolnville, Camden, and Rockland will provide ample opportunity to go shopping or to explore the many fine local restaurants. There is an excellent informal lobster house

right near the entrance to the ferry at Lincolnville Beach, where you can eat inexpensive shore dinners on picnic tables outdoors or in somewhat more formal settings inside. Visitors to the island are warned, however, that the ferry schedule is strictly adhered to, and it is possible to be stranded on the wrong side of the bay if you let time slip by unnoticed. No pets permitted. *Room Rates:* Rooms are from $40 (with shared bath) to $50 per person per day, MAP. *Driving Instructions:* Take U.S. 1 north of Rockland through Camden and to Lincolnville Beach. Board the ferry there; upon disembarking on Islesboro Island, take the first three right-hand turns in a row. There is a sign on the tree at the third right.

Kennebunkport, Maine

Kennebunkport is a typical Maine seacoast harbor town. Much of the village has remained untouched for more than a century. This area has long been a favorite of vacationers and is somewhat crowded during the summer months because of its proximity to Massachusetts. The village houses the *Seashore Trolley Museum* with its collection of more than a hundred trolleys from all over the United States and Europe. Part of a visit to this museum includes an exciting and educational ride on some of the restored old trolleys. Kennebunkport is famous among afficionados of odd festivals for its *Dump Week*, when garbage is turned into "dump art" and the town picks "Miss Dumpy," who then presides over the festivities, including a

"Dump Parade." There is indoor tennis at the *Meadows* and golf at the *Arundel Golf Course*. *Rachel Carson Wildlife Refuge* offers peaceful birdwatching and hiking. The *Brick Store Museum* in neighboring Kennebunk has a fine display of items from local history, a carriage collection, and maritime memorabilia.

THE CAPTAIN LORD MANSION

Pleasant Street, Kennebunkport, ME. Mailing address: Box 527, Kennebunkport, ME 04046. 207-967-3141. *Innkeepers:* Beverly Davis and Richard Litchfield. Open all year.

The Captain Lord Mansion is one of the finest examples of nineteenth-century craftsmanship in current use as an inn in the state of Maine. Built in 1812 by a skilled crew of ships' carpenters idled by the British blockade of the harbor, the mansion is an extremely impressive structure with multiple chimneys and a cupola large enough to hold a group of people. Captain Lord clearly could spend as much as he wished to perfect the details of this three-story gem. The front door with its elaborate leaded-glass fanlight opens onto an unusual three-story unsupported elliptical staircase of great strength and grace. The wide-board pine floors have been restored to their original warmth, and the walls of the mansion's common rooms and guest rooms have been covered with carefully selected reproduction wallpaper. The entire restoration of the mansion was accomplished by a Herculean effort on the part of Jim Throumoulos, the former owner. The inn was just recently purchased by the new innkeepers, the Litchfields.

The entire mansion is carefully appointed with lovely antiques. There are twelve working fireplaces, five of which are in the guest rooms. The beds in the rooms are antiques and include a 12-foot-tall black walnut four-poster, two intricately carved Victorian beds, a massive brass four-poster, and a cannonball king-size bed. Plants, steamer trunks, handmade quilts, and old rugs add personal touches to the rooms.

The romantic qualities of this grand old home are certain to appeal to those who seek a quiet retreat. From the octagonal cupola, guests can enjoy the sunset, gaze at the stars, or watch the boats on the Kennebunk River. Flower gardens and giant chestnut and elm trees grace the inn's grounds. Guests are served country-style breakfasts around the big kitchen table. No other meals are served. The

serene atmosphere over-all at the inn makes one feel like a guest in a wonderful village home of yesteryear. No pets permitted. Families with children are welcome, but there are no special facilities for children. *Room Rates:* Rooms are $40 to $60 per couple year-round. The fourth night is free following three nights at the above rates from November 1 through April 30. *Driving Instructions:* Take exit 3 off Route I-95 and follow signs to Kennebunkport's Dock Square. At the square, turn right onto Ocean Avenue and go 3/10 mile to Green Street. Take Green Street (left) uphill to Pleasant Street. The inn is on the corner.

THE CHETWYND HOUSE

Chestnut Street, Kennebunkport, ME 04046. 207-967-2235. *Innkeeper:* Susan Knowles Chetwynd. Open all year (guests should be sure to check first).

The Chetwynd is a small guest house built in the middle 1800s by Captain Seavey of Kennebunkport and recently redecorated. The blue-shuttered white clapboard house is situated in the heart of Kennebunkport just a few blocks from restaurants, art galleries, and craft shops on Dock Square. Across the street from the Chetwynd is the busy Kennebunk River which empties into the ocean one-half mile away. There are two sandy beaches and the rocks of the breakwater are a wonderful place to sit and watch the parade of fishing boats and graceful sailboats heading for the sea. Another relaxing place is the garden at the Chetwynd. The four guest rooms share two baths. Susan Chetwynd serves a delicious breakfast with melon, strawberries, freshly squeezed orange juice, and—if a guest fancies it—oyster stew! Tea and coffee are available anytime. No pets permitted. Children are permitted but not encouraged. *Room Rates* (1978): Single rooms are $18; double rooms are $26 to $30, breakfast and beverages included. Off season, rooms are $14 to $26. *Driving Instructions:* At Dock Square, go two blocks toward the ocean.

Monhegan Island, Maine

Monhegan Island is accessible only by ferry from Port Clyde or by private boat. The island is quite unimproved by man, although it does have electricity and a moderate supply of drinking water. Do not expect tourist attractions or entertainment. This is a place to relax and withdraw from the hectic pace of city life or even from the comparatively lively life in the coastal Maine tourist centers. Enjoy nature at its finest here and reacquaint yourself with the sea.

ISLAND INN

Shore Road, Monhegan Island, ME 04852. 207-372-9681. *Innkeepers:* Robert and Mary Burton. Open June 18 to September 18.

Just getting here is half the fun. The drive down from Thomaston to Port Clyde is one of our favorites, and then in the tiny, old-fashioned fishing village of Port Clyde, you must board a ferry for a half-hour ride out to the island. Long a favorite of Andrew Wyeth's, Monhegan Island has loyal devotees who are not put off by the somewhat barren, rocky surroundings.

The Island Inn, perched 40 feet above the island's only harbor and wharf, has thirty-eight rooms, most of which share baths. It was built in 1850, and additions in 1907 and 1927 brought it to its present size, with its many dormers and rooftop cupola. The inn has simple, comfortable furnishings, but its main attraction is clearly the setting. Life on Monhegan is as simple as any life can be, with few vehicles, few telephones, limited electricity, and virtually no entertainment other than that provided by Mother Nature and one's own ingenuity. This is an ideal retreat and an unusual vacation experience. The dining room serves three meals of well-cooked Maine food and is open to the public as well as the guests. Neither children nor pets are permitted. *Room Rates* (1978): $21 to $28 per person per night. *Driving Instructions:* Take Route I-95 to Brunswick, Route 1 to Thomaston, then Route 131 to Port Clyde and the Monhegan Ferry.

Spruce Head and Owls Head, Maine (including neighboring Thomaston and Rockland)

The village of Spruce Head is a small island connected by bridge to the St. George Peninsula outside of Thomaston. It consists of a summer colony of cottages and a modest year-round population including a number of fishermen and lobstermen who work out of the local harbor. There is a rockbound lobster pound that can be seen from the road through the island. There are several antique shops in the area, as well as one of our favorite bookstores, the *Lobster Lane Bookstore*, which has a great many used books and magazines.

Owls Head is a favorite summer vacation spot, with many full summer residents as well as the weekly rental and transient trade. The *Owls Head Lighthouse* is one of Maine's most beautiful. Across from the tiny general store in Owls Head is a wonderful antique store crammed to the ceilings (literally) with antiques, memorabilia, and junk, all of which has spilled into the shop's front yard, making this a wonderful place to browse on an otherwise gloomy day.

Rockland is a small city best known for its *Seafood Festical* held the first weekend in August each year. Tons of lobster, shrimp, and french fries are consumed annually at this fest. The *Farnsworth Library and Art Museum* has an unusually good collection of nineteenth- and twentieth-century art, including works of Wyeth and other Maine artists.

Lining its Main Street, Thomaston has some of the most prestigious homes in midcoast Maine. It is the home of *Montpelier*, the reconstruction of General Knox's mansion, now open as a museum during the summer months. The Maine State Prison is here, and trusted inmates under supervision operate a *Prison Workshop Store* with a variety of well-made wooden furniture in the front and an inmates' craft gallery in the rear. Inmates will be happy to answer questions about products in the shop.

THE CRAIGNAIR INN

Clark Island Road. Spruce Head, ME 04859. 207-594-7644. *Innkeepers:* Terry and Norman Smith. Open all year.

The Craignair is an unpretentious seaside country inn. Dotted with islands, the coastline in this part of Maine is very picturesque and removed from the bustle of the more populous resort areas.

Originally built to house quarry workers, the Craignair is located at the end of the road that leads to Clark Island. Ospreys nest on the disused quarry poles. The plain white, unshuttered building has sixteen guest rooms; most share hall baths. Set above the ocean and Clark Island as well as the local cove, the dining room and many of the guest rooms have an unobstructed view of the sea. A deck at the seaside allows guests to relax in the sun while watching the lobster boats at work and, closer to the shore, the sea gulls and other shore birds. Many guests like to hike on Clark Island, open to guests of the inn. This is not an inn with fancy surroundings or myriad resort-style activities. It is likely to appeal to writers, naturalists, artists, beachcombers, and anyone seeking relaxation and an opportunity to reaffirm one's inherent connection with the sea. Dinner is a single-entrée affair, with the meal of the day chosen from a menu that changes daily. Entrées range from the ubiquitous New England

clambake to a Chinese buffet to shish kebab to lasagna to shrimp scampi. Breakfasts are hearty, with bacon and eggs or pancakes among the morning offerings. *Room Rates:* Rooms are $12 to $17 per person, lodging only; $14 to $19 per person, EP; $19 to $24 per person, MAP. *Driving Instructions:* From Thomaston, drive south on Route 131 5½ miles to Route 73 East, then 1 mile to Clark Island Road and down 1½ miles to the inn.

Tenants Harbor, Maine

Tenants Harbor is a small lobstering village with a modest summer tourist population. Its seclusion on the peninsula running from Thomaston to Port Clyde has meant that its New England character has remained generally unchanged. It is one of seven villages within the township of St. George and was settled in 1605. The village area was once a major source of granite. Its inhabitants also supported themselves by fishing and lobstering. For many years, the village was a major shipbuilding center, and many large vessels were built in Tenants Harbor. At low tide several wrecks can still be seen here. Day trips to Port Clyde (and from there by ferry to Monhegan Island) and to the neighboring communities of Spruce Head, St. George, South Thomaston, Thomaston, Owls Head, and Rockland provide the visitor to this area with a taste of the same fine scenery and seafaring life that inspired so many of Andrew Wyeth's paintings when he lived nearby.

THE EAST WIND

Tenants Harbor, ME 04860. 207-372-8800 or 372-8908. *Innkeepers:* Tim Watts and Ginnie Wheeler. Open all year.

Snuggled in a corner of the peaceful village of Tenants Harbor is The East Wind, built in 1890 and restored in 1975. The inn is within walking distance of the village library and post office and a short drive from all the attractions on the St. George Peninsula, stretching from Thomaston to Port Clyde. The inn was built as a sail loft and ship chandler's operation. The gracious old white frame structure has sixteen guest rooms, two with private baths. The first floor contains a large kitchen, pantries, a dining room that overlooks the harbor, a spacious lobby, office, and manager's room. The rooms are

simply decorated with wall-to-wall carpeting throughout, and many antiques, including brass beds. Three meals are served daily to guests. Dinners feature seafood including lobster prepared three ways, haddock, clams, scallops, and a shore dinner, with steaks and chicken Kiev for those who don't care for seafood. Prices for full dinners range from $3.95 to $15.95 (for the shore dinner); most with seafood and steak cost $5.95 to $7.95.

There are no traffic jams, no noise, no pollution, and no fast-food restaurants here. There is, instead, fresh sea air, four-season recreation, and congenial hosts at one of Maine's newest old inns. *Room Rates:* From June through September, rates range from $18 for a single room to $36 for a two-room suite. Off-season rates are $6 to $8 less. *Driving Instructions:* From U.S. 1, just east of Thomaston, take Route 131 south 9½ miles to Tenants Harbor, then turn left at the post office and continue straight to the inn.

Wiscasset, Maine

As you drive north through Wiscasset on Route 1 and you have left the central village, look to the right at the harbor and you will see one of the most eerie yet romantic sights of coastal Maine. There, at the shoreline, lie the remains of two grand old schooners. Gray, shadowy reminders of the glory of sailing days gone by, these majestic giants are now lying on their sides, slowly being reclaimed by the sea they once sailed.

Wiscasset is a much visited and photographed coastal village.

There are many antique and craft shops here and several small, pleasant restaurants. Among the museums in the area are the *Lincoln County Fire Museum* with its collection of antique fire trucks, hearses, and carriages; the *Lincoln County Museum* and old *Lincoln County Jail*; the *Maine Art Gallery* with its collection of work by Maine artists, including art for sale; and, finally, the *Music Museum*, displaying a wide variety of old musical instruments.

THE SQUIRE TARBOX INN

Westport Island, ME. Mailing address: RFD 2, Box 318, Wiscasset, ME 04578. 207-882-7693. *Innkeepers:* Elsie White and Anne McInvale. Open mid-May through mid-October.

The Squire Tarbox is a rare find in Maine—an old country inn in an incomparable setting. It is located on a 10-mile-long island near Wiscasset, linked to the mainland by bridge. Westport Island has one main road, Route 144, running the length of it. At the end of this road is an old house, part of it dating from 1793. The larger main building was added later. Today the property consists of a main house and a barn, with connecting smaller sections between. In this way, the farmer and his family were able to walk from their house to the barn to do chores without the necessity of going out into the bitter cold winter weather.

The house was carefully restored some years ago, and it retains the original floors, carvings, moldings, fireplaces, wainscoting, and old glass windows so characteristic of a home of the early nineteenth century. This is not a large inn; the eight guest rooms are almost always occupied. Each summer, guests are drawn here by the crisp, clean Maine air. This is a place for people who love old things and do not require the organized activity of larger inns or resorts.

Meals are absolute heaven at Squire Tarbox. Every evening (except Sunday) dinner is served with a choice of two entrées, one of them a fish or shellfish. Lobster is not served at the inn, because it is the innkeepers' personal belief that lobster is best enjoyed "in the rough" at one of the places nearby specializing in boiled lobster. The entrées include flounder, sole, haddock, or any of the native shellfish served in a variety of wonderful sauces. Each meal contains three vegetables, all freshly picked that day from the inn's own garden, and delicious, unusual soups, such as apple soup or Portuguese tomato soup. Dessert might be a chocolate mint pie with whipped

cream and almonds or an apple cake with whipped cream. Guests are served a complimentary breakfast, and dinners are served to the public and guests alike. *Room Rates:* Rooms are $30 for a double and $20 single. A charge of $5 is added for each additional person. *Driving Instructions:* Take Route 1 north from Bath. Turn right on Route 144, and follow it for 8 miles.

INLAND

Bethel, Maine

Bethel is a lumbering and farming center located along the Androscoggin and Sunday rivers in the Oxford Hills, adjacent to the foothills of the White Mountains and within a short distance of the immense *White Mountain National Forest*, a portion of which lies within the state of Maine. The combination of the area's rolling hills and the backdrop of the White Mountains provides some of Maine's most memorable interior scenery. Visitors to Bethel in the winter can enjoy downhill skiing at the *Sunday River Skiway* and at *Mount Abram*, and cross-country skiing at the *Sunday River Inn* and along trails in the *White Mountain National Forest*.

The grandeur of the mountains is no less evident in the summer, when hiking along well-marked forest trails and shopping for antiques and crafts take over as leisurely activities. Bethel also has a covered bridge over the Sunday River.

THE SUDBURY INN

Main Street, Bethel, ME 04217. 207-824-9308. *Innkeepers:* Douglas and Sharon Scott. Open all year.

First open to the public in 1873, this inn was initially an overnight stopping place for nineteenth-century businessmen. Now it serves tourists who visit the area in all four seasons, especially since travelers have discovered that inland Maine offers fine winter sports with fewer crowds than in neighboring New Hampshire and Vermont. The inn offers accommodations in sixteen rooms, three with private baths. Rooms are generally large, with solid country furniture very much in keeping with a nineteenth-century inn that appeals to twentieth-century tastes. The inn's restaurant serves three meals daily to guests and the public and is particularly proud of its scallops Newburg, lamb shaslik, and chicken orange. The Clark Street Pub lounge has a fireplace and copper bar and comfortable chairs for those who want to read quietly after a day on the ski slopes or hiking through the forest. *Room Rates:* Double rooms are from $15 to $22, depending on bath location. *Driving Instructions:* The inn is on Main Street, one block south of Route 26 in Bethel.

SUNDAY RIVER INN

Sunday River Skiway Access Road, Bethel, ME 04217. Mailing address: RFD 2, Box 141, Bethel, ME 04217. 207-824-2410. *Innkeepers:* Steve and Peggy Wight. Open October to May.

The Sunday River is not an old country inn. It is included here, however, because it is a small, family-oriented inn with a special devotion to skiers in an area that has relatively few inns of any sort. Furthermore, the inn is run by a young couple who encourage all their guests to take full advantage of the area's resources.

The Sunday River Inn is located at the edge of a large tract of wilderness managed for timber production by paper companies and private tree farmers. The inn operates the Sunday River Ski Touring Center on the premises with its 25 miles of groomed and maintained trails and hundreds of miles of unmarked logging roads. Equipment and instruction are available, as are a waxing and warming room, guided tours, and night skiing lit by kerosine lamps on Friday nights. The Outward Bound School uses the inn as the expedition launch-base for its winter program.

The inn itself is a simple building, with the ski shop in an attached small barn. Built in 1965 and given later improvements, the inn has inviting stone fireplaces in both the living and dining rooms. There are fourteen guest rooms, of which two are new housekeeping units with private baths while the rest share baths. In addition to the guest rooms, two sleeping-bag bunk dorm-rooms are popular with teenage members of families. Meals, too, are simple here, with only one entrée served family style to guests and public alike. Breakfasts are also served to the public. No pets please. *Room Rates:* Double rooms are $21 per person, MAP; bunk rooms are $15 per person during peak seasons. Off season, the rates are lower (off season being October 1 to November 15 and April 15 to May 15). *Driving Instructions:* Take Route 2 East from Bethel for 2 miles. Turn left at the sign for the Sunday River Ski Area; then go 3 miles to the inn.

The Forks, Maine

The Forks is a sparsely populated area of northwestern Maine along Route 201. This highway runs from Waterville toward Quebec and was the route used by Benedict Arnold and his men for their assault on that fortress city during the Revolutionary War. The road is absolutely spectacular, with wonderful vistas at every turn. Four companies now offer white-water rafting trips down the *Kennebec River* through the Kennebec Gorge and also down the Dead River. Both rivers are also very popular for kayaking and canoeing. In mid-August there are annual white-water canoe races on the *Dead River* and a bicycle race from Jackman to Waterville. The area offers fine hunting, fishing, snowmobiling, and cross-country skiing. Guides are available through the local town office or *Crab Apple Acres*.

CRAB APPLE ACRES

Route 201, The Forks, ME. Mailing address: P.O., West Forks, ME 04985. 207-663-2218. *Innkeeper:* Eleanore Evans. Open all year.

Crab Apple Acres is an 1853 farmhouse overlooking the Kennebec River in a rather remote section of Somerset County. Mrs. Evans offers seven guest rooms, which share two baths. The farmhouse has many old-fashioned features, including the original fanlight over the door, Dutch-oven fireplace, wide pumpkin-pine floorboards, original Christian-cross doors, and old hinges and thumb latches. The inn is quite popular with people seeking a peaceful retreat, and with hunters, snowmobilers, and those on canoe trips. The nearest formal recreational facilities are at least 25 miles away, so this farm is definitely for those content to enjoy the entertainment provided by the natural setting itself.

Meals at Crab Apple are served family style, mostly to guests, but the public is welcome by reservation. Mrs. Evans takes great pride in the home-style food served. One of her specialties is chicken pie. Homemade jams and jellies are always served at breakfasts. Liquor is not served, but guests are welcome to bring their own to the table. *Room Rates:* Rooms are $18 to $20 per person, AP. Lodging, no meals, is $7 per person. *Driving Instructions:* Take Route I-95 to the Skowhegan, Quebec exit, then take Route 201 to the farmhouse in The Forks. Quebec City is about 140 miles north of here.

Greenville, Maine (Moosehead Lake Region)

The greater Moosehead Lake region is a true wilderness. Maine's North Woods have a pervasive atmosphere and a history of logging. The area away from the lake is owned by giant paper companies, and logging is still very much in evidence. The woods and the water are open to everyone. This is the country of Henry David Thoreau, who described it in detail in *The Maine Woods*, based upon his travels in the area in the mid-1800s. At that time this was Indian land, but control later passed to industry.

Moosehead is the largest lake in Maine. It is about 40 miles long and 20 miles wide at its widest point. Here you can see not only the moose for which the lake was named, but deer, bear, and a multitude of smaller mammals, as well as numerous game and other birds. The Moosehead Lake region boasts over 200 miles of groomed snowmobile trails and the *Squaw Mountain Ski Area*, a ski resort for all ages that emphasizes family winter vacations. This is a great region for hunting and fishing, with many sports-lovers flying in to their preferred sections by seaplane. There are several outfitters who rent boats and canoes and will supply guides for trips to the more remote sections. Canoers who plan to explore without a guide should beware of sudden squalls and high winds.

FROST POND CAMPS AND CAMPGROUND

Star Route 76, Frost Pond, Greenville, ME 04441. Telephone: Two-way radio contact with Folsom's Air Service in Greenville. Messages may be left with Folsom's by calling 207-695-2821 before 4:00 P.M., seven days a week. *Innkeepers:* Eric and Judith Givens. Cabins are available May 15 through November 30 and in winter months with advance notice. After December 15, access is by ski or snowmobile.

Frost Pond is so wonderful and remote (40 miles from the nearest town, Millinocket) that we had to include it. Frost Pond Camps are best described as rustic, and that is their attraction. It is a comfortable but rugged wilderness camp on a quiet lake surrounded by forests of spruce, fir, maple, birch, and beech. There are eight cabins equipped with gas stoves, refrigerators, electric lights, and wood stoves. Seven others have no electricity or water, but water may be obtained from the well. The one larger cabin has hot and cold running water, shower, and indoor toilet. The cabins accommodate from two to eight people. Frost Pond is a brook trout haven, squaretails over 1½ pounds are not uncommon, and the Givens have seen some weighing close to 4 pounds. Boats, canoes, and outboards are available for rent or you can launch your own. The North Woods teem with wildlife—moose, bear, fox, and snowshoe hare, to name a few. It's a bird lover's paradise with great horned owls, bald eagles, ducks of all sorts, loons, and many species of warblers and finches. The 200,000-acre *Baxter State Park* 15 miles away offers a variety of trails for hiking and mountain climbing. Mount Katahdin, Maine's highest peak (5,267 feet), is located in the park and is visible from Frost Pond.

If guests wish to eat out there are restaurants in Millinocket (40 miles away) and Greenville (50 miles away). *Cabin Rates:* The rates vary according to length of stay, ranging from $6.50 to $8.00 a day per person. *Campsites:* $3.50 a day or $21.00 a week. *Driving Instructions:* Take Route I-95 north to the Medway exit, then take Route 157 west to Millinocket. Follow Baxter State Park road northwest past the park entrance to its junction with Great Northern Paper Company Road. Follow this road to Ripogenus Dam (drive carefully; the road is heavily used by trucks hauling tree-length logs). The camp is 3 miles beyond.

WILSON'S ON MOOSEHEAD LAKE

Route 15, Moosehead Lake, East Outlet, ME. Mailing address: Star Route 84, Greenville Junction, ME 04442. 207-695-2549. *Innkeepers:* Ron and Jane Fowler. Open all year.

Wilson's consists of a group of fifteen housekeeping cottages, which sleep up to eighteen people, grouped around an old colonial house

with an interesting history. The original house was built prior to 1865 by Henry Wilson, a dam keeper on Moosehead Lake. He was asked to be the dam keeper at East Outlet, and he agreed on the condition that he be allowed to bring his house with him. The old house was then floated across the lake and placed on the shore at East Outlet. Later, an inn and a water tower were attached to the original Wilson house. The result is a rather unique assemblage of buildings with many floors, passages, and stairways to wander through and explore.

The old hotel has five big, old-fashioned guest rooms available in summer only. It is also used as the office and recreation area.

Most of the cottages on the property are log cabins, all with housekeeping facilities, furnished with pieces from the hotel and newer furniture. Many have fireplaces. The inn has its own beach, dock, boats, and canoes (there are additional charges for use of the boats and canoes). There is fine fishing in the lake or in the Kennebec River, which begins near the cabins. This is a year-round place, and many visitors come in the winter for skiing and snowmobiling. Pets are permitted. *Room Rates:* The hotel rooms are $10 to $15 a night. No meals are served. The cabins range from $20 to $50 (for the eighteen-person lodge) a day, with $25 a typical figure for a cabin that sleeps four and has a fireplace. Weekly charges for this cabin would be about $145. *Driving Instructions:* Take the Maine Turnpike to the Newport exit, Route 17 to Corinna. Then take Route 7 to Dexter and Route 23 to Guilford. Take Route 15 to Greenville, 6 miles past Squaw Mountain.

Kingfield, Maine

Kingfield is a remote but popular Maine village located about 50 miles from the Canadian border in the Carrabassett River valley about 40 miles west of Rangeley Lakes. The village is a short drive to *Sugarloaf, USA,* Maine's largest ski area and now one of the East's important year-round recreational resorts. There are a number of important ski-touring centers in the area, including the *Deer Farm Ski Touring Center* in Kingfield and the *Carrabassett Valley Ski Touring Center.* The *Appalachian Trail* passes nearby, as does the Arnold Trail. This area is receiving increasing recognition as a fine area for fall foliage viewing, especially as Maine's popularity during this season increases in proportion to the increasing crowding on the highways of the more western or southern New England states.

THE WINTER'S INN

Box 44, Kingfield, ME 04847. 207-265-5421. *Innkeeper:* Michael Thom. Open all year, with full restaurant facilities from December 15 to April 15 and from July 1 through October 15.

In the late 1800s, A. C. Winter and his friends the Stanley Brothers (inventors of the Stanley Steamer) returned from a day of hunting and, being at a loss for something to do, designed a house to be built on a hill overlooking the lovely little village of Kingfield. The result of their musings was the Winter's mansion, a wonderful example of Georgian colonial revival architecture, complete with pillars, pilasters, bold vertical lines, and classic details. The building is now in the National Registry of Historic Places, having been impeccably restored by owner-innkeeper Michael Thom. A handsome entrance of etched glass and oak welcomes guests to the Grand Salon, a high-ceilinged, wide hall where a fire burns cheerily in one of the inn's three matched fireplaces. Presiding over the salon is the Winter's Chickering box grand piano, which had been in the original music room. From the hall, the grand staircase ascends to a huge Palladian window on the landing and continues up to the curved maple bannister on the second floor. The entire mansion is furnished with antiques and oil paintings of the period and, in the second-floor guest quarters, big brass beds. The guest rooms on this floor range from two-room suites with private baths to a large single room that shares a bath with one other room. High-style bunk rooms for skiers are on

the inn's third floor. There are sixteen guest rooms in all, four with private bath. Both upper floors have comfortable sitting areas.

On the main floor, off the Grand Salon, are the dining rooms of the inn's elegant restaurant, Le Papillon, serving haute cuisine française by candle and firelight to guests and public. The windows of these rooms overlook meadows, streams, and the nearby mountains. Breakfast is served only to the inn's guests. Across the hall is the former music room, now a fireside lounge bar. The original Winter's barn has been redone and houses Balthazar's, a pub with a working fireplace and dart board. The pub is named in honor of Balthazar, a fifteen-year-old cat, the ultimate authority at the inn. Another less tangible presence at Winter's Inn is a ghost (of "Winter's past," naturally) who appears occasionally. The inn has tennis courts and a swimming pool for guests' enjoyment. A seasonal ski shuttle is provided to nearby *Sugarloaf, USA,* Maine's giant ski resort. Pets are not permitted; children are permitted but not encouraged. *Room Rates:* During ski season and summer, rates range from $28 to $38 per person, MAP. Off-season rates are $21 to $26 per person. *Driving Instructions:* Take Route 27 north from Farmington to Kingfield. Take a left on Depot Street to the intersection with School Street (at Tranten's General Store). Turn right up the hill to the inn.

Moose River—Jackman area (Maine's north woods)

Located deep in Maine's north country—not far from the Canadian border—are the towns of Moose River and Jackman. The area is northeast of Moosehead Lake, Maine's largest lake and one of the most beautiful in the east. The two towns are situated on the Moose River, with the border mountains rising around them and scores of lakes and streams filled with landlocked salmon and trout. This is perfect terrain for cross-country skiing on abandoned logging trails, hiking, and hunting. There is also excellent fishing, boating, and canoeing in the area. Fly-in trips can be arranged in Greenville and at other airports. Jackman has seaplane facilities; Moose River has an airport at Sky Lodge. Boats and canoes can be rented in the towns. Guides are recommended for treks into the remote areas around the towns; arrangements can be made through the lodges and in towns. It is generally dangerous to attempt extended trips into the wilderness without guides. This applies to canoers—there are many white-water areas and falls, as well as wooded portages. There are lodges and fishing camps in the towns and the surrounding area for a real wilderness vacation any time of the year.

SKY LODGE AND MOTEL

Route 201, Moose River, ME 04945. Mailing address: Jackman, ME 04945. 207-668-2171. *Innkeeper:* E. R. Landgraf. Open from May 28 through November 22.

Sky Lodge is the largest all-log lodge in the northeast. Built in 1929 on the spot where the original settlers of the Jackman–Moose River area built their homes, the rustic lodge sits high on a clearing in the remote, unspoiled north woods, surrounded by the breathtaking panorama of the Maine border mountains, lakes, and pine forests. The 200 acres offer a world of outdoor activities—hiking and exploring the pine woods and lakes—and near the lodge shuffleboard, archery, horseshoes, badminton, and also swimming in the pool. A golf course is adjacent to the lodge grounds; boating, canoeing, and fishing in the remote Maine waters are all within a mile. The main room of the inn is a big, two-storied affair with two enormous stone fireplaces and curving stairs leading up to the bearskin rug-draped balcony and the guest rooms. These rooms are all furnished with

handmade pine furniture and "snowshoe" chairs (snowshoe furniture can be purchased in the gift shop). The eleven guest rooms in the lodge and fourteen in the motel down the hill all have private baths. Six of the lodge's guest rooms have working stone fireplaces—one even has a fireplace in the bathroom. The Sky Lodge dining room is open to the public for all three meals. The large picture windows offer a spectacular view of the countryside. Good, hearty American food is featured, and the menu is changed daily. On a typical evening one could have a Swiss Cheese omelet, grilled pork chops with Dutch apples, Maine lobster, or a fresh poached salmon in egg sauce. The freshly baked breads and homemade desserts are plentiful. There is also a congenial cocktail lounge complete with one of the giant stone fireplaces. For pilots, there is a fine 1,750-foot grass strip and 100-octane fuel is available at the lodge's airport. Pets are permitted at the lodge's discretion. *Room Rates:* Current rates were not available at the time of publication. Reservations are advisable. *Driving and Flying Instructions:* Driving—Take Route 201, 2 miles north of Jackman. Flying—Sky Lodge Airport is on the Montreal sectional aeronautical chart.

Index of Inns

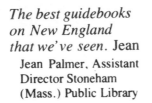
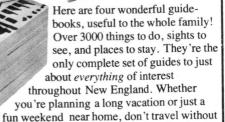

All over America, travelers are discovering the special delight of America's historic country inns.

For a friendly welcome . . . for a taste of local color . . . for a restful, homelike atmosphere . . . for a scenic location . . . and, frequently, for the best food in town, you can't do better than an Inn.

Wherever you travel in America, the *Compleat Traveler's* Companions are your best guide to hundreds and hundreds of little known, out of the way inns, lodges, and historic hotels where you can escape the daily humdrum and feel like an honored guest.

So experience a refreshingly new, remarkably old, way to travel—there's a Country Inn waiting for you now!

The Compleat Traveler's

COUNTRY
INNS OF AMERICA